D1553609

David Pallister, Sarah Stewart
and Ian Lepper

SOUTH AFRICA INC.

THE OPPENHEIMER EMPIRE

Revised and Updated Edition

YALE UNIVERSITY PRESS
New Haven and London

Originally published in Great Britain 1987
by Simon & Schuster Ltd.
Paperbound edition published in Great Britain 1988
Corgi Books by Transworld Publishers Ltd.
First published in the United States 1988
by Yale University Press.

Printed in the United States of America.

Library of Congress catalog card number: 88–50650
International standard book number: 0–300–04251–5

The paper in this book meets the guidelines for
permanence and durability of the Committee on
Production Guidelines for Book Longevity of the
Council on Library Resources.

2 4 6 8 10 9 7 5 3 1

To the black miners of South Africa

★ ★ ★

In crossing the river I become a new man,
Different from the one I was at home.
At home I was secure
But now that I am on this side
I am in a place of danger,
Where I may lose my life at any time.
So prepare me for my death . . .

   From *Another Blanket*, Sotho migrant labourers' song

★ ★ ★

I believe that we are today crossing the Rubicon. There can
be no turning back . . .

   President P.W. Botha, 15 August 1985

David Pallister is an investigative journalist on the *Guardian* with a long-standing interest in South Africa. He has also travelled throughout the rest of Africa.

Sarah Stewart is a writer and editor on international affairs. She has been a corporate researcher for Counter Information Services, the International Longshoremen's and Warehousemen's Union and the Data Center, and is co-author of a book on Nicaragua.

Ian Lepper is a corporate analyst and the development officer for Twin Trading, a London-based trading house for the Third World. He has written widely on companies and Southern African issues for Counter Information Services, including *Black South Africa Explodes* (1977) and *Partner in Apartheid* (1986).

Contents

Preface and Acknowledgements

The Dutch first came to South Africa in 1652, when Jan van Riebeeck founded a small settlement at the Cape of Good Hope as a way-station to the East for the Dutch East India Company, but it was not until two centuries later that the region began to be of real interest to Europeans. In 1867 diamonds were first discovered there and in 1884 the first South African goldfields were opened. The so-called Randlords who exploited the fabulous underground riches came from England, Germany and Russia. Many of them were anglophile Jewish émigrés, and the first great mining houses were based in London. They combined a brutal capitalism with a colonialist fervour that sought to secure South Africa's wealth within the British Empire. In their scheme of things the Boers, who spoke the 'kitchen language' of Afrikaans, were rural primitives; the tens of thousands of Blacks who worked the mines were dispensable units of production who could only be 'civilised' by a long association with European culture. The Boer War, at the turn of the century, decimated the Boer republics of the Transvaal and the Orange Free State and in 1910 the Union of South Africa was established.

The second generation of Randlords included the Oppenheimer brothers, who came from a wealthy merchant family in Germany. Sir Ernest Oppenheimer founded the Anglo American Corporation of South Africa in 1917. It became the largest company in South Africa and, in many respects, the dynamo of the apartheid economy. For the past fifty years the family has enjoyed an unprecedented control of the West's supplies of diamonds, gold and platinum. Sir Ernest's son, Harry, was known around the world as 'The King of Diamonds'. With their money and power, their rise to pre-eminence has paralleled and at times complemented the development of the South African state. Sir Ernest and Harry welded together an empire of huge and sprawling proportions that has penetrated the economies of six continents. Yet the empire is so complex that it is never recognised as a single entity.

The family themselves, and the corporate image, have presented a face to the world as South Africa's leading white opponents of apartheid. Both father and son have been opposition politicians as well as leading capitalists arguing against the more restrictive practices of apartheid. Yet the mines on which their wealth rests provided the economic impetus for some of South Africa's most vicious legislation – the Pass Laws, the Group Areas Act and the migrant labour system where thousands of men live in compounds away from their families. The system was already in the making even before the Afrikaner nationalists took power in 1948 and imposed their ideological racism on the country.

Cautiously and assiduously, the Oppenheimers have honed a mystique about them that has so far defied critical examination. To be sure, Sir Ernest and Harry have inspired three biographies over the past twenty-five years, all of them from admirers and the last in 1978. Nevertheless we owe them a debt, as their approach guaranteed access to privileged family information. The structure of the secretive Anglo American Corporation and the De Beers diamond monopoly has been pondered over by countless economic commentators. But the true picture of the Oppenheimer dynastic empire has always remained elusive and partial.

Here, for the first time, is an attempt to redress the balance. This book began as a research project by Counter Information Services (CIS), which has a fifteen-year history of exposing the workings of multinationals. It has produced four reports dealing directly with South Africa, including its first on Rio Tinto Zinc and in 1977 a study of the Soweto uprising, *Black South Africa Explodes*. In late 1985, as the political situation in South Africa became more critical, it was decided to expand the project, then well advanced, into a book.

Our researches have taken us to Johannesburg, most recently in 1986, into the citadels of the Anglo American empire and down the gold mines. We have unearthed matters which the empire would prefer to have remained hidden, and resuscitated events which it would prefer were forgotten. The result is neither biography nor corporate history but, we hope, a synthesis of a family and its fortunes which illuminates some of the most important political developments in southern Africa this century. In unravelling the complexities, we have avoided the strict chronological method. Rather as a diamond cutter we have selected each facet as a face of the whole. There is, though, a detailed appendix showing the group's interests around the world.

As we have written, the unfolding struggle for black liberation in South Africa has quickened and events are being daily overtaken by the battles in the townships. New power relationships are evolving within the white and black communities. The sanctions debate is raging unresolved, as yet reluctant to tackle the core of the apartheid regime's strength – gold. But whatever may happen in the coming months, we hope that this book assists an understanding of South Africa's most loyal ally, the Oppenheimer dynasty. Nelson Mandela summed up the Oppenheimers' strategy nearly twenty-five years ago, writing in the June 1953 issue of the monthly magazine, *Liberation*: 'Rather than attempt the costly, dubious and dangerous task of crushing the non-European mass movements by force, they [the Oppenheimers] would seek to divert it with fine words and promises and divide it by giving concessions and bribes to a privileged minority (the "suitably qualified" voters perhaps).' They are still, against all the odds, pursuing the same course.

The Counter Information Services project was launched with the support of the J. Roderick MacArthur Foundation of Niles, Illinois. The project led first to a report and campaign in Britain against Consolidated Gold Fields.

We would like to thank all those who have helped us with our work on this book, including the Anglo executives who gave us interviews and the staff of the Data Center, Oakland, California. In particular Jonathan Bloch, Duncan Brewer, David Brooks, Margaret Busby, Martin Cleaver, Brian Hackland, Jeremy Herbert, Anne Koch and Pat Sidley, and those in the trade unions in South Africa, were generous in their assistance to us. We would also like to thank the Joseph Rowntree Social Service Trust, the Fund for Tomorrow, the World Council of Churches, Christian Concern for Southern Africa, the American Committee on Africa, and the Institute for Policy Studies, who gave their support to the CIS project.

London
February 1988

Abbreviations

AAA	Australian Anglo American
AAC	Anglo American Corporation of South Africa
ABF	Associated British Foods
ABI	Amalgamated Beverage Industries
ACT	Advanced Corporation Tax
AECI	African Explosives and Chemical Industries Limited
AFL-CIO	American Federation of Labor–Congress of Industrial Organizations
AHI	Afrikaner Handelsinstitut
AJV	Ashton Joint Venture
AMAX	American Metal Climax Inc.
Amaprop	Anglo American Properties Limited
Ambras	Anglo American Corporation do Brasil Limitada
Amcar	Amcar Motor Holdings
Amcoal	Anglo American Coal Corporations Limited
Amgold	Anglo American Gold Investment Company Limited
AMIC	Anglo American Industrial Corporation
AMWU	African Mine Workers' Union
Amzim	Anglo American Corporation Zimbabwe Ltd
Anamint	Anglo American Investment Trust Limited
ANC	African National Congress
Anglo	Anglo American Group

Anglo-Vaal	Anglo Transvaal Mines Consolidated
APS	Association of Private Schools
Armscor	Armaments Corporation of South Africa
Assocom	Association of Chambers of Commerce
Barnat	Barclays National Bank
BOSS	Bureau of State Security
BSAC	British South Africa Company
CDM	Consolidated Diamond Mines of South West Africa
Charter	Charter Consolidated
CIA	Central Intelligence Agency
CMS	Consolidated Mines Selection Company
CNA	Central News Agency
Consgold	Consolidated Gold Fields
COSATU	Congress of South African Trade Unions
CPSA	Communist Party of South Africa
CSO	Central Selling Organization
De Beers	De Beers Consolidated Mines Limited
DPTC	Diamond Purchasing and Trading Corporation
ERGO	East Rand Gold and Uranium Company
Escom	Electricity Supply Commission
FCI	Federated Chambers of Industry
FOSATU	Federation of South African Trade Unions
FRELIMO	*Frente da Libertacão de Moçambique* (Mozambique Liberation Front)
FSH	Freight Services Holdings
GE	General Electric Company
Gencor	General Mining Corporation
GFSA	Gold Fields of South Africa Limited
GWU	General Workers' Union
ICI	Imperial Chemical Industries Plc
IDAF	International Defence and Aid Fund for Southern Africa
IGC	International Gold Corporation
ILO	International Labour Office
IMF	International Monetary Fund
IQM	Industria Quimica Matiqueira
Iscor	Iron and Steel Corporation

JCI	Johannesburg Consolidated Investment Company Limited
JMB	Johnson Matthey Bankers
MATS	Management and Technical Services
MAWU	Metal and Allied Workers' Union
MDC	Marine Diamond Corporation
Minorco	Mineral and Resources Corporation Limited
MLL	minimum living level
MPLA	*Movimento Popular da Libertacão de Angola* (Popular Movement for the Liberation of Angola)
MNR	Mozambique National Resistance Movement
MWU	Mine Workers' Union
Nafcoc	National African Federated Chambers of Commerce
NASA	National Aeronautics and Space Administration
NUM	National Union of Mineworkers
OAU	Organization of African Unity
OFSIL	Orange Free State Investments
PAC	Pan Africanist Congress
PFP	Progressive Federal Party
PP	Progressive Party
RDM	*Rand Daily Mail*
RFS	Rennies Freight Services
Rhoanglo	Rhodesian Anglo American
RTZ	Rio Tinto Zinc
SAAN	South African Associated Newspapers Limited
SAB	South African Breweries Limited
SACTU	South African Congress of Trade Unions
SADCC	Southern African Development Coordination Conference
SAF	South African Foundation
Safmarine	South African Marine Corporation Limited
SALDRU	South African Labour and Development Research Unit
Samcor	South African Motor Corporation

SANLAM	South African National Life Assurance Company
SAP	South African Police
SASOL	*Suid Afrikaanse Steenkool, Olie en Gaskorporasie* (South African Coal, Oil and Gas Corporation)
Scaw	Scaw Metals
SLA	Southern Life Association
SOFIN	Sociedade Financeira Portuguesa
Soweto	South-Western Townships
SWA	South West Africa
SWAPO	South West Africa People's Organization
TEBA	The Employment Bureau of Africa
UCT	University of Cape Town
UDF	United Democratic Front
UNITA	*União para a Independencia Total de Angola* (Union for the Total Independence of Angola)
UP	United Party
Zamanglo	Zambian Anglo American
ZANU	Zimbabwe African National Union
ZAPU	Zimbabwe African Peoples' Union
ZCCM	Zambia Consolidated Copper Mines
ZCI	Zambia Copper Investments

Chronology

1652:	Dutch arrive in South Africa, founding settlement at Cape of Good Hope.
1836:	Great Trek of Afrikaner settlers.
1866:	Gold discovered in Boer republic of the Transvaal.
1866, 13 July:	Bernhard (Bernard) Oppenheimer born in Friedberg.
1867:	Diamonds discovered in Kimberley in Northern Cape.
1870, 30 September:	Louis Oppenheimer born in Friedberg.
1872:	Anton Dunkelsbuhler arrives in Kimberley.
1878:	Dunkelsbuhler and Co. set up.
1880, 22 May:	Ernst (Ernest) Oppenheimer born in Friedberg.
1880:	First Anglo-Boer (Afrikaner) war.
1884:	First South African goldfields opened.
1886:	Witwatersrand goldfields opened.
1899–1902	Anglo–Boer War.
1902, November:	Ernest Oppenheimer arrives in Kimberley.
1906:	Ernest Oppenheimer marries May Pollak.

1908, 28 October:	Harry Frederick Oppenheimer born in Kimberley.
1910:	Union of South Africa constituted from the Cape, Natal, the South African Republic and the Orange Free State.
1910:	Frank Leslie Oppenheimer born.
1912, 6 January:	Native National Congress (NNC) formed.
1912:	Ernest Oppenheimer becomes mayor of Kimberley (till 1915).
1913:	Native Land Act passed, confining Africans to 88 per cent of the land.
1917:	Anglo American Corporation of South Africa founded.
1918, March:	100,000 African miners strike unsuccessfully for higher wages.
1920:	70,000 workers on Witwatersrand gold mines strike, stopping production on 21 mines for 3 days; troops sent in but wage increase agreed.
1921:	Communist Party of South Africa formed.
1921:	Ernest Oppenheimer knighted.
1921, 13 June:	Bernhard Oppenheimer dies.
1924:	Ernest Oppenheimer becomes member of South African Parliament (till 1938).
1925:	NNC renamed African National Congress (ANC).
1934:	Lady May Oppenheimer dies.
1934:	United Party formed.
1935:	Frank Oppenheimer dies.
1936:	Sir Ernest Oppenheimer marries Caroline (Ina) Harvey.
1943:	Harry Oppenheimer marries Bridget McCall.
1945, 8 June:	Nicholas Frank Oppenheimer born.
1946:	70,000 to 100,000 African mine-

	workers on the Witwatersrand strike for higher wages; troops called in to drive them back to the mines.
1948:	Afrikaner National Party win elections.
1950:	National Party government bring in Population Registration Act, classifying people as White, Coloured or Native (later Black).
1951:	Opening of Anglo's first Free State gold mine, Welkom.
1954:	J. G. Strijdom becomes South African Prime Minister.
1955, 5–6 March:	South African Congress of Trade Unions (SACTU) founded.
1955, 26 June:	Freedom Charter adopted at Kliptown, Transvaal.
1956, 19 January:	Louis Oppenheimer dies.
1956, December:	156 members of Congress Alliance arrested and charged with High Treason.
1957:	Sir Ernest Oppenheimer dies.
1957:	Ghana becomes independent.
1958:	Verwoerd becomes Prime Minister.
1959:	Progressive Party formed.
1960:	Chief Albert Luthuli awarded Nobel Peace Prize.
1960, 21 March:	Sharpeville massacre, when peaceful demonstrations against Pass Laws fired on by police, leaving 69 dead and 178 wounded.
1960, April:	ANC banned.
1961, March:	Treason Trial ends with acquittal of last defendants.
1961, 16 December:	Umkhonto We Sizwe (Spear of the Nation) launched, dedicated to a strategy of political and economic sabotage, with Nelson Mandela as its Commander-in-Chief.

1961:	South Africa leaves the Commonwealth to become a republic.
1962:	Uganda, Burundi become independent.
1962:	Tanganyika become independent.
1963:	Kenya becomes independent.
1964, 11 June:	Nelson Mandela and other leaders sentenced to life imprisonment.
1964:	Malawi becomes independent.
1964:	Zambia becomes independent.
1964:	Zanzibar joins Tanganyika to form Tanzania.
1965:	Rhodesian settler government declare unilateral independence (UDI).
1966:	Basutoland becomes independent as Lesotho.
1966:	Bechuanaland becomes independent as Botswana.
1966, 6 September:	Verwoerd assassinated; John Vorster succeeds as Prime Minister.
1968:	Swaziland becomes independent.
1975:	Mozambique and Angola become independent.
1976, 16 June:	Soweto uprisings, in protest against compulsory use of Afrikaans in African schools.
1976, November:	Urban Foundation started.
1977, 12 September:	Steve Biko dies in detention.
1978:	Vorster resigns. Botha succeeds as Prime Minister.
1979:	Botha's first conference with business leaders at Carlton Centre, Johannesburg.
1980:	End of settler government of Southern Rhodesia: Robert Mugabe becomes prime minister of Zimbabwe.
1982:	Southern African Development Coordination Conference (SADCC)

	established with Angola, Botswana, Lesotho, Malawi, Mozambique, Swaziland, Tanzania, Zambia and Zimbabwe.
1982:	Harry Oppenheimer retires as chairman of Anglo.
1983:	National Union of Mineworkers (NUM) recognised by Chamber of Mines.
1983:	Botha becomes State President.
1984:	Harry Oppenheimer retires as chairman of De Beers.
1984:	First official NUM strike.
1984:	Bishop Desmond Tutu wins Nobel Peace Prize.
1984, March:	Nkomati Accord.
1985, 20 July:	SA government declares state of emergency.
1985, 13 September:	Gavin Relly meets ANC leaders in Zambia.
1985, December:	South African economic blockade of Lesotho, leading to coup overthrowing Chief Jonathan.
1986, 13 June:	SA government declares state of emergency.
1986, 24 November:	Barclays Bank in South Africa sells out to Anglo.
1987, May:	White elections.
1987, 10 August:	NUM strike results in 40,000 sackings.

1
A Day Out to Carletonville

The young black security guard stands in the Johannesburg street, dressed in his immaculate peaked cap and shiny leather belt, an oval badge on his left breast carrying the inscription 'Anglo American Property Services'. Swinging his baton against the palm of his hand, he is guarding the Carlton Centre, the pride of the city and the largest commercial property complex in Africa. It is dominated by a fifty-storey office block which is joined to the thirty-storey Carlton Hotel by a huge glasshouse dome, where exclusive boutiques sink two floors below ground level in a pit of luxuriant vegetation. Among the shoppers and visitors, well-dressed Blacks move easily and confidently through the Centre and the hotel lobby. On the hotel's notice board – a week before the Soweto Day state of emergency was announced in June 1986 – is a reminder that the British Tourist Authority has hired a convention room to sell the Old Country.

Today we are taking an unusual guided tour through the American-style grid streets of downtown Johannesburg, into the northern suburbs, with their spacious walled villas, and then out on the modern highway, past the smoky expanse of Soweto, to the first gold mines which created this city on the high inhospitable veld one hundred years ago. Evidence of the old rapacious Randlords who discovered and exploited the hidden treasures of diamonds and then gold is not hard to find. The slag heaps of the old city gold mines still stand as their testament. But we are seeking out the estate of their successor, Harry Frederick Oppenheimer, patriarch of the Anglo American group, usually known as Anglo. Everything we pick out on the way is part of the Anglo empire, including those dumps which Anglo is re-treating to extract the last vestiges of gold and uranium. At the other extreme is our Ford car, bought at one of the McCarthy showrooms and insured with Eagle.

Through busy downtown Johannesburg, past the Civic Towers/ICL House and the Devonshire Hotel and a dozen other office buildings, people are going about their daily business: shopping in the upmarket Edgars department store, buying South African Breweries beer, Fanta soft drinks and Boschendal wines from Solly Kramer's liquor store and food in one of the OK supermarkets. You could choose Farm Fare eggs and chickens, Olé sunflower oil, Yum Yum peanut butter, Carmel pickles and Denny mushrooms and asparagus. Cake could be picked up from the Blue Ribbon bakery chain, Jenny Wren fabrics at Scott's clothing store, Hush Puppies at the nearest ABC shoe shop, and any number of choices in paints, wallpapers and furniture.

At the other end of the financial district stands a huge mirror-plated lopsided pyramid with a spire at one end and the front curtain wall cut like the face of a diamond. Number 11 Diagonal Street was designed for Anglo American Property Services by the Chicago architect Helmut Jahn, a disciple of Mies van der Rohe. Inside the heavy plate-glass doors the multi-faceted, mirrored walls of the foyer angle up to a peak five storeys above. A broad plume of water illuminated by coloured lights falls down a sculpted, stainless-steel slide. When the sun shines, the light and heat are reflected onto the Johannesburg Stock Exchange, where half the dealings are in Anglo shares. Some yards away is an imposing sandstone building with high panels of stained glass over the ornate main doors. It has the grandeur of a 1930s cathedral, but in keeping with Anglo's passion for discretion the only identifying sign is

engraved below a frieze of elephants at the foot of the steps:
44 Main Street. This is the Anglo group's headquarters that
Harry Oppenheimer, though formally retired and an octo-
genarian, still visits every morning of the working week.
Occasionally at lunch time his slightly hunched diminutive
figure can be seen strolling down to the Rand Club, a young
minder walking a few paces behind with a bulge in the
jacket of his well-cut lounge suit.

There are other, more obvious signs of the Oppenheimers' all-pervasive influence in the city. Several minutes
from Main Street is the Market Theatre arts complex. The
donation plaque in the foyer records the generosity of the
Sir Ernest Oppenheimer Memorial Trust. In Gold Reef
City, a tourist toy-town celebration of the old mining
houses, is the Oppenheimer Conference and Banquet Hall.
Heading north to the suburb of Parktown, an unmarked
side road has been specially cut through the high embank-
ment of the De Villiers Graaff Motorway. On the other
side, a road leads to a pair of tall metal gates, electronically
operated by the uniformed black guard in his gatehouse.
This is the entrance to Brenthurst, the Oppenheimers'
beautiful family home, situated within 50 acres of the most
manicured piece of real estate south of the Limpopo. Set on
the side of a tree-covered ridge, Brenthurst isolates its
residents from the geographic and political reality surrounding it. The northern suburbs are also home for some
of South Africa's most prestigious private schools, many of
which have been supported by Anglo and the other large
mining houses. Harry Oppenheimer himself went to Parktown Prep School in the 1920s; its aim, according to the
prospectus, was 'to prepare the sons of gentlemen for
admission to Eton, Harrow and other leading public
schools'.[1] As we shall see, the élitist English public-school
ethos has for decades informed the Oppenheimer family
and its closely knit senior management.

Johannesburg is still growing, and it is hard to miss the
tower cranes of the LTA construction company as we head
south-west for the motorway that curves through the gold
towns of the Witwatersrand. *Business Day*, which we picked

up at CNA stationers, says that the enfeebled rand is steadying against the dollar; still good news for the gold mines. As the new road sweeps up and round Soweto, LTA's Komatsu construction equipment can be seen finishing off the project. Our Ford competes for popularity with the Peugeots and Citroëns and Mitsubishis. Great mounds of rock and earth litter the countryside, the detritus of a hundred years of goldmining.

A farmer is feeding his crops with AECI fertiliser. He has a new Ford tractor. On either side of the road, large signs at the gates of driveways tell us we are entering gold country. The tree-lined drive to the mine looks inviting. The verges are neatly cut, and off to one side is the cricket pitch and bowling green. On Sundays both are well-populated with Whites in their whites.

A little further on, a single-storey building and a club house are set among the trees and lawns. This is mine administration territory, and as we get closer to the mine-head the grass becomes unkempt, brown and shrivelled. High fences, industrial buildings and piles of stores start to appear. The enclosed hostel compound, where thousands of black miners live, has towering steel gates with guardhouses. Only residents may come and go. Everyone else, including wives, are trespassers.

At the minehead there is more evidence of the group. Big drums of Haggie steel cable winch the cages down the shaft, built by LTA. Kitted out in the miners' white overalls, rubber boots and sweat rag, visitors are crammed into the low, dark cage. In the winch room the operator throws the switch and the needle on the great disc before him slowly starts moving round as the cage gathers speed. It plunges down the first of three mile-deep shafts at 11 metres a second; the wet rock walls flash by in the gloomy light of the miners' lamps. Down in the heat and the noise and the spray, the Boart drill bits with industrial diamond tips from De Beers, the group's world diamond cartel, are making holes for the AECI explosives and fuses. The ore broken out by the explosion will eventually be grounded down with Scaw crushing balls.

The list could go on. Even including just a few of its mainstays – AMIC, Amaprop, Charter, Consgold and JCI – the Anglo group can claim over 1,350 subsidiaries and associated companies. The growth of Anglo since the Second World War to become South Africa's largest and most influential corporation is largely the story of the South African political economy, for it has done more than any other business to contribute to the country's wealth and to the power of the white minority. It has become within South Africa the key private enterprise whose mines, industry and commerce, along with the South African state's economic interests, make up the core of the country's economy. The old adage that what is good for General Motors is good for the United States is far more apposite to Anglo and South Africa. Certainly Anglo controls a far greater proportion of the South African economy than General Motors could ever hope to achieve in the USA. At the same time, Anglo has built up a diverse and powerful overseas empire spanning six continents and with a web of secret companies to take advantage of international tax agreements.

You will not find the Oppenheimer business featuring in any league table of top multinationals. This is because no one will admit formally that it exists, and legally in fact it does not. Technically there are simply two major South African publicly quoted companies, the Anglo American Corporation of South Africa (AAC) and De Beers Consolidated Mines, with an admitted close working relationship and various cross-holdings with other companies. Because the boards of AAC and De Beers present their companies as independent entities on stock exchanges and to business partners and governments around the world, they can never formally admit that the two operate as inseparable twins. This means that those who recognise this reality have no solid base from which to describe Anglo as a whole. It is not possible just to add together the investments listed in the annual reports of AAC and De Beers to get the whole and those who try, like the publisher of the South African *Who Owns Whom*, are treated with scorn and derision by senior

Anglo executives. The two halves have to be taken apart, dissected and put back together again to arrive at what is a multinational ranking about twenty-fifth in the world – bigger than Unilever, ITT, Nissan, Siemens or BAT.

Even then, the difficulty of accounting for a myriad of different companies in industries as diverse as banking and wattle harvesting, added to the lowly exchange rate of the South African rand, can understate Anglo's true scale. One measure is the number of people who work for the group. Including the finance houses it controls, Anglo employs 305,000 people in the gold mines alone; 25,000 in the diamond business; probably 100,000 in other mines, including platinum and coal; 150,000 in manufacturing; 140,000 in the food, beverage and retail industry; and perhaps 50,000 in sundry other enterprises. Outside South Africa there are about another 30,000, including the large and poorly paid Latin American workforce. Altogether, then, the group has some 800,000 workers, most of them earning miserable wages at the very heart of apartheid, producing the minerals, goods and services that are essential to keep white South Africa rich.

Another approach is to examine South Africa's mineral reserves on which the economy is almost entirely dependent. The country, including illegally-occupied Namibia, is the Western world's biggest producer of gold, platinum, uranium, gem diamonds, chrome, manganese ore and vanadium (which is used to make high-grade steel for oil pipelines). The value of its minerals is exceeded only by the United States'; together they account for about 60 per cent of all exports, and gold alone provides nearly a half. South African gold mines produced 640 tons of gold in 1986, just over half of Western production. Coal is reputedly the second largest foreign-exchange earner, from a production of 170 million tons a year. South Africa is the world's leading exporter of steam coal and ranks fourth in total coal exports. Until the advent of European sanctions, it supplied 50 per cent of France's needs, and 60 per cent of the 36 million tons exported in 1984 went to the EEC, including to Britain during the miners' strike. Even in the post-sanctions era, South Africa managed to export 45 million tons in 1986, partially by cutting its prices, and was expected to sell around 40 million tons in 1987. But the exact breakdown of exports is unknown, because figures for minerals such as platinum, vanadium and uranium are classified as state secrets. Platinum group metals in particular are a vital export and may well exceed coal in value.

As the premier South African mining organisation, incorporating three mining houses, Anglo's contribution to the economy is second to none. The principal house, the Anglo American Corporation, administers mines which produce 41 per cent of the country's gold, 57 per cent of its uranium and 22 per cent of its coal; De Beers mines the bulk of South Africa's diamonds. When the other houses are taken into account, the group's control of South Africa's gold and uranium rises to over 70 per cent, with a slightly smaller but still dominant position in coal and platinum.

The group structure has developed from the more clearly defined system of 'administered' companies. Until relatively recently the AAC annual report attempted to explain this:

> The term 'group' has a wider meaning in the South African mining industry than its statutory definition . . . the parent [mining] house not only administers companies that are not necessarily subsidiaries, but provides them with a full range of technical and administrative services, and is able to assist them in finding capital for expansion and development.[2]

This is a polite way of saying: 'We do not formally own these companies but we decide everything they do.' Or, as Harry Oppenheimer once admitted: 'When I say control I don't necessarily mean 51 per cent.'[3]

This system of administered control was originated on the goldfields at the end of the last century. Lacking local capital to finance new mines, the mining houses would raise it in the USA or Europe by floating new companies in which they would retain a minority stake. They would then appoint their own directors and negotiate renewable management contracts.

We can also identify three other types of company within the group. Besides subsidiaries wholly owned by either AAC or De Beers, there are the jointly controlled subsidiaries such as the mining house Johannesburg Consolidated Investment and the international investment giant, Minorco. Then there are the controlled associates such as the African Explosives and Chemical Industries (AECI) and South African Breweries, where a strong minority interest and boardroom representation allows effective strategic control. A stage more remote are the related companies, often based in America or Europe, which are additionally tied to the group by a long historical association, mutual interests or a holding so significant that no rivals exist. Such are the Engelhard Corporation in the USA and Charter Consolidated in England. Finally there are the straightforward investments spread through every other major industry in the country.

The most striking aspect of the South African economy is the degree to which it is dominated by just a few large companies, with the state and the private sector jointly controlling strategic areas such as transport, freight, engineering and shipbuilding. The trend towards monopoly began with the needs of the mining houses. The expansion of the gold mines provided both the market and some of the capital to develop industry and commerce locally. As the mines were expanded, the state met the demand for an infrastructure of transport, water and electricity. At the same time, the state's protection of local industry by import controls encouraged the growth of local production, using foreign expertise and capital.

In Western industrial terms, South Africa was and still is a small economy, and this has tended to encourage mergers and monopolies in order to compete with imports. In the 1950s an expansion of South Africa's money market and its growing sophistication primed the pump. Anglo played a crucial role in this transformation by opening its own merchant bank in 1955, Union Acceptances Ltd, a hugely successful venture that in the next few years came to dominate the money market.

In the next decade, the value of Anglo's industrial investments increased by nearly 500 per cent to 290 million rand. During the 1960s, South Africa had one of the fastest-growing economies in the capitalist world. In the first three years of the decade, gross domestic product rose by 9.3 per cent, more than in any country in Europe or North America. Anglo made a substantial contribution to this growth by helping to staunch the withdrawal of investment from the country following the Sharpeville massacre of sixty-nine Blacks in 1960. The group's gold mines were deeper and more dependent on foreign technology than the other mining houses. All of them depended on the electrical, hydraulic and mechanical engineering and expertise that the local subsidiaries of US and European companies provided, as well as imported components and equipment. Without them the mines would at best be less profitable and at worst be forced to shut down. The threat of disinvestment and sanctions provided both the motive and the opportunity for Anglo, growing fat on its Orange Free State gold mines, to move into South African industry in a big way. The aim was vertical integration of the mining industry, from the banks that supplied the loans to the plantations that made the wooden pit props. To facilitate this, Anglo created a new vehicle, the Anglo American Industrial Corporation (AMIC), to centralise and coordinate its expansion with one of the group's other companies, the De Beers Industrial Corporation. With its foreign partners and foreign technology, the group began its long march through every aspect of South African economic life and the formation of some of the giants of South African industry. In many cases they were tied to the strategic needs of state, including defence, as much as to the health of the group and its shareholders around the world.

It began with the creation of the Highveld Steel and Vanadium Corporation, which is now the largest private steel producer in Africa. This was designed by Davy United of Sheffield in England, and an American junior partner,

Newmont, provided technological expertise. It soon became one of the biggest quoted industrial concerns in the country.

In 1964, Anglo acquired Scaw Metals, which gradually developed its steel products with the help of American and British technical aid. Scaw became one of South Africa's leading exporters of manufactured goods and suppliers of grinding balls and high-tensile wire to the gold mines. It won an international reputation for its steel and foundry products, and in America supplied undercarriages for railway freight cars.

Another success story for Anglo was its Boart International group, set up in the 1930s and growing to be the world's pre-eminent manufacturer of diamond- and tungsten carbide-tipped mining drills, with subsidiaries in a score of countries. Boart is the name given to rough non-gem diamonds; the company's supplies came, of course, from De Beers' mines. The gold mines needed explosives in vast quantities. The African Explosives and Chemical Industries (AECI), originally jointly owned by De Beers and ICI of Britain, came into the group with the Anglo take-over of De Beers in 1929. It is the largest producer of commercial explosives in the world. In 1986 it ranked eleventh by assets in the South African top 100 league table and seventh by profits. With the continuing partnership with ICI, it has created South Africa's chemical industry, helped with the development of uranium extraction for the nuclear industry and is involved in the production of methanol-petrol substitute. It is the leading producer of fertilisers, plastics and ferro-silicon for the group's steel-making. A measure of its lasting importance to South Africa was given in the *Financial Mail* some years ago: 'If AECI shut down tomorrow, the repercussions to South Africa would be far more serious than those of the recent coal miners' strike to Britain. All mining and much of industry would come to a standstill; agricultural output would dwindle miserably. If the shut-down continued for long, we'd be in danger of starvation.'[4]

As with some other Oppenheimer activities, there is a

darker side to AECI. It also set up, with ICI machines and personnel, South Africa's munitions industry. A published history of the company recorded that 'as early as 1937 the South African government, reviewing its resources, decided that it needed an ammunitions factory and entered into negotiations with ICI. The outcome was an agreement by which ICI undertook to supply the necessary machines for making the components in a plant that would produce 100,000 rounds of ammunition in a thirty-six-hour week, while AECI were to produce the cordite and the percussion caps.'[5] In the next thirty years AECI set up three more munitions factories to supply the army and the police, all of which were taken over by the state in 1970. But that was not to be the end of Anglo companies co-operating in the armaments business. After the Soweto uprising it was revealed that AECI made the tear gas which is used by the police and the mine security forces against demonstrators and strikers.

Another company was involved in a grander and more covert operation. In the late 1970s, South Africa acquired the technology and the machine parts to develop a long-range 155mm howitzer capable of propelling a shell thirty kilometres. It was the most advanced artillery system in the world, developed by a joint American-Canadian company called Space Research Corporation. The system was of immense importance to the South African Defence Force. In the invasion of Angola in 1975/6, the Russian artillery used by the Popular Movement for the Liberation of Angola (MPLA) had easily outmatched the South African guns. In the following two years, more than 50,000 155mm shells, gun barrels, a radar guiding system and sophisticated testing equipment were supplied to South Africa.

The period coincided with the signing of the United Nations mandatory arms embargo against South Africa. American customs documents, revealed at the subsequent trial of Space Research executives, showed that an Anglo freight company had been involved in at least one of the shipments. On 3 February 1977, South African Airways flight 210 left John F. Kennedy airport in New York for

Johannesburg with a highly technical cargo. This included
a piezzotronic gauge, a textronic scope and a velocity coil –
all for measuring gun-barrel pressure and shell speed. The
shipper was named as Aero Marine Freight Services,
Johannesburg, 50 per cent owned by Anglo.[6]

A heavyweight piece in the industrial jigsaw was provided in 1965 with the formation of LTA, one of the
construction giants of southern Africa and a group subsidiary. Oppenheimer was for years the chairman of the board.
Leading different consortia, it has built the Orange-Fish
River Tunnel, the huge Cabora Bassa Dam in Mozambique, Johannesburg's Jan Smuts airport, as well as roads,
bridges and railways. Another group subsidiary, Shaft
Sinkers – set up and controlled by Anglo – digs the group's
mine shafts, a key role in developing mines because of the
huge expense that must be incurred before the mine can
start earning money. Shaft Sinkers' expertise is such that it
can now win tunnel and shaft contracts abroad.

This remarkable expansion of vertical control in heavy
industry, often linked to mining, was reproduced in other
areas. The Mondi Valley Paper Company was formed in
1967. As usual, a foreign company brought in the technology: the British Bowater Paper Co., which took a 13 per
cent stake. During the 1970s, the integration of the paper
industry was made complete. Anglo owns plantations, saw
and pulp mills and five plants manufacturing paper and
cardboard. It has an assured domestic market through the
group's large minority interests in the two leading English-
language newspaper groups, Argus and South African
Associated Newspapers (SAAN).

The Anglo group's aggressive acquisitiveness has not
been daunted by recession. As with the post-war import
controls, the weakness of the economy in the mid-1970s
actually encouraged Anglo to greater centralisation. In the
motor industry it originally held only a minority share in
South Africa's largest distributor, McCarthy. But in 1976 it
merged Illings and Chrysler South Africa, taking 75 per
cent of the newly-named Sigma Motor Corporation, making it the third largest motor manufacturer. But with too

many competitors in a small market it was losing large amounts of money – an estimated 200 million rand in 1984. Anglo's solution was to get bigger. In 1985, then renamed Amcar, it was merged with the Ford Motor Company of South Africa, leaving Anglo with 58 per cent control. Nor has divestment hindered its progress. After Ford pulled out in 1987, Anglo took over another 18 per cent of the newly-named Samcor, and now controls a company second only to Toyota in its share of the auto market. Its recent acquisition of the divested Barclays and Citibank operations means that it is also the top South African banker, an achievement which brought Anglo to the remarkable position of controlling or having a major stake in eleven out of twelve of South Africa's market leaders.

In the property business, Anglo American Properties Ltd (Amaprop) is in the top four, with the highest amount of equity funds at 343 million rand. Besides the Carlton Centre and 11 Diagonal Street, it wholly owns major developments in most major cities in South Africa, including the McCarthy Chrysler Building in Durban, Transvaal House in Pretoria, the Southern Life Centres in Cape Town and Krugersdorp and the huge Killarney shopping mall in Johannesburg. For good measure, Anglo has also acquired the largest chain of travel agents.

A more indirect route was chosen to consolidate the group's grip on the food and drink industry. Until 1983, its main food company was the Tongaat-Hulett Group, the twelfth largest firm in the country. South Africa's most powerful industrial group after Anglo, Barlow Road, had already begun to strengthen its food interests at a time of a growing black consumer market. The financial takeover of the Premier Group in 1983, leaving executive power in the same friendly hands, perfectly illustrated Anglo's economic clout and unrivalled connections.

Premier, then South Africa's second largest food company, was built up by the Bloom family, Jewish émigrés from Russia at the turn of the century. Tony Bloom, the 45-year-old chairman, had a small minority holding through a family trust. Unusually for a South African businessman, he has a special dispensation from the Soviet Union to visit his relatives there and to check that they receive their dividends.[7] Educated in law at Johannesburg's Witwatersrand University, then at Harvard and the Stanford Business School, he has won a reputation as one of South Africa's more progressive business leaders. He has spoken out against the detention of trade-union leaders and is one of the few businessmen who openly support the African National Congress's vision of 'one person, one vote' in a unitary state.

In 1983, Bloom decided to South Africanise the business, just in case the largest shareholder, Associated British Foods (ABF) of the UK, decided they had other plans for Premier and his position in it. ABF, owned by the Weston family of Canada, may well have been planning a pull-out, especially after the lifting of exchange controls in February that year.

In any event, Bloom's choice of partners was an easy decision to make. For many years he had been a close friend of Gordon Waddell, the then chairman of Johannesburg Consolidated Investment (JCI), one of Anglo's most important mining finance companies, which held 4 per cent of Premier. Waddell, a bluff and ambitious Scot, had a formidable place in South African business. He was a member of what has been called 'the royal balcony' – the small group of financiers who have the resources and the contacts to make or break companies in which they have a minority holding. Harry Oppenheimer was its unchallenged king. And Gordon Waddell used to be Harry's son-in-law from his marriage to Mary Oppenheimer in 1965. Since their divorce he remained a member of the inner cabinet of the Anglo American Corporation until his sudden announcement of retirement from JCI and departure to the UK in early 1987 (see Chapter 6). Like several senior Anglo men (women have no place in this traditional hierarchy), Waddell spent some time in parliament for the Progressive Party. His campaign manager in 1974 was Tony Bloom, the godfather of his children.

Bloom's other choice was another close business colleague, Donald Gordon, the head of the big insurance company, Liberty Life, who had built up a stake of 11 per cent in

Premier. At this stage a decision was taken by Anglo's inner
cabinet to move in, bringing Gavin Relly, Anglo's chairman, into the direct negotiations. The result caused a major
upheaval in Johannesburg boardrooms and, at a stroke,
transformed the controlling interest of the South African
consumer retail business.

The JCI/Liberty/Anglo consortium not only purchased
52 per cent of Premier, they also consolidated their one-
third holdings in South African Breweries (SAB), the
fourth largest industrial concern in the country, and
transferred the lot into a new Premier holding company.
The consortium was then the largest shareholder. SAB
was blue-chip: the first industrial company to be listed
on the Johannesburg Stock Exchange in 1893. When
chief executive Dick Goss heard of the consortium's
plans, he was livid. The entire board threatened to
resign with him at the prospect of having to play second
fiddle to the young upstart from Premier. In the end,
after all-night negotiations which ended up at the only
hotel in town still serving food and drink, the Land-
drost, Goss agreed to the merger on the understanding
that Relly would be chairman and he and Bloom deputy
chairmen.

But after fifteen years of running SAB and defending its
beer monopoly with what one close observer called the kick
to the crotch delivered with aplomb and stunning accuracy,
Goss had no stomach for his new masters. He quietly
resigned, leaving Bloom as chairman. Shortly afterwards
Waddell moved onto the SAB boardroom and took over the
chair. The board of SAB was still able to report that, to the
best of their knowledge, no company or individual had a
controlling interest in the company. It was a convenient
fiction for all concerned. But as Tony Bloom, in his
sumptuous new headquarters in the northern suburbs,
admitted: 'You don't do things that are going to antagonise
your major shareholders.'[8] Between them, JCI and Anglo
now control 47 per cent of Premier and its SAB stake; this
makes Anglo the financial mediator in the huge chain of OK
Bazaars supermarkets, the ubiquitous CNA Gallo record

and book shops and numerous other interests, from furniture to fishing.

The ability of Anglo to maintain control over many companies without taking majority shareholdings depends to a large extent on its position in the financial markets. A worsening economic climate in the 1970s led to a series of calculated mergers in banking and insurance that left Anglo virtually impregnable. In particular, its network of alliances created a buffer against any threats from Afrikaner capital, which still harboured resentments against the size and influence of English-speaking business, despite some closing of ranks after the 1976 Soweto uprising.

Central to this reorganisation of the country's financial institutions was Anglo's relationship with the country's banking giant, Barclays National (Barnat), in which the group became the largest single South African shareholder. With 14.1 per cent, Harry Oppenheimer sat on the board, a position that caused him considerable embarrassment when it was revealed in 1975 that Barclays had invested £6.5 million in South African government defence bonds. Under anti-apartheid pressures in Britain, Barclays started to hand over control of the South African operation to Anglo in 1985. Peter Leslie, the UK general manager, said it was a purely 'commercial decision'. The effect was to reduce Barclays' holding in the South African bank to 40 per cent, increase Anglo's stake to 30 per cent and allow for its name to be changed. 'This will be consistent with our own long established policy that the Barclays name should not be attached to a business when we cease to be the controlling shareholder.'[9] Among Anglo's other collaborators were Liberty Life, ranking third in the life assurance league, and Southern Life (SLA), the fourth largest life assurance company with assets of 4.5 billion rand, over which it took control in 1984 with Barclays as a minority partner. In addition, Anglo held large minority interests in the huge South African Eagle Insurance Company and in the Discount House of South Africa.

In November 1986 Anglo's grip on Barclays became complete. In a dramatic and unexpected move, Barclays

announced that it was finally pulling out of South Africa.
The chairman, Sir Timothy Bevan, again said that the
decision was 'basically commercial'. It was clear that the
bank's business was being badly hit by the student boycott
in Britain and there were fears that its huge investment
plans in the United States would also be jeopardised by the
South African connection. The shares of Barnat, now called
First National, were transferred to the Anglo group, with
22.5 per cent going to Anglo American, 7.5 per cent to De
Beers and 25 per cent to Southern Life. For the Oppenheimer empire it was a hugely advantageous deal, with the
shares going for 18 rand compared with the 23 rand price on
the Johannesburg Stock Exchange. For a stake of 527
million rand, Anglo acquired control of a bank with assets
of 23 billion rand and deposits of 16.86 billion rand. In
addition Barclays in London promised that the credit lines
would remain open as well as the relationship on training
and technology. Chris Ball, the South African managing
director, who adhered to the Anglo political camp, promised that no one would lose their jobs and that the new bank
could look forward to opening foreign branches and investing abroad.

Monopoly in the private sector has led to four corporations representing 81 per cent of the shares quoted on the
Johannesburg Stock Exchange, with Anglo accounting for
60 per cent. It is, in effect, a cartel economy with room for
only a few suppliers. The government has not been anxious
to challenge this concentration. Indeed, it operates some of
the largest enterprises in transport, electricity, the mail and
the iron and steel industry. Many of these grew out of the
need to provide the infrastructure necessary for the mining
houses. The Electricity Supply Commission (Escom), for
example, was formed when it became clear that private
electricity generation was not enough to service the bur-
geoning gold mines. Now Anglo provides the bulk of
Escom's coal. The railways were also developed for the gold
mines, linking the Reef mines to the ports in the Cape,
Natal and Mozambique. 'There is a cartel for everything
and anything in this country,' one businessman remarked.

But where Anglo treads, formal cartels are not necessarily required. Its grip on South Africa's private sector is such that it can dictate to whole industries. Its incredible control becomes apparent when you look at the *Financial Mail* list of the largest companies, ranked in terms of total assets, the so-called SA Giants. Out of the top fifty, Anglo controls sixteen, with combined assets of 98.8 billion rand: AAC, De Beers, Amgold, Gold Fields of South Africa, OFSIL, Freegold, JCI, Vaal Reefs, Driefontein, Barclays (now First National), Southern Life, AMIC, SAB, Premier, AECI and Tongaat-Hulett. Neck and neck with Anglo is the state, with 98.1 billion rands' worth of assets in the form of the electricity and transport utilities, the Post Office, the Reserve Bank, the SASOL oil-from-coal operation, the Iscor steel corporation, the Industrial Development Corporation and Armscor, the government's weapons manufacturer. With Anglo controlling 25.7 per cent, and the government another 25.6 per cent of the SA Giants' total assets, there's not a lot of room for the competition. The pack is a long way back: Old Mutual Group (Nedbank, SA Mutual, Barlow Rand and CGS Food) comes in third, with two other insurance groups, SANLAM and Liberty Life, trailing far behind. Although these figures do include some double counting of assets, this can be justified since each part of a group can operate separately, borrowing money 'independently' to gear up, for example, for an assault on the stock market.

The picture is essentially one of a relatively small economy with three main pillars: the state, the three insurance-based groups which slug it out with each other, and Anglo. Small wonder then that Anglo is the final arbiter in the private sector and that the Oppenheimers inspire awe in their own community.

2

The Oppenheimer Dynasty

It is twenty years since Harry F. Oppenheimer, at the time in his mid-fifties, was credited with being one of the ten richest men in the world, along with Paul Getty, Howard Hughes, Daniel Ludwig and the man who invented the Polaroid camera, Dr Edwin Lang.[1] Oppenheimer was not only a shrewd businessman blessed with an inheritance of the richest goldfields in the world. In his time he has been an opposition MP and an apparently staunch opponent of apartheid policies; an ex-officio international apologist for the slow pace of reform; and a surrogate diplomat for American, British and South African interests in black Africa. He has friends and relatives in the highest echelons of American finance and politics, as well as in the aristocratic oligarchies of the City of London.

Anglo – the accepted shorthand for the group – has never lacked influential friends, ever since Harry's father Ernest founded the company in 1917 with the help of a mining financier who was later to become the president of the United States, one Herbert C. Hoover. British knights litter the boardrooms of Oppenheimer's principal companies, and both British and French branches of the Rothschild family are represented on the board of De Beers. Both Oppenheimer's father, Ernest, and his uncle, Bernhard, were knighted for their services to the British Empire in the First World War; and when Sir Ernest visited London for

his seventy-seventh birthday there was lunch at Bucking-
ham Palace. The Royal Family and the Oppenheimers, by
chance, share the same stockbrokers, Rowe & Pitman; in
1984 Anglo added a special sheen to its tiara by taking a
substantial stake in the firm before it merged into Mercury
Securities in 1986, one of the big financial services groups
gearing up for the deregulation of the City of London.
Whether in Washington or Africa, Harry Oppenheimer is
received by heads of state. He travels in a private Gulf-
stream jet. Visiting VIPs to Johannesburg invariably end up
at his table. On the evening before the British Prime
Minister Harold Macmillan made his famous 'winds of
change' speech he dined with the Oppenheimers at
Brenthurst. But whenever the winds threatened to blow
down to the Cape, it was Harry Oppenheimer, more than
anyone else, who repeatedly came to the rescue of the South
African state in its most beleaguered times.

Control of his vast organisation rests ultimately with a
handful of individuals, the board members of a small
private company registered in Johannesburg under the
name E. Oppenheimer and Son. It is through this company, set up by Sir Ernest in 1935, that the family and its
friends has maintained its unchallenged position. The
family directors are Harry, his son Nicky, his British
cousin, Sir Philip Oppenheimer, the American Henry
(Hank) Slack, the third husband of Harry's only daughter,
Mary, and her first husband, the ex-Lions Scottish rugby
player, Gordon Waddell, until he left the country. Then
there are the trusted colleagues. Julian Ogilvie Thompson is
the son of a former chief justice of South Africa and
chairman of De Beers. He joined the Anglo London office
in 1956, fresh from Oxford University as a Rhodes scholar
with a degree in politics, philosophy and economics. Gavin
Relly, the chairman of the Anglo American Corporation
who steered the group's interests in Zambia, Canada and
New York, has been an Anglo man for close on forty years.
Sir Albert Robinson, a former United Party MP, ran JCI
until Waddell was ready for the job. Grey Fletcher was a
troopleader colleague of Harry's from the South African 4th

Armoured Cars. Murray Hofmeyr, who succeeded Waddell as chairman of JCI in 1987, was another Rhodes scholar at Oxford, where he earned a double blue for rugby and cricket. He worked with Relly in Zambia in the 1960s before becoming chairman of Anglo's London arm, Charter Consolidated. Sidney Spiro, another former chairman of Charter, was a long-standing member of the AAC executive committee and still sits on the Minorco board. Like Hank Slack, Minorco's president, Ogilvie Thompson and Relly both spent some time as Harry's personal assistant and are considered to be part of the 'family'. Only Mary takes no active part in the running of the business. Within the select circle there is a more powerful inner cabinet that takes the most sensitive and important decisions: Relly, Ogilvie Thompson, Slack, Hofmeyr, Nicky and, to a decreasing degree, Harry Oppenheimer himself.

This then is the Oppenheimer dynasty, as powerful and tightly knit as anything to be found in the oilfields and haciendas of Texas. The key to the family's control and its personal wealth lies in the relationship between E. Oppenheimer and Son and the two core companies of the group, the Anglo American Corporation of South Africa Limited (AAC) and De Beers Consolidated Mines, which has run the formidable diamond cartel for three-quarters of a century. AAC and De Beers own just over a third of each other's interests, while E. Oppenheimer and Son owns about 8.2 per cent of AAC's shares, an unknown amount of De Beers and 6.5 per cent of the group's international investment company, Minorco, which is nominally based in Bermuda. The family firm also has the right to exercise a 5 per cent option on any new business. The exact holdings of E. Oppenheimer and Son are a secret as closely guarded as South Africa's nuclear capacity or its oil trade. But they could be worth billions of dollars.

Within South African society, or at least the white, English-speaking part of it, the Oppenheimers enjoy a status verging on the regal. Their births, marriages and deaths are an endless source of media fascination. During the 1950s, Johannesburg newspapers would solemnly

announce: 'Mrs Harry Oppenheimer will leave Johannesburg for London on Friday, January 18, by Sabena to take
her two children back to school.'[2] Johannesburg Whites
will long remember Mary's first wedding in 1965, when a
riot took place among the thousands of people fighting for a
glimpse of the young bride, fresh from her debutante
season in London. There were 500 bottles of champagne for
the 1,000 guests, not one of whom was an African. The only
non-White, apart from a couple of black journalists, was
Mrs Violet Padayachi of Durban, an Indian social-worker
friend of Mary's, who lent a safe touch of exoticism with her
resplendent sari. Friends of Mary say that she wanted to
invite some of her associates on the executive committee of
Union Artists, a group which promoted black theatre. Her
father disapproved; he did not want to cause any 'controversy'.[3] Harry's present to his son-in-law was a Maserati
sports coupé, the first such car in Africa.

The family have always spent their wealth with tasteful
ostentation. For the sixtieth birthday of Bridget, Harry's
wife, in 1981, 450 invitations were sent out in her racing
colours of black and yellow; their horses had carried off
some of the classics of the South African turf. The Peter
Duchin band was flown in from New York for the occasion
and played in a marquee on Mary's country estate; the
band's normal nightly fee was $10,000. Taking tea with
Mrs Oppenheimer in the 1960s was a gracious business.
Gibson, one of the twelve black indoor staff (not including
the housemaids), would lay the table with lace and silver,
dressed in white with a scarlet shoulder sash. Two other
servants, similarly dressed, would clear away afterwards.
The atmosphere was redolent of Empire, the same which
can still be found today in certain British ambassadorial
residences in the Third World. The servants, of course, are
treated with punctilious politeness.

Although originally Jewish from Germany and living in
South Africa, the Oppenheimers liked to consider themselves quintessentially English. Indeed, half the family –
Ernest and his brothers – took British nationality when they
first arrived in London in the late nineteenth century, hence

their eligibility to receive knighthoods. In the 1930s Sir Ernest quietly converted to Anglicanism, as did a number of his Jewish contemporaries in order to conform with the prevailing culture of the anglophile Randlords. Both business and family relations became entwined with the English aristocracy, which often led to some bizarre, if remote connections. Sir Ernest's nephew, Sir Michael Oppenheimer, married a daughter of Sir Robert Harvey, whose second daughter married Baron Balfour of Inchrye, a Conservative MP and a junior minister for air during the war. (Balfour's second marriage was with the sister of John Profumo, the secretary of state for war whose political career ended with a spy scandal in the early 1960s.) After Sir Michael's death his widow, Caroline (Ina), married Sir Ernest, and Sir Michael's son married a daughter of another Conservative MP, Sir Hugh Veer Huntly Duff Lucas-Tooth. There was something contagious about the breed. Ogilvie Thompson married into the family of Viscount Hampden, a judicious choice of father-in-law as he happened to be managing director of the merchant bankers, Lazard Brothers, a close Anglo friend. On the business side some of the blue bloods of the city's old-boy network joined Anglo. Esmond Baring, related to the bankers, Baring Brothers, joined the company in London after a spell at Rowe & Pitman in 1951. Esmond's son Oliver, a partner in R&P, had Harry Oppenheimer as a godfather. Another R&P partner, Hughie Smith, the son of Lord Bicester of Morgan Grenfell, one of Anglo's bankers, joined in Johannesburg. One can begin to understand that the credit-worthiness of the Oppenheimers in the City was not just based on the lucre beneath the high veld on the Witwatersrand.

The most admired qualities of British life were those which had built and sustained the Empire. They were replete with apparent contradictions. A certain arrogance was tempered with a studied modesty; courtesy masked ruthless self-interest; a patronising élitism was disguised with conviviality. The ethos, above all, was that of the English public school.

Both Harry and his heir Nicky followed the celebrated
route of Charterhouse and Harrow respectively, then on to
Christ Church, Oxford. While the very rich went to
England, the merely wealthy were catered for at home.
Ever since the 1840s, South Africa had Anglican schools
modelled on the great English institutions, and ever since
the discovery of gold in 1886 the mining houses have been
their main source of funds.[4] In the 1950s, Harry Oppenheimer donated £7,500 for a new sixth-form block at
Michaelhouse, the leading Anglican school in Natal. W. D.
Wilson, a former AAC deputy chairman, was an old boy
and a member of the Michaelhouse Trust. Highbury, the
old preparatory school in Natal, received 15,000 rand from
the Anglo American Chairman's Fund in 1969. The Sir
Ernest Oppenheimer Trust gave 30,000 rand to Waterkloof
House preparatory school in Pretoria. In 1962, Kearsney
College in Natal opened its science laboratories, the Oppen-
heimer Building. A year later, Anglo financed a new
Anglican school at Welkom primarily for the children of
white employees on the Free State gold mines.

The church schools and their national organisations were
notoriously exclusive and conservative. Jewish and Roman
Catholic schools were treated with suspicion and disdain
and it was not until the 1970s that they were allowed as
observers to the two main coordinating bodies, the Head-
masters' Conference and the Association of Private Schools
(APS). In 1976, the APS confirmed that member schools
should provide Christian teaching and worship, continuing
the exclusion of the twenty-three Jewish schools, though
allowing Catholic ones to qualify. Senior Anglo executives
such as W. D. Wilson and M. C. O'Dowd were leading
lights in the formation of the APS in 1974 and Wilson and
Harry Oppenheimer inspired the formation of the Industrial Fund, which improved science facilities and financed
study trips to England for teachers. It was not until the
1970s that black pupils were allowed into the schools. The
Catholic schools took the initiative in the Cape, Natal and
even the Boer heartland of the Transvaal, where the
authorities consistently rejected all black applications for

admission; they simply ignored the law. For the Anglican schools, agonising about the morality of denying multi-racialism yet wanting to preserve their white cultural identity, the process took much longer and with a few exceptions they still remain predominantly white.

The Oxford connection, however, remains the strongest at Anglo. In 1984, six of its eight divisional heads were Rhodes scholars. Senior executives display a remarkable degree of uniformity and, like Harry Oppenheimer, have managed to excise all but a hint of their South African accent. Only half in jest, Gavin Relly says: 'We did have occasionally the odd itinerant Cambridge man. They didn't stay for very long.'[5]

Relly himself illustrates another Anglo practice which derives from the clubbiness of the group. Appalled by the Nationalist Party victory in 1948, he decided to work for the opposition United Party: 'I must say not from any vast conviction that that was the way to spend one's life, but I didn't know what to do next.'[6] Working for the UP leader Sir Villiers Graaff, he met Anglo's Albert Robinson at a political meeting. Learning of Relly's uncertainty about a career, Robinson invited him to have lunch with Harry Oppenheimer, then a rising MP in the United Party. A month later Oppenheimer sent him a letter inviting him to see the company secretary in Johannesburg, a man whom Relly recalls was most unpleasant. Nevertheless, he started work in the records department for £17 a month and by the end of 1950 was working as Harry Oppenheimer's personal political assistant. Relly's current personal assistant, a young graduate from the Sorbonne, was recruited in almost exactly the same way. An Anglo director suggested over dinner that he call by the personnel department the following Monday. When he did, he was met by the personnel director.

The Oppenheimer management philosophy strives to be unobtrusive. It sees the group in terms of interests it can control, rather than in the formal relationships to be found in other corporate balance sheets. In most multinationals there is an explicit chain of command from the top down.

This is not the case with Anglo. Only at the highest levels of managment does it operate as an integrated whole, based at AAC headquarters at 44 Main Street, Johannesburg. All major group investment decisions originate or must be approved here by the inner cabinet. For AAC, decisions are then endorsed by the fifteen-man executive committee which meets every Tuesday and Thursday. Until his retirement from Anglo American in 1982, and from De Beers in 1984, Harry Oppenheimer, like his father, held an autocratic power of veto and initiative. He still remains a director of De Beers and his advice is regularly sought on important decisions. Below, there is a disguised power structure with day-to-day management coming from executives in apparently separate companies. The resulting effect is broadly the same as in any other multinational, though the appearance is very different.

An example from the gold mines will give a good indication of the complexity of the system. Western Areas in the Far West Rand is administered by Johannesburg Consolidated Investment (JCI), which has a direct holding of only 6.4 per cent. Anglo's gold investment company, Amgold (48.6 per cent owned by AAC), holds 2.5 per cent of its shares. AAC directly has 2.2. per cent. A company called Elsburg Gold Mining has a 48.7 per cent stake, but Elsburg is 26.6 per cent owned by JCI and 10.6 per cent by AAC and Amgold. The majority of the other investors, as with all the gold mines, are spread out among Americans, Europeans and South Africans. In formal AAC terms, Western Areas is strictly investment; in reality it is controlled and managed by the group.

The system of hidden control extends from gold into industry and commerce. As long as the separate companies – called associates – perform well, then Anglo takes a back seat and reaps the dividends. When they are in danger of foundering, or when the group goes on an acquisition binge, then the awesome might of the empire's financial strength is rapidly unveiled.

The question of the succession to Harry Oppenheimer is still not resolved. He had the foresight to set up an inner cabinet to replace his autocratic rule and to ensure continuity of family control whatever the abilities of his son. The advantage of the present system is that it obviates the need for the direct heir to run the business in the same overt fashion and Nicky has yet to demonstrate the tough ambition that would project him into the hot seat. Gavin Relly, who took over the Anglo chair in 1982, expects to remain there for several years. When he does leave, it is likely that Ogilvie Thompson, a few years his junior, will succeed him. Then it could be Nicky Oppenheimer's turn, if he wants it. Given current political developments in South Africa, however, it is a moot point whether he will be celebrating the centenary in 2017.

3
Early Days

As a well-connected German Jew who had become a naturalised Briton, Ernest Oppenheimer was not at first sight destined for great things in South Africa. He had all the characteristics likely to cause resentment and envy among the white population. He arrived on the diamond fields of Kimberley in November 1902, five months after the end of the bitterly fought Boer War which brought the Afrikaner republics of the Orange Free State and the Transvaal into the British Empire. Although Kimberley, in the Cape Colony, was anglophile, rural Afrikaners disliked the foreign mining capitalists who were threatening to take over economic power.

Added to the militant trade unionism and racism of the white mine-workers from Europe was a strain of anti-Semitism that caricatured the many German Jewish mining magnates as 'Hoggenheimer' – a name actually derived from a musical comedy that came from London in the same year. In that production, its connotations were of the reputation which the earlier Randlords had acquired as greedy exploiters of workers and political manipulators of governments. In London they flaunted their enormous wealth, with grand houses in Park Lane and Belgravia, while their black miners were corralled in compounds and treated little better than animals. Foremost among these Randlords was Cecil Rhodes, the man who amalgamated the diamond mines into the powerful De Beers company and set up the diamond-selling syndicate in London which has controlled the world's market ever since. To his many enemies, who considered him no more than a cynical opportunist, he was also the man who engineered the fiasco of the Jameson Raid into the gold-rich Transvaal republic in 1895. As the Prime Minister of the Cape Colony, he also lent his support to the notorious Masters and Servants Act, commonly known as the 'Every Man to Wallop his Own Nigger Bill'.[1] In South Africa the silk-hatted bloated character of Hoggenheimer, with strong Semitic features, came over the years to personify the hated capitalist in both communist and later nationalist socialist propaganda. Although the name was not initially aimed at Oppenheimer, as the family rose to their pre-eminent position in the diamond and gold business it was to stick to them for decades.

Despite these obstacles, the Oppenheimer empire grew and prospered. For, at every critical point in the rise of Anglo, the Oppenheimers and the South African state co-operated in each other's survival. Like distracted lovers, they may not have always enjoyed each other's company but they were bonded by inseparable interests. The power of the white mine-workers was bloodily curtailed by the state, a plentiful and disciplined supply of cheap non-White labour was organised, the hostility towards foreign capital was overcome and gradually the Afrikaner was drawn into the mainstream of industrial growth. Even the Nationalist victory of 1948 and the consolidation of apartheid – already well advanced – did not impede the progress.

Ernest Oppenheimer had a head start when he arrived in Kimberley at the age of 22, to run the office of the London diamond-buying firm of A. Dunkelsbuhler. It was all in the family. They were part of the general Jewish exodus from the turbulence and growing anti-Semitism in Central Europe that led to the wider diaspora in New York, London and Johannesburg. Oppenheimer's older brothers Louis and Bernhard had been working on the diamond fields more than a decade earlier for their cousin by marriage, Anton Dunkelsbuhler. Louis had been the firm's Kimberley representative and soon became a partner. Bernhard had signed the 1890 diamond syndicate agreement on behalf of Dunkelsbuhler, which created in London the first efforts at setting up the world diamond cartel.

Ernest came from a large family of six boys and four girls. His father Eduard was a prosperous cigar merchant, descended from a Jewish family in Reichenbach, now in East Germany near Karl Marx Stadt, where his great-grandfather Baer Loew Oppenheimer was president of the Jewish community and the only Jewish property-owner to be exempted from land and property taxes.[2] At the time of Ernest's birth, the family had lived in Friedberg near Frankfurt for many years, but the income from cigars could not sustain such a large family. At an early age the children were obliged to find their fortunes elsewhere. Bernhard left home at 13, and at the age of 16 in 1896 Ernest went to London to be apprenticed in Dunkelsbuhler's office. By the turn of the century, five brothers were in London and all working in the diamond business. Ernest and Otto were both sorting diamonds at Dunkelsbuhler's and Louis was a senior partner in the firm. Gustav had arrived for a brief spell in the industry and Bernhard had moved on to handle the diamond interests of the family firm of Lewis and Marks. Then there was another first cousin, Gustav Imroth, an employee of Dunkelsbuhler who went on to become the head of the JCI before it was absorbed into the group. Of all the brothers Ernest's relationship was closest with Louis, ten years his senior, who stayed in London to manage first the family's diamond interests and then its copper mines in Rhodesia.

*   *   *   *   *

Kimberley, at the turn of the century, had been transformed from a rough, shanty mining settlement into a substantial town of 10,000 people, with several fine public buildings, theatres, well-kept white suburbs and its own golf course. But it was still a company town, dependent on the employment and benefaction of De Beers, the leading diamond-producing company. In Ernest's first year it was recovering from the shock of the death in March 1902 of Cecil Rhodes, who had been associated with the town for thirty years. Ernest first lodged with the London syndicate's main representative, Fritz Hirschhorn, a director of De Beers, and yet another cousin on his mother's side.

A quiet and industrious young man, Ernest quickly made his mark on Kimberley society and the diamond world, having already chosen a wife with auspicious London society connections. In June 1906 he married Mary (May) Pollak, the daughter of a wealthy London stockbroker and a past president of the London Stock Exchange. Joseph Pollak lived in one of London's most exclusive streets; his mansion in Kensington Palace Gardens is now the embassy of the Royal Nepalese government. The couple had met at the wedding of Ernest's brother Louis and May's older sister, Charlotte. In 1908, the year that May presented Ernest with an heir, Harold Friederich, he was elected to Kimberley council. Frank was born two years later. In 1912, when the town achieved the status of an Anglican cathedral city, he became the mayor.

Meanwhile, the fortunes of A. Dunkelsbuhler were thriving. The company, on Ernest's advice, had taken a substantial stake in one of the new diamond finds, the Premier mine. In 1905 it formed a close association with Consolidated Mines Selection (CMS), one of the handful of early mining finance houses. CMS had interests throughout the British Empire, but its main potential lay in the mineral rights it owned on the Far East Rand, where gold had been discovered deep below the surface. It was first found in boreholes by the Transvaal Coal Trust and, although there were doubts about the expense of developments, CMS bought up Trust properties and opened two small mines.

By that time, too, the system of recruitment and supply of African mine labour that was to serve the mine-owners so well for the next fifty years was firmly in place. In 1913, the Chamber of Mines, set up in 1889 by the mining houses to guarantee a regular supply of low-cost labour, finally established control inside South Africa, as well as in Mozambique and the three high-commission territories of Bechuanaland, Basutoland and Swaziland. The Chamber's success was achieved with the help of Generals Louis Botha and Jan Smuts, the leaders of the Transvaal colonial government after the Boer War, and of the Union after 1910, when South Africa was united within the British Empire.

The generals, formerly Boer guerrilla commanders, were not, however, entirely accommodating to mining interests, since they were caught between conflicting ideologies and interests. After the Boer War, they had reconciled themselves to the British connection and wanted to heal the rift between the Afrikaners and the English-speakers. They also had to balance the interests of the powerful and militant white miners and the mine-owners. With the shortage of labour worsening as more mines were sunk, the white miners wanted a rigid job colour bar to protect their skilled jobs. Anxious to keep wage costs down, the owners on the other hand wanted to be able to introduce non-Whites to some lower-skilled jobs. For its part the government had to ensure that revenue from the mines was sustained and balanced against the needs of Afrikaner farmers, who were also competing in the same labour market.

A combination of administrative and legislative measures provided an uneasy compromise. The mine-owners reluctantly paid high taxes and were obliged to tolerate a government inspectorate overseeing the conditions of the mine labour compounds. After a white miners' strike in 1907, the Transvaal government agreed to a fixed ratio of 'civilised labour' to black labourers. In addition, the Union government regulated wages and prohibited the poaching of African workers by other mining companies. But, most significantly, the Native Land Act of 1913 gave legal effect to the confinement of Africans in 8.8 per cent of the land, establishing the permanent labour reserves that were later institutionalised as the bantustans. Finally, the Pass Laws regulated the entry of Africans into 'white areas' to work. The relationship between these measures was far from settled, but at the outbreak of the First World War the big mining houses were poised for their next great leap forward.

Ironically, the hostility felt towards Germany by South Africa's empire loyalists provided one impetus for the creation of the Anglo American Corporation. From the outbreak of the war, Oppenheimer was the victim of a growing campaign against his German origins, even though he showed his loyalty to the Crown by helping to raise a second battalion of the Kimberley Regiment. One handbill distributed around the town carried a story from the *Rand Daily Mail* entitled 'Lesson in Manners for Mr Oppenheimer'.[3] It reported the resignation of the German-born mayor of Coventry. The U-boat attack on the liner *Lusitania* off the coast of Ireland in 1915, with the resultant loss of 1,300 lives, persuaded Ernest Oppenheimer to resign. During the anti-German riots that broke out in Kimberley, the police had to protect the Oppenheimer home from an angry mob. Oppenheimer's car was stoned. He decided to evacuate his wife and their two sons to Cape Town and a few weeks later the whole family embarked for London.

It was not long before Ernest was back again in South Africa. There were pressing matters to be dealt with. CMS, with one-third of its shares in German hands and with four German directors on its board, was coming under attack in South Africa and in the British press; there was a possibility that the Custodian of Enemy Property would take the company over. Oppenheimer returned to Johannesburg with the intention of disposing of the CMS assets, but its holdings on the potentially rich deep levels on the Far East Rand convinced him otherwise. The CMS board agreed to Oppenheimer's taking a half-share in any new ventures in the area. Although he could have relied on capital from Dunkelsbuhler, he decided that such a huge investment called for money from abroad.

The way in which the Anglo American Corporation was put together gives a graphic insight into the far-flung connections the Oppenheimers had already cultivated. Ernest's first move was to contact William L. Honnold, a former American managing director of CMS, who had gone back to the US in 1915 and was active in fund-raising on behalf of the American Commission for the Relief of Belgium. Having long been enthusiastic about the potential of the Far East Rand, he readily agreed to help. He approached the Commission's chairman, a man with lengthy experience of mining as an engineer, Herbert C. Hoover.

When Hoover and Oppenheimer met in London to discuss the plan, Ernest was accompanied by his friend Henry Hull, the Minister of Finance in Botha's first cabinet. Hoover was sold the idea and together with Honnold arranged for the finance. Back in South Africa, Hull and Oppenheimer explained their plan to Smuts, who had reservations about the Americans moving in for a fat profit. He was much assured by the fact that Oppenheimer intended to register the company in South Africa, rather than in London like all the other houses. There was a slight problem about the name originally proposed: Honnold disliked 'African American Corporation' because he felt it 'would suggest on this side our dark-skinned fellow countrymen and possibly result in ridicule'.[4]

The Anglo American Corporation of South Africa Limited was eventually formed in September 1917 with an issued capital of £1 million. Its board and shareholders were a heavyweight affair. William B. Thompson was the founder of the giant American mining combine, the Newmont Mining Corporation. C. Hamilton Sabin of the important US group, Guaranty Trust, represented the interests of another major shareholder, the J. P. Morgan banking firm of New York. From the National Bank of South Africa came an MP, Hugh Crawford. With General Smuts' blessing, Hull took his seat and Ernest Oppenheimer made up the six.

There were, in addition, committees in London and New York which included Louis Oppenheimer and several CMS directors. Ernest had set out his ambitions for the new company a few months earlier, in a letter to Honnold in May 1917:

The first object I have in view is to secure for our company a fair share in the business offering on the Far Eastern Rand. Once this is accomplished I shall steadily pursue the course of bringing about an amalgamation of Mines Selection and Rand Selection with our own company. We have already travelled some considerable distance towards an amalgamation between Mines and Rand Selections. . . . Taking all the facts into account it does not seem too optimistic to think . . . that we shall be able, within a reasonable time, to bring about a willing combination of the three Eastern Rand holding companies, which would straightaway make us the most important gold group in Johannesburg.

There is, moreover, no reason why our new company should not grow in other directions than in gold development. It may for instance be possible for our company eventually to play a part in the diamond world. What South Africa wants [for diamonds] is enterprise and money and I believe our new company will supply both.[5]

The amalgamation did take place, although Ernest Oppenheimer nearly did not live to see the day. On a trip from London to South Africa in the closing days of the war, he was aboard the liner *Galway Castle* when it was struck by a U-boat torpedo two days out of Plymouth. He and the other survivors in his lifeboat were picked up at nightfall by a British destroyer.

Once back in Johannesburg, Oppenheimer continued with his grand plan, though it was another ten years before he achieved hs ambition of being the King of Diamonds.

Anglo American was still a relatively junior-ranking mining house. The Oppenheimer axis of AAC, Consolidated Mines Selection and Rand Selection had a combined paid-up share capital of £1.4 million. The three giants, Central Mining/Rand Mines, the Barnato Brothers group and Consolidated Gold Fields, each had over £4.2 million. All four, which were to play an important part in the

opening of the new goldfields, began with diamond money.
Consolidated Gold Fields was launched by Cecil Rhodes.
Central Mining was the gold-mining legacy of two of the
most famous Randlords, Alfred Beit and Julius Wernher,
who died in 1906 and 1912 respectively. Their diamond
interests were taken over by the firm of L. Breitmeyer,
whose representative in South Africa was Oppenheimer's
cousin and De Beers director, Fritz Hirschhorn. Oppenheimer's relentless assault on De Beers and the London
syndicate was finally to estrange him from the man who had
welcomed him to Kimberley fifteen years before. Barnato
Brothers, on the other hand, turned out to be an ally. This
group was in the hands of Solly Joel, the nephew of the
legendary Barney Barnato. Born Barnet Isaacs, the son of a
second-hand clothes dealer from London's East End,
Barney became one of the first four life directors of De
Beers Consolidated Mines. After Barnato's suicide in 1897
(by throwing himself overboard from a mail steamer), Solly
Joel was the pre-eminent diamond man. When AAC was
formed he was the largest shareholder in the three main
diamond producers – De Beers, Premier and Jagersfontein
– as well as having substantial gold interests in Johannesburg Consolidated Investment.

Oppenheimer's first coup against the elderly De Beers
monopoly was to buy up all the rights to the rich alluvial
deposits in South West Africa, which the League of Nations
had given to South Africa to administer. For this, he
needed his two main props again: the South African
government and the Americans. Both were amenable.

Oppenheimer's contact with Smuts had grown into a
friendship, and he was invited to go with the general to the
Versailles peace conference. Approached by the invaluable
Hull, Botha also had no objection, although a clause in the
contract stipulated that the new company, Consolidated
Diamond Mines (CDM), operate 'with due and proper
regard to the interests of the Union Goverment and of the
Territory of South West Africa'.[6] J. P. Morgan, as well as
the family firm A. Dunkelsbuhler, helped raise much of the
£3.8 million capital. The acquisition was a major coup, for

CDM was producing 16 per cent of world output. On the strength of its combined interests, in 1919 Anglo American was made a senior partner in the London selling sydicate. This success was not made without creating family rancour. Fritz Hirschhorn deeply resented Anglo's intervention. Despite Oppenheimer's attempts to placate the old man, Hirschhorn never forgave him, and there was more bitterness to come. Oppenheimer's objective of breaking the De Beers control of the syndicate and making himself King of Diamonds was undiminished. In his scheme of things, family sentimentality and loyalty had no place. His ambitions, however, had to wait on other pressing developments on the gold mines.

Working costs on the mines had increased by a third between 1917 and 1920, and the Chamber of Mines decided that the only way to deal with critically narrow margins was to cut white miners' wages and to use Africans in jobs otherwise reserved for Whites. Smuts sided with the Chamber, and in 1922 the white miners responded with the Rand Revolt. Hundreds of them were killed in the artillery and aeroplane bombardments that Smuts launched against them. It was, in the event, a pyrrhic victory. The strikers' political allies, the Nationalist and Labour parties, came together in the general election of 1924 to form the first government systematically to entrench white privilege at the expense of the black majority. The authoritarian police state of modern apartheid was in the making.

Sir Ernest Oppenheimer, who had been knighted in 1921 for his early recruiting efforts in Kimberley, was elected as a member of Smuts' South African Party, representing the town that had so violently rejected him nine years earlier. For the next ten years, Oppenheimer maintained an uneasy relationship with the Nationalists in government. There was talk within Nationalist circles about a state take-over of the diamond and gold mines. Yet by the late 1930s Oppenheimer had completely taken over De Beers and the London marketing syndicate; Anglo massively increased its interests in the gold mines which were making huge profits, and new, even richer finds were on the horizon in the

Orange Free State. In addition, the company expanded its operations in industry and mining throughout southern Africa. Such hostility as existed across the floor of the South African parliament never seriously restricted Anglo's growth.

Oppenheimer's vaunting ambition to impose an iron grip on the diamond business was achieved within five years. To his stake in the London syndicate and the CDM mine in South West Africa he added the right to market stones from Angola, the Congo and West Africa with Barnato Brothers as a partner. When in 1925 the syndicate refused to increase CDM's annual producers' quota of 21 per cent, Oppenheimer withdrew, taking with him Solly Joel. Together the two men made a bid for the entire production of De Beers through a new and rival syndicate which included Oppenheimer's reliable backers, J. P. Morgan in New York and Morgan Grenfell in London. In the next year Oppenheimer's strengthened interests won him a seat on the De Beers board. It was another humiliation for Fritz Hirschhorn.

The South African government had been watching these unstable developments with increasing concern. It introduced the Diamond Control Act, with wide powers to take over the sale and production of diamonds. The intention was to use these powers only as a last resort if the producers could not agree on their quotas. The industry as a whole was horrified and launched a fierce attack. But Oppenheimer used more diplomatic tactics. As an opposition MP he was able to secure an amendment which ensured that, in any dispute, preference would be given to producers registered in South Africa.

In the following three years the pressures on De Beers and the diamond syndicate increased. The discovery of alluvial diamonds in Lichtenberg in the Western Transvaal and then in Namaqualand on the bleak Atlantic coast of the Western Cape drove prices down, since the diggers who rushed there were supported by the Nationalist government of Hertzog. Many of the diggers were Afrikaners and in legislation the interests of the 'small man' were protected.

Hertzog also created state diggings and proposed a South African diamond-cutting industry, which was seen as a threat to the syndicate's control of marketing through a single, European channel. Oppenheimer's answer was a proposal to rationalise the entire industry, from point of production in South Africa to selling in London. Members of the Syndicate were sympathetic, as well as some of the more forward-thinking members of the De Beers board. In London, Oppenheimer secured the support of the Rothschild group and in December 1929, two months after the Wall Street crash drove the world into depression, the board of De Beers finally capitulated to his demand for the chair. At the end of the month, Fritz Hirschhorn resigned.

The new chairman's initial task was to reorganise the whole business. First, Anglo American's controlling interest in CDM and Solly Joel's holding in the Jagersfontein mine were transferred to De Beers in return for De Beers shares, giving Anglo control of De Beers, which also had a controlling interest in the other main producer, Premier. The syndicate, with its stocks and contracts to buy South African production, was replaced in London by the Diamond Corporation, with Oppenheimer as chairman. The Corporation, then controlled by De Beers, Anglo and Dunkelsbuhler, was given the power to buy diamonds from all other sources. The grand design of Cecil Rhodes, De Beers' first chairman, had been completed and the stage was set for Ernest Oppenheimer to show that he could take on a hostile government and win.

The Depression had made it more and more difficult to sell diamonds, both as jewellery and in industry. The stockpile was growing fast, and De Beers was running out of cash. Production had to be cut back. Oppenheimer warned that the whole industry would collapse unless the mines were closed. The South African government protested, not least because of the unemployment such a move would cause among white miners. Oppenheimer brought over De Beers directors from London to argue the case. Adrian Fourie, the Minister of Mines, was unimpressed:

We have had the spectacle in South Africa that there is one man who is chairman of all the producing companies in South Africa, that the same man is chairman of the Diamond Corporation. He alone is the centre of the whole diamond industry and, moreover, he advocates his own case in this House. The fact is that the Hon. Member for Kimberley can juggle, manipulate and deal with all the diamonds he pleases, and all the men whom he brings over from overseas amount to nothing, because he turns them all round his thumb. It is necessary for the government to take this great industry under its protection and that the interests of the public in general should not be lost sight of.[7]

Oppenheimer ignored the protests, and deep-mine production throughout South Africa was closed down in March 1932. Fourie set up a commission to investigate the industry. Anglo contemptuously refused to give evidence, and the commission was withdrawn.

Oppenheimer's ability to disregard the government was based on several interconnecting factors. In the first place, South African English capitalists, although seen as a threat by sections of the Afrikaners, were the main source of government revenues. The gold mines contributed one-third. When South Africa eventually followed Britain off the gold standard in 1932, gold profits and state revenues sharply increased.

Secondly, as a member of Smuts' opposition South African Party, the second largest party in the House, Oppenheimer had considerable influence at the political centre. He was the party's frontbench spokesman on mining finance. In 1933, as the Depression deepened, General Hertzog, the Nationalist prime minister, and Smuts formed a coalition to create a united white response to the economic difficulties and to push ahead with legislation, requiring a two-thirds majority, to protect white jobs from black competition. A year later the coalition was formalised into the United Party, with 19 Nationalist MPs staying on the opposition benches for their long haul to government in

1948. Oppenheimer stayed in parliament, though without portfolio, until 1938. His lack of office, however, was no disability. The appointment of a new Minister of Mines, sympathetic to Anglo, resulted in the government and the administration of South West Africa joining De Beers in a producers' association which took a half-interest in the London Diamond Corporation. Until the Nationalist electoral victory of 1948, Anglo had few quibbles with South African government policies and the stigma of 'Hoggenheimer' was not a serious threat. Although anti-Semitism was rife among poorer Afrikaners, much influenced by events in Germany, leading Nationalists had so far resisted it. General Hertzog stated in 1929: 'Where it concerned nationalism, love of people, hatred of oppression, the Jew and the Afrikaner always stood together.'[8] Even Dr D. F. Malan, one of the hard-line Afrikaners who later identified with the Nazi cause, was saying in 1930: 'I think the people of South Africa, generally, belonging to all parties and sections, desire to give to the Jewish people in this country full equality in every respect . . . full participation in our national life, and I am glad to say that we are still in that position today in South Africa to appreciate, and appreciate very highly, what the Jews have done for South Africa.'[9]

Finally, although Ernest Oppenheimer and the Chamber of Mines wanted the job colour bar to be relaxed, other measures ensured that they had a plentiful supply of cheap black migrant labour from neighbouring African countries. The control and suppression of the black working class was a crucial development in the separation of the races and in keeping labour costs down. Oppenheimer shared the general white view, prevalent as much in ruling circles in London as in Johannesburg, that the African needed to be 'civilised' before he or she could take part in responsible society. Political participation by Africans was not even contemplated. There were few, among them a handful of white trade unionists, who departed from an acceptance of racism and the efforts of the Nationalist-Labour government, between 1924 and 1933, entrenched White privilege. Some of the legislation irked the mine-owners; some of it assisted them. In the end, both the mine-owners and the government benefited, at the expense of the Africans. A black African, the 1922 Stallard Commission stipulated, should only be in the towns in order to 'minister to the needs of the white man and should depart therefrom when he ceases to minister'.[10]

The first priority was to exclude Blacks from skilled jobs. The government's 'civilised' labour policy absorbed Whites into the state sectors such as the railways, replacing non-White workers. The Job Reservation Act and the Mines and Work Act of 1926 made certain categories of work for Whites only. Through the Industrial Conciliation Act of 1924, the legalised trade unions could exclude Africans, Indians and Coloureds by the closed shop and control of entry to apprenticeships. In some of the newer light industries, white unions insisted, in order to protect their own job security, that non-Whites should be paid the rate for the job. Others co-opted non-Whites for different reasons, as the secretary of the Typographical Union explained:

> Up to 1927 we refused to have Indians in the Typographical Union. They then commenced negotiating separately, and eventually eliminated the European printer from the Natal. We then took them into our union to stop that. The result is . . . they have been almost eliminated. That happened because we took them into the union. But when they were separate, they practically eliminated us. That tells a story.[11]

The 1925 Customs Tariff Act made it a condition of the protection it offered that employers take on a 'reasonable proportion of civilised workers'.

Africans were more strictly curtailed in every aspect of life. The Pass Laws, which meant that Africans were obliged to carry documents giving them permission to be in 'white areas', were more rigorously enforced with fines and prison sentences. Within the towns the Urban Areas Act of 1933 curtailed the rights of residence for black people. The Native Service Contract Act of 1932 made it a criminal offence for Africans to leave the mines or farms without their employers' consent. Growing militancy by the African National Congress (formed in 1912) and a nascent black trade-union movement, unregistered but not illegal, was savagely suppressed by new powers in the Native Administration Act of 1927 and the Riotous Assemblies (Amendment) Act of 1930. The Hertzog-Smuts coalition after 1933 accelerated the process with the 1936 Land Act by which 14 per cent of the land was permanently allocated to Africans, who represented 70 per cent of the population.

The government encouraged the mine-owners to recruit further afield. Amendments to the Immigration Act allowed them to open recruitment offices north of latitude 22 degrees, a line which cuts present-day Angola and Mozambique in half. The proportion of foreign workers – about half of the 318,000 on the mines – steadily rose. Throughout the period, the wage ratio of white miners to black was 12 to 1.

★   ★   ★   ★   ★

The Oppenheimer family, meanwhile, had established themselves in the grand style of the so-called 'Randlords'. In 1924, they bought a mansion standing in fifty acres of parkland and called it Brenthurst. The two boys, Harry and Frank, went to a private school nearby and thence to Charterhouse public school in Surrey, England. In a smaller house on the estate – Little Brenthurst – Ernest Oppenheimer built up his famous library of books, manuscripts and maps. He acquired a gallery of Dutch and Flemish old masters and a couple of Goyas, although, by all accounts, his own appreciation of them was subordinate to his pleasure in showing them off to visitors. The atmosphere at Brenthurst was formal and genteel, reminiscent of the country seat of the minor English aristocracy. At home Ernest was a doting father, and when young Harry went up to university at Christ Church, Oxford, he financed his son's taste for champagne picnics in the country. He even turned up for Harry's twenty-first birthday party bringing with him his old friend General Smuts.

In the mid-1930s Ernest Oppenheimer suffered several personal tragedies. In 1934, his wife died at the age of 46 and his nephew Sir Michael, Bernhard's son, was killed in a plane crash. The following year, his own younger son Frank, who was moving up through the company after graduating from Trinity College, Oxford, drowned in a municipal lido while on a holiday in Madeira. The day after the funeral, Oppenheimer was baptised into the Christian faith. Although many Jewish financiers sought to become Anglicised through Anglicanism, Oppenheimer's specific reasons have remained a mystery. It has been argued that after the death of his wife and son he turned to the Bible for solace. Others have tentatively suggested a more cynical motive – that Germany, just like the Allies, needed diamonds for their machine tool industries and Hitler would not have traded with a Jew.[12]

Whatever the reasons for his conversion, Ernest was certainly in a state of shock and went to London, where he married Michael's widow, Ina, in 1936. Harry was one of the witnesses. (In a curious way, this marriage was typically Oppenheimer; throughout their lives both Ernest and Harry liked to bring relatives and friends into the business. The head of the Anglo American Corporation until his death in 1934 was Leslie Pollak, the brother of Ernest's first wife.)

Brenthurst, with a new young hostess, became the hub of Johannesburg high society. Bridge was the preferred game, and dinner continued to be a black-tie occasion, served on gold plate. The family car was a Rolls.

Unfailingly courteous, to the point of diffidence in public life, Ernest Oppenheimer was also uncommonly vain. He sat for numerous portraits of himself, as if he had a keen sense of his place in history, and when attacked in parliament he would pose as the South African patriot grossly maligned. When criticised for his plan to close the diamond mines during the Depression, he told the Minister of Mines: 'I look forward to the time when it can be said in the House that De Beers company under my guidance kept its people employed while everybody else retrenched. It will be some acknowledgement of what I am doing. . . . There will be some satisfaction in knowing that the Government at least says, "Here is a South African who stands up for the country and sticks to his guns and who tries to see things through."'[13] But the real businessman in him emerged when he warned about the need to cut back on production: 'I am not going to be pointed out as the chairman of De Beers company who saw it brought to bankruptcy and who kept their Europeans employed to ruin the shareholders.'[14] Like his hero Cecil Rhodes, to whom he constantly referred, Ernest Oppenheimer was an autocratic empire-builder, brushing aside, for example, shareholders' objections to the way in which he spent De Beers' profits for gold and industrial developments. In business from an early age he also exhibited Rhodes' ruthless ambition. Both men asserted, long before it was a practical reality, that they would come to control the diamond trade. Although Oppenheimer resisted the virulent racism of Rhodes (who described how Anglo-Saxons could benefit those parts of the world inhabited by 'the most despicable specimens of human beings'[15]) he did subscribe to Rhodes' theory of 'equal rights for all civilised men'. Business often kept him away from parliament; in some sessions during the late 1930s, when the government presented no threats, Oppenheimer did not make any speeches. He could be generous; he spent millions of rand on good works, not least the building of houses in the black township of Soweto.

These characteristics of both the public and the private man were reproduced in Ernest's son Harry to an uncanny degree, and, although tempered by changing attitudes to apartheid and black militancy, have remained at the centre of the Oppenheimers' philosophy and the empire they have built.

★　　★　　★　　★　　★

The war against Germany marked another watershed in Anglo's fortunes. While Harry went off to join the South African forces, fighting with the British Eighth Army in

North Africa as a brigade intelligence officer, Ernest directed the group's expansion into gold.

Prospecting in the Orange Free State had discovered a fabulously rich goldfield. Anglo at first was in a weak position, holding only minority interests in two smaller mining companies. But in the next five years Ernest went on an intensive share-buying spree. Despite opposition and competition from other mining houses, the complex system of interlocking shareholdings on which the mining industry was founded allowed him to build up substantial minority stakes.

By 1945, Anglo had taken over the two companies which held the richest deposits: SA Townships and Lewis and Marks. These provided eight of the fourteen new gold mines subsequently developed in the province, seven of them directly controlled by Anglo. The group was able to finance its acquisitions largely from its own reserves, which had increased spectacularly in the late 1930s with the recovery of the diamond business. In 1937 alone, diamond sales brought in £17.7 million.

Before Anglo could reap the benefits of the Free State, however, the questions of labour costs and black workers' militancy had to be dealt with.

During the war, working profits on the mines declined. Inflation pushed up the costs of manufactured goods they used, as well as white miners' wages. The South African state imposed a war tax on profits amounting to 71 per cent. At the same time, the real wages of black miners were kept down. Government policy of encouraging internal migrant labour had impoverished the reserves where most of the Africans lived and where the remaining families had to eke out a subsistence living. Between the years 1933 and 1939, some 135,000 African peasants sought work on the mines, a 50 per cent increase of African labour. Many other African workers, deterred by the low mining wages, were attracted to the greatly expanding industrial sector, where black wages rose by over 50 per cent during the war. The influx of Africans into the urban and mining areas sparked off a new wave of militancy organised around trade unions.

The mine-owners did not want black mine unions. The Chamber of Mines remarked: 'Trade unionism as practised by Europeans is still beyond the understanding of the tribal Native.' The Trades and Labour Council, which did not object to coloured workers joining unions, argued that black Africans had 'not yet reached a stage of mental and cultural development in which they can be entrusted with the rights and duties involved in recognition of their unions.'

All the non-white groups, especially the Indians of Natal, were active in forming unions, some of them mixed. In Transvaal in 1941 a Council of Non-European Trade Unions was set up, which claimed 158,000 membership in 1945 in 119 unions. This was equal to 40 per cent of the 390,000 African workers in commerce and manufacturing. The Council's inaugural meeting was presided over by Moses Kotane, a member of the African National Congress (ANC) and of the Communist Party of South Africa (CPSA).

The ANC was a different organisation then from now. Meetings were opened with a prayer and a hymn, a mace represented respect for parliamentary procedures and there was a strong commitment to non-violence. The White-dominated CPSA had only just emerged from years of internal conflict to reverse its racist position according to which only Whites could lead the revolutionary vanguard. With support from the Transvaal African National Congress, the African Mine Workers' Union (AMWU) was formed in 1941. By 1944 it claimed to represent 25,000 workers, despite the hostility to recruitment from the mining companies. Organisers took jobs in the mines and held night meetings in the compounds. Women food vendors secretly distributed union leaflets.

A wave of strikes in several industries and in the Natal coal mines in 1942 was followed in January 1943 with a strike by the African Gas and Power Workers' Union against the Victoria Falls Power Company, which supplied electricity to the mines. Smuts appointed a commission of inquiry, the Witwatersrand Mine Natives' Wage Commission, under Justice Lansdowne.

The Commission reported at the end of the year that

African mine-workers could not survive on their wages and
that it found that over three-quarters of the 308,374
Africans were paid less than the Chamber of Mines' 'average daily wage'. The Commission report concluded that the
reserves were deteriorating and impoverished, and recommended an annual wage increase of between £10 and £12, or
about 30 per cent a year – the calculated shortfall between
income and expenditure of a family on the reserves.

But the Commission rejected the AMWU demand for
recognition, saying that African miners had 'not yet reached
the stage of development which would enable them safely
and usefully to employ trade unionism as a means of
promoting their advancement'.

The Smuts government refused to accept the Commission's recommendations, although small wage increases
were implemented. A recent history of trade unionism in
South Africa notes:

> Chamber of Mines' policy was to get rid of anyone
> trying to organise African workers. Spies were planted
> in the Union and the government added to War
> Measures Acts (which already prevented Africans
> from striking) Proclamation 1425, prohibiting gather-
> ings of more than twenty persons on mine property.
> This made the holding of meetings virtually impos-
> sible, and also meant a great reduction in the finances
> of the Union as dues could not be easily collected and
> new members could not be recruited.[16]

The crisis on costs and labour relations came to a head in
1946, when the AMWU demanded a minimum wage of 10
shillings a day and a repeal of War Measure 1425. After the
Chamber of Mines ignored the demands, between 70,000
and 100,000 African mine-workers struck on twenty-one
mines.

General Smuts sent the police and troops to drive the
men back to work. In all, twelve were killed and 1,200
injured. Several strike leaders and the Johannesburg district committee of the Communist Party were arrested and
given nine-month suspended prison sentences. The entire

executive of the CPSA was also charged with sedition, a case which was eventually quashed two years later by the Supreme Court.

From an early stage, Anglo was keenly aware of the huge investment costs involved in developing the Free State mines and the need to keep black wages down. In 1943, an unsigned memorandum by an Anglo official warned:

> Any increase in Native wages will be considered as an unfavourable factor, as it must affect the cost of work in every department involved – exploration, expenditure on equipment and its installation and, ultimately, actual working costs. If conditions are made more onerous the danger will be that capital will fight shy of an enterprise like this which is still very much in the unproved stage.[17]

Concern about attracting capital was finally dispelled in early 1946, when Ernest Oppenheimer told the shareholders of the Orange Free State Investment Trust that borehole Number 1 on the boundary between farms Geduld and Fridersheim would yield gold worth £1,600 a ton of ore – a fabulous 500 times more than the payable limit on existing mines. Stock exchanges in London, Paris and New York rushed for Free State shares. In the next four years, Anglo raised £48.3 million in loans from British and European banks, and De Beers ploughed £16 million into the Free State mines.

The official biography of Ernest Oppenheimer, a 600-page monument by Sir Theodore Gregory, published in 1962, makes no mention of the 1946 strike, or of Oppenheimer's reaction to it. What does come across from his letters and speeches of the period is a belief in racially separate housing, the continuation for the foreseeable future of the compound system and the provision of sufficient amenities for Africans to guarantee the mines a stable and acquiescent labour force. In 1947, at a ceremony to open the sinking of a gold-mine shaft, Oppenheimer spoke of the need to develop the sparsely populated Free State mines efficiently:

When I speak of 'efficient' I do not just mean the
lowest possible working costs on the best possible
tonnage, but also that we pay special attention to the
welfare of our employees and to the development of
the region as a whole. . . . It is our aim to have the
best possible housing conditions for our European
population, and to improve their amenities of life to
the greatest possible extent.[18]

As for the Africans:

I have on many occasions referred to our aim of
materially improving the housing conditions of our
Native population. When I think of our Native problems I am, of course, influenced by the conditions in
Northern Rhodesia, where we have a large population
of married Natives with their families who are separately housed. Then again I think that in our coal-
mining enterprises in Natal we have married and
single quarters. It is essential to make a careful study
of the whole problem. . . . Personally I am convinced
that it is in the interests of the Natives and of the
mines to establish villages for married Native people,
and also to improve on the present compound structure and general arrangements. In this connection it is
obvious that where large numbers of Natives coming
from territories outside the Union are employed by the
mining companies the compound system must be
continued for some time to come, but I feel sure our
ultimate aim should be to create, within a reasonable
time, modern Native villages from which the mines
will ultimately draw a large proportion of their Native
labour requirements.[19]

Faced, as ever, with competition for African labour in
other industries, Oppenheimer told the 1951 annual meeting about the efforts to attract labour to the mines:

While the gold-mining industry has always devoted
great care to the welfare of its Native employees, we
believe that there is scope for a further advance in the

direction of providing greater facilities and amenities on a somewhat higher civilized standard for our Native employees. With this end in view we have introduced central dining-halls in the midst of double-storied dormitory blocks and we have applied new standards of nutrition, hygiene and control in these hostels. Some doubts have been expressed whether the Natives would really appreciate these innovations: but there is an accumulating weight of evidence to show that they are popular with Natives. This evidence is not only in the form of verbal expressions of approval and gratification; current statistics also show that a very high percentage of our native employees in the Free State consist of those who have sought employment in our mines. This is an attitude of mind on the part of Natives seeking work which should be encouraged and developed in the general interests of the gold-mining industry.[20]

Conflicts with the Nationalist government after 1948 over labour policy prevented the Oppenheimers from implementing their plans for settled mining villages for Africans. But in the Rhodesias, where the rigidity of apartheid had not been fully imposed, Anglo was able to bring some of its policies towards black workers to fruition.

The Oppenheimers, father and son, were dismayed by the growing tide of black nationalism sweeping across the African continent. Their disapproval for anything that smacked of majority rule stayed with Harry right through his business life. Anglo's operations in the copperbelt north of the Limpopo showed how ingrained their paternalism had become.

Anglo had first invested in the Rhodesian copperbelt (most of it in present-day Zambia) in 1924. This was the same year in which Cecil Rhodes' British South Africa Company transferred its thirty-year-old administration of Northern Rhodesia to a legislative council that excluded Africans. By the end of the Second World War, Anglo was producing nearly half of the area's 233,000 tons of ore.

Ernest Oppenheimer took pains to reassure Britain, as the colonial power, that the mining operations in the territories would remain within the imperial sphere of influence, rather than fall to the Americans as the leading experts in world copper production. After Anglo incorporated its Rhodesian holding company, Rhodesian Anglo American (Rhoanglo), in London in December 1928, the deputy chairman R. B. Hagart wrote to the company's Rhodesian manager:

> Sir Ernest has asked me to mention to you that he would be glad if you would take the first opportunity of giving the Governor an outline of the position of the new company. As you are aware, from the very outset of developments in Northern Rhodesia, a great point has been made of the fact that there was being developed a big and practically the only copper field in the British Empire, and the political importance of this fact has been emphasised on several occasions. This being so, we feel it is extremely important to avoid giving the slightest impression that this great national asset is passing into foreign hands. From the figures I have given you above you will see that the capital of the new company is being provided almost entirely by British interests, the only American interest involved being the Newmont company whose co-operation it was desired to obtain as it was felt essential that we should have on the technical side some large American copper group interested. You will be able to assure the Governor, therefore, that the Rhodesian Anglo American Limited is a British company with almost entirely British capital.[21]

In 1953, Anglo and the other British and American mining companies enthusiastically supported the creation of the Central African Federation (the two Rhodesias and Nyasaland, now Malawi) which the Conservative government in Britain set up to perpetuate white settler rule. On the new electoral roll in 1953 the income and educational

qualification requirements meant that there were 423
African voters out of an African population of 7 million.
Less rigid separation of the races, however, allowed the
companies to build mining villages to stabilise their
workforce. Despite opposition from the white miners'
union, the black miners, well organised in their union,
also won the right to fill several categories of jobs previously reserved for Whites. Oppenheimer circulated the
employees of Rhoanglo with a statement setting out the
group's objectives:

> Half a century ago the population of the Copperbelt
> lived in savagery and fear – helpless victims of slave-
> raiding anarchy and disease.
> Their progress in half a century has been phenom-
> enal – a rate of progress unsurpassed in the world's
> history.
> This progress has been solely due to the order and
> leadership of the European. Its continuance is still
> completely dependent on this leadership and will be
> so for the foreseeable future.
> African progress in Rhodesia must continue. It is
> the duty of the European leadership to see that it
> does so; and the copper companies are constantly
> introducing improvements in African housing, pay,
> leave and working conditions generally. This, how-
> ever, is not enough. The African has learnt to use
> simple European tools and to perform tasks that,
> until a generation ago, he would have regarded, if he
> thought of them at all, as far beyond his ability. The
> African must be allowed to develop these skills and
> he must be helped to develop them through Euro-
> pean teaching. It is the whole basis of the policy of
> the new Federation that the African should play a
> fuller part in the industrial economy of the country of
> which he is a citizen.[22]

Two years later, Harry Oppenheimer echoed his father's
concern about keeping Whites in control. Applauding the

formation of the black miners' union on the copperbelt, he
went on:

> Recently, however, there has been an unmistakable
> tendency for this African union to allow itself to be
> used as the instrument of black nationalists, whose
> objective is not a fair participation of Africans in a
> multi-racial society, but the transformation of Rho-
> desia into an exclusively African country.[23]

The Oppenheimers were proud of their infrastructure
investments in the Federation and of their efforts to keep
the copperbelt within the sphere of influence of the British
Empire. The Anglo group joined in the £20 million contribution from the mining companies to help build the Kariba
Dam; a loan of £1 million was made to Rhodesia Railways,
and another £5 million was spent on buying 20,000 new
trucks, which were then leased to the railways for twenty-
five years.

This investment outside South Africa attracted criticism
from the Nationalist Prime Minister, J. G. Strijdom.
Harry, who had followed his father's trail into parliament in
1948, parried the attack by revealing just how lucrative the
copperbelt was. During the previous ten years £5.6 million
had been invested, but £10.7 million had been returned. In
1955, Ernest reported that £35 million had been invested in
opening up the mines, and £45 million of profits had been
returned for expansion and services.

The Oppenheimers' glowing accounts of African
advancement, however, concealed some more pertinent
realities. Most of rural Northern Rhodesia remained
impoverished, not least because the mines attracted able-
bodied men away from the villages. There was no attempt
to provide social services and still less education. In 1958,
out of a population of about 3 million there were fewer
than 1,000 African children attending secondary schools,
and only one of these schools provided entrance to
university.

A more revealing insight into Ernest's policy of improving conditions for Africans is contained in a letter he wrote

to Harry in 1941. The de facto colour bar imposed by the white miners' union, he believed, had embarrassed the government into forcing the mining companies to spend more than they otherwise would on black housing. He resented it:

> The people entrusted with the opening of this enter-prise [the N'Kana mine] did not create a mining camp, nor even a mining town, but a mining Utopia. The layout of the town, the houses, the amenities, the free services to our employees do not exist anywhere else. The whole thing is a dream town, something which – if mining is carried on in Paradise – one imagines it to be like. . . . Then again what has been the effect on our management: extravagance. Anyone might have imagined that our workmen who had all these favours *forced* [his emphasis] upon them would be loyal. Not a bit of it. The vulgar display of wealth made them an easy prey to Bolshevik propaganda. Why should we not supply more homes, more benefits, when our managers lived in palaces, when we kept a beautiful guest house for the benefit of directors, who pay an occasional visit?[24]

Ernest Oppenheimer died in 1957, a revered figure in white South Africa. Shortly before his death, his official contribution to South Africa was recognised by the Minister of Mines at a special luncheon given in his honour at the Diamond Producers' Association. 'Almost all the countries in the world have their industrial kings and mining magnates,' the minister began. 'In the United States the names of Carnegie, Rockefeller and Ford are well known to every schoolchild. In Germany you have the famous Krupp family, and in England the Lever Brothers. As Sir Ernest is a world figure it is perfectly natural that I should compare him with those I have mentioned.'[25] Oppenheimer's contribution to the majority of South Africans is more difficult to assess. It was only in 1956 that he visited for the first time and saw the appalling conditions in the south-western townships (later known as Soweto) outside Johannesburg.[26] He was shocked at what he saw and arranged for a 3 million rand loan through the Chamber of Commerce to help rebuild some of the worst slums. As a final gesture of philanthropy, it proved to be too little, too late.

4

The Importance of Being Harry

The transition from father to son was a seamless operation, the more so because Harry Oppenheimer had grown up and matured as a mirror-image of Sir Ernest, who, in his later years, had progressively taken a less active part in running the business.

Harry had joined the boards of Anglo American and De Beers in the 1930s. He worked closely with his father in the same office and in the two years he was away during the war received long and detailed letters from Ernest about the group's fortunes: producing as much copper for the war effort as possible, buying into the rich Free State goldfields, and placating the allies in their insatiable demand for diamonds, the cutting tool of war munitions.

He returned to South Africa in July 1940, having been offered a job on the staff of the new Coastal Command, headed by Ernest's friend General Pierre de Villiers. On a posting to Robben Island, the future site of the notorious prison for nationalist leaders, he met Signals Lieutenant Bridget McCall. Not surprisingly, given the small white South African élite, their parents had known each other long before in Johannesburg. They married in 1943, Bridget having resigned her commission and Harry following a few months later. Back at 44 Main Street he was made managing director of Anglo American. Within two years they had two children, Mary and Nicholas. The dynasty was assured.

Harry also began to establish himself as a formidable public figure in his own right, once again the Hoggenheimer scourge of the Nationalist Afrikaners. Only this time they had the potential power to clip his wings. It had always been Ernest's ambition that his son would enter politics as he had done. In the 1948 elections, at the age of 39, Harry decided to stand in his home town of Kimberley for Smuts' United Party, to become the second 'Member for De Beers'. There was one small problem, he lived 300 miles away in Johannesburg. The solution was quickly found: he decided to take up the sport of the Randlords, racehorse breeding, and bought the old De Beers stud at Mauritzfontein, just outside the city.

The Nationalists' surprise victory, on the platform of separate development for the races, did not at first completely demoralise the opposition, although Smuts lost his seat, as he did in 1924 when Ernest was elected. But the Nationalists moved quickly to consolidate their power. Their strength was rooted in the countryside with the isolationist Afrikaner farmers, and with the poor urban Afrikaners, who had found themselves in increasing competition with Blacks during the industrial boom of the war years. The United Party, largely the mouthpiece of English and Jewish mining and finance, retained the support of demobbed servicemen, many of whom were horrified with the prospect of the country being run by erstwhile sympathisers of Hitler. One of the first acts of the new government was the release of Nazi supporters from prison.

Harry Oppenheimer quickly adopted his father's mantle and became a leading opposition front-bench spokesman on economic affairs. Nationalist ideology of separate development, which restricted the labour market, and the danger of nationalisation, posed a serious threat to his business. His response was characteristically brisk, providing funds for the United Party as well as supporting extra-parliamentary opposition in the shape of the anti-fascist Torch Commando group.

Led by the South African Battle of Britain ace, Group Captain 'Sailor' Malan, the commando was formed from war veterans who clearly saw the comparisons between Hitler's Germany and apartheid. Their fears were aroused by the pace of the Nationalists' programme. By 1950, the government had removed the indirect Indian representation in parliament, established a register of everyone's race in the Population Registration Act to exclude so-called Coloureds from passing as Whites, outlawed mixed marriages and sexual relations between Whites and non-Whites, and set about creating ghettos for urban Blacks under the Group Areas Act.

The Torch Commando was principally inspired by the plan to exclude coloured persons from the electoral roll in the Cape, where about 50,000 registered coloured voters (out of a potential 120,000 who qualified under the property franchise) had a significant influence in a handful of seats. Besides wanting to unite the two sections of the white community, the United Party had consistently viewed the coloured population as allies. That did not prevent the commando from having grave doubts about admitting coloured people as members. It was first agreed that non-Europeans could form separate units, just as they did in the war. Then the commando executive committee restricted membership to those who had the franchise – male Cape Coloureds who met literacy and economic standards.

The coloured ex-servicemen decided the issue. At the end of 1951, their representatives declared that they had no wish to join. 'The commando's fight is the white man's fight to re-establish the integrity of his word, and in this work the Coloureds obviously have no part.'[1]

The commando adopted Malan as its national president when he returned to a hero's welcome in South Africa. He was also given a job, offered to him in London shortly before. He became personal assistant to Harry Oppenheimer. While the commandos marched in the streets in their thousands, the Nationalists launched a concerted attack on the £1 million United South Africa Trust Fund which Oppenheimer had set up with other group executives to support the United Party's work. In parliament he was

accused of setting up a secret fund to finance a Torch
Commando putsch on the lines of the abortive Jameson
Raid in 1895. Oppenheimer, one Nationalist MP accused,
'has practically swallowed up three-quarters of the country
and will swallow up the other quarter as well if we allow
him'.[2]

Prime Minister Malan (no relation of Sailor Malan)
joined the assault:

> What we have against us is money power, principally
> under the leadership of Oppenheimer. He has become
> a power in the land. Oppenheimer – the one who sits
> in parliament – has control of millions of pounds, and
> he puts this at the service of our opponents in this
> struggle. Oppenheimer with his millions exercises a
> greater influence than, I think, any man in South
> Africa has ever had.[3]

Harry Oppenheimer defended himself in parliament. The
fund was no secret; its address and number even appeared
in the telephone book. It was simply a group of like-minded
people putting their money together to support legitimate
political ends: in this case the United Party.

Despite the heated exchanges in parliament, the government recognised a golden goose when it saw one. From the
very beginning, the Nationalists worked closely with
Oppenheimer on the establishment of a strategic uranium
industry for the atomic weapons programme in the United
States and Britain. Uranium was extracted as a side product
of gold, and Anglo's deputy chairman, R. B. Hagart, was
appointed to the new Atomic Energy Board in 1948. Anglo
provided one of the two pilot plants at its Western Reef gold
mine, and by 1952 five of the group's mines were desig-
nated by the government as uranium producers. In agreement with the government, the Combined Development
Agency, representing the USA and Britain, provided loans
to start up production. The profits for Anglo were
immense. Between 1953 and 1958, the Chamber of Mines
estimated, working profits from uranium rose from £1.8
million to £37.7 million.

Similarly, Oppenheimer's criticisms of the government were less than fundamental. In throwing his money and his support behind the United Party, he was certainly not mounting a challenge to the principle of white supremacy. The party preferred to call it 'white leadership', and it resisted his idea of a common electoral roll even with a very limited franchise.

'We do not need to go in for some kind of head-counting democracy,' he told parliament, 'which, in the long run, will turn over the government of the country to Blacks who would be just as nationalistically inclined as we Whites. What we must do plainly, definitely and unequivocally is to recognise the non-European population as a permanent part of our urban population and give them a sense of permanence and of belonging.'[4] Although he unsuccessfully pressed for permission to build mining villages for married black workers, such as the 'paradises' on the copperbelt, he was by no means an advocate of Blacks and Whites living alongside each other:

> I think all of us in this House will agree that we must maintain the standard of living of the European people, and it certainly would not help the Natives to lower that standard. I think people would also agree that it is very desirable to have residential segregation. I think everyone in this House is agreed that it is most undesirable to put political power into the hands of uncivilised, uneducated people, as far as we can help it.[5]

Oppenheimer returned to the theme in a speech in 1956, in which he recognised that Africans would eventually have to become integrated into white society. But, he emphasised:

> Until they are able on the whole to do that – and it will take many years – it will not be possible to avoid – and, indeed, it will be essential to maintain . . . a substantial measure of social and residential separation of the races. This separation, however, while in practice it will correspond broadly with the racial division and must inevitably, I am afraid, be reinforced by racial

prejudice, is in its essence not a question of race but of culture, or, if you like, of class.

. . . It does not make for racial harmony if people of widely different habits and cultural standards are required to live in close social relations with one another. If we are wise, therefore, we will accept the desire of the Europeans in Southern Africa for a measure of social separation as something that corresponds with the realities of the situation.

He justified his support for a qualified franchise:

The only way it may be possible to reconcile parliamentary government as we understand it, with participation by Africans in political power on a basis which involves no race discrimination, is by limiting the right to vote to people who can reasonably be expected to be sufficiently educated and sophisticated to work a parliamentary system. . . . I would not deny that universal adult suffrage is an end to be worked for, but it cannot – anyhow in areas of permanent white settlement – be adopted without incurring unacceptable risks until the standards of education and living are far higher than they are today.[6]

He has, in fact, never denied his innate conservatism. After joining the new Progressive Party in 1959, he spoke at the final election rally of Helen Suzman in October 1961. He had decided to vote for the party, 'because I am really a conservative. The Progressive Party is opposed not only to White domination but also to Black domination. We can oppose Black domination successfully only if we are able to win the sympathy of people outside the country. And we can win their sympathy only if we can make it clear to them that we are not seeking to defend white domination, but civilisation.'[7]

Many years later he remarked: 'In a South African context I may seem to be liberal, but at heart I'm just an old-fashioned conservative.'[8]

That was in 1984. Oppenheimer has at least been consistent. In the same interview, he said that granting universal suffrage would lead to 'chaos and disorder'. He would give votes

> to all those, both black and white, who had reached a certain level of education. It might even be feasible to restrict the vote to those who owned their own home. It would be a fascinating experiment!
> . . . It would be a good idea to pick out capable young blacks while they are still at university and systematically groom them for greater things – deliberately turn them into an élite.

Any voting system, he concluded, would have to 'provide cast-iron guarantees for the white minority'.

Perhaps the most telling comment on Harry Oppenheimer's politics was in 1973, just before the resurgence of black militancy, in a book written with the approval and co-operation of the family. Despite the author's efforts to romanticise the Oppenheimers' contribution to South Africa, he felt at ease to write:

> Harry had never subscribed to the view that apartheid was morally wrong. In his view it was at root an honest attempt to cope with overwhelming racial problems. 'The government policy is not an attempt to repress but to find a solution. The assumption is that the two races can't get along, and that the black areas will eventually emerge as independent states.' Verwoerd and his successors had tried to 'give it a go', as he put it, but had based their whole approach on the false premise that it was physically possible to separate black from white, when it was manifestly too late. His chief objections to apartheid, then, were on practical grounds: South Africa had gone so far with all her races together that it was not simply foolish but actually dangerous to interfere with the *status quo*.[9]

Oppenheimer was demonstrating the dilemma that all South African businessmen face: the repression which has offered today's riches is also the force which is jeopardising its profit-making abilities and ultimately its survival in

private hands. Most businesses have been content to focus
on short-term financial goals, leaving the wider questions of
how to contain the threat of black expectations up to the
government. But Anglo, along with a few other large
'English' corporations, has been keenly aware of the contradictions. The fact that it too did little about them in practice
until forced to do so by black militancy and international
pressure suggests that for two decades, at least, the antago-
nisms between business and government were no more than
sparring games.

Anglo's vision is of a South Africa brought into the
twentieth-century world of a modern industrial society, free
of the constraints of apartheid, with a free labour market
and greater flexibility for business. Informal restrictions on
the black population – income, education and opportunity,
for example – would take the place of apartheid's overt
racial controls. The force of law and the institutions would
replace the provocative use of the police and some form of
political rights, in a federated state with guarantees for the
white and other minorities, would be granted. An individual meritocracy would form the basis of a black urban
bourgeoisie to guarantee the survival of capitalism.

Promoting these views has been the crusade of almost all
Anglo top executives. Two of them – Gordon Waddell and
Zach de Beer – have also been Progressive Party MPs. No
one has been more committed to the crusade than Harry
Oppenheimer himself. This may at first seem surprising,
given his position as the richest man in South Africa, who
stood to gain so much from co-operating with the apartheid
regime and exploiting its repression of the black workforce.
On the other hand, his very wealth meant that he could
afford to have unpopular views and that he had more to lose
than anyone else. The international nature of the group
from its early days also meant that he could see the dangers
more clearly as the movement towards independence from
colonial rule gathered pace. Ghana was the first to gain its
independence in 1957.

In South Africa during the 1950s the rising tide of black
protest, and state repression, concentrated Oppenheimer's

mind on the need for a less complacent approach to an increasingly unstable society. The response of the African National Congress to the Nationalists' victory in 1948 was to transform itself from an ineffectual talking shop for moderate intellectuals into a mass movement of resistance. In this it was spurred on by its Youth League, whose members included Nelson Mandela, Walter Sisulu and Oliver Tambo. The League's Programme of Action for boycotts, demonstrations and civil resistance was adopted at the 1949 congress together with their own candidate for president – Dr James Sebebuijwasegokgoboontharile Moroka, a doctor and landowner. His name meant: 'I have come at last, having been criminally enslaved, but will bring rain, peace and freedom to my people.' The Defiance Campaign, which faltered in 1952 after the arrest of 8,500 people, gave the ANC a new confidence. Action rather than resolutions also radicalised its leaders, who began to analyse society in class terms for the first time. Closer ties were established with the Communist Party of South Africa. Sisulu visited the Soviet Union and China, where he was deeply impressed by Mao's peasant revolution. In 1955, 3,000 delegates to the ANC's Congress of the People gathered in a fenced enclosure in the village of Kliptown, near Johannesburg, to approve the Freedom Charter. It began:

We, the People of South Africa, declare for all our country and the world to know: that South Africa belongs to all who live in it, black and white, and that no government can justly claim authority unless it is based on the will of all the people; that our people have been robbed of their birthright to land, liberty and peace by a form of government founded on injustice and inequality; that our country will never be prosperous or free until all our people live in brotherhood, enjoying equal rights and opportunities; that only a democratic state, based on the will of all the people, can secure to all their birthright without distinction of colour, race, sex or belief.

Even these minimum and unremarkable demands were anathema to Oppenheimer's thesis of a 'civilised' society. But, for him, there was worse to come. 'The national wealth of our country, the heritage of all the South Africans, shall be restored to the people,' the Charter went on. 'The mineral wealth beneath the soil, the banks and monopoly industry shall be transferred to the ownership of the people as a whole.' These were subversive ideas for the state, headlong into its programme of separation of the races, and for Oppenheimer, who was about to embark on the huge financial and industrial expansion of Anglo with Free State gold profits. They underlined the threat Anglo faced if Nationalist policies inflamed political tension to the point where the white minority could no longer retain control of the country. The state's initiative was clear enough; in the following year, Mandela was among 156 dissidents arrested and put in the dock for the marathon five-year Treason Trial. Oppenheimer and his friends chose the long road of deflecting black liberation by trying to co-opt a pliant black middle class.

The Progressive Party was formed by a small group of liberal professionals from the Cape who believed that race was the central issue in South African politics and that the United Party was failing to mount a credible alternative to apartheid. Oppenheimer did not inspire the breakaway, but he was consulted throughout the period by Zach de Beer, Colin Elgin, another liberal Cape MP, and Harry Lawrence, the chairman of the United Party caucus. His acquiescence, and certainly his money, made it all the more feasible.

In his annual statement as chairman of AAC in 1959 he had already signalled a decisive break by calling for African participation in government. 'It seems to me that, from whatever angle one approaches this complicated problem, one comes back to the conclusion . . . that constitutional changes are essential by which both Europeans and Africans would be guaranteed against the passing of unfair discriminatory legislation based on race.'

The split occurred during the United Party congress at Bloemfontein in August 1959 when eleven dissidents, including Zach de Beer, decided to resign. De Beer's first move was to travel to Johannesburg to canvas Oppenheimer's support. It was readily given, but before he announced it on 2 September it was felt necessary to secure the backing of Harry Lawrence, who was somewhere in Europe. Both sides were desperate to recruit him and a pile of letters accumulated at a *poste restante* in Rapallo on the Italian riviera, the only address known to his family. 'By sheer chance,' de Beer recalled, 'I was lunching with Oppenheimer at his house, here, and Wallace Strauss [a former UP leader] was there and a number of other men. We were standing on the stoep having drinks before lunch, when Harry Oppenheimer was called to the phone and we could hear him in the distance shouting, "Yes, Harry, yes, I can hear you. Yes, Zach is here. I'll call Zach, Harry, he's here." And so it went on. Eventually he put the phone down and he came out and he said, "Gentlemen, that was a call from Rapallo."'[10]

Nearly twenty years later Oppenheimer put forward in an unpublished interview his reasons for favouring an alternative party:

I think it presents itself, to us in the first place, but perhaps to business in an ever widening circle, that Nationalist policies have made it impossible to make proper use of black labour. This is felt to be dangerous in two ways: a danger because it's necessary in order to get economic growth, to make use of black labour, because unless you keep the economy extremely small you can't man the skilled jobs with white people. On the other hand, it's felt that, if you are going to operate business successfully, you want to do so in a peaceful atmosphere, and the only way to have a peaceful atmosphere is to enable black people to do better jobs and to feel part of this economic system. I think it's because the Nationalist Party was felt to prevent these things happening that it was looked on as a danger.[11]

As for the United Party: 'Really – what did it do? It provided a home for the really old-fashioned people who didn't want to face up to the issues. . . . The United Party just sat there, thinking that it could solve this problem by appeals to white unity, and by a sort of kindliness in relation to black people, which the Nationalist Party simply didn't have. And this simply wasn't enough.'[12]

The central tenet of the Progressive platform, as formulated at the first party congress in 1959, was 'to enable the peoples of South Africa to live as one nation in accordance with the values and concepts of Western civilisation'.[13] The proposed constitution would allow citizens 'of a defined degree of civilisation' to participate 'according to their ability to assume responsibility'. No-one holding the vote would be disenfranchised, so qualifications would only be demanded of Blacks. White fears were allayed by the promise that no one group would dominate another. The underlying assumptions were of cultural and racial superiority and these were specifically bolstered with the pledge to continue to support separate schools, housing and other facilities. Economically, the party differed little from the United Party. It supported free enterprise and called for better training and education for skilled workers, a minimum unskilled wage, social security and unions for skilled and semi-skilled workers. Only in one area, business and commerce, were Blacks to be allowed to compete freely. The party's 'main principles and policies' document did not attack apartheid *per se*; it advocated segregation to maintain racial peace and it was staunchly anti-communist. The main difference was that it recognised that black demands, first, existed in a coherent form and, secondly, had to be acknowledged if stability was to be achieved.

Stanley Uys, the parliamentary correspondent of the Johannesburg *Sunday Times*, summed it up like this:

> If anyone thinks the Progressives have come on to the scene as saviours of the non-Whites, they can promptly put that idea aside.
>
> The Progressives, if anything, will be saviours of the

Whites. There is nothing starry-eyed about them. Their purpose in switching the emphasis from race to civilisation is to preserve as much of the white man's civilisation as possible.

In return for political concessions, they hope to gain the non-Whites' support for the white man's way of life, particularly his economic order.

That is why their policy pays so much attention to economic and labour issues – and that is why it is so attractive to industrialists.[14]

Although Oppenheimer personally financed the party, he did not permit any direct corporate support, knowing the risks involved. But there was a recognition that his support would aid the company: 'I felt that the advancement of these sort of policies and an attempt to get them adopted in South Africa was very much in our interests as a business, as well as our interests as South Africans.'[15]

The Progressive Party bore the Oppenheimer imprint from the start. Before its first congress, for example, Harry Lawrence sent Oppenheimer draft position papers on the the urban African, economic policy and labour policy. These were returned to the national steering committee on the day before the congress met in November, with Harry Oppenheimer on the platform. Many of Oppenheimer's detailed amendments, written in his characteristically over-cautious style, were adopted. A clause in the labour policy calling for the removal of all restrictions on the productivity was dropped because he was concerned about alienating white trade unions. References to the undesirable and uneconomic migrant labour system were excised from the explanatory note.[16]

We have got to be jolly careful [he wrote] not to give our political opponents any opportunity to say that we're going to take steps to stop migrant labour. Consider the position of the gold mining industry which employs getting on for 400,000 migrants. In principle this may be a bad thing, though it must be remembered that the life of the gold mining industry is limited and, as compared with the life of a nation, very short indeed. It may therefore be questioned on this ground whether it would be right to settle the entire labour force it uses permanently in the urban areas. Quite apart however from any question of whether it's right or wrong, it would obviously be utterly impossible. . . . I feel, therefore, that the emphasis should be on creating a settled African population, and that we should not express opposition to the migrant labour system as such. There would, however, be no objection to saying that every opportunity would be given to the mining industry to employ a larger proportion of settled Africans than they do at present.

On the policy for urban Africans, though, the party sought to discourage migrant labour – a recognition that manufacturing business, as potential allies, needed a stable, skilled labour force. Oppenheimer disapproved, but he got his own way on the question of trying to bridge the wage gap between Whites and Blacks. A scheme for job reclassification was dropped because of the difficulties he saw in either bringing white wages down and alienating a large section of the electorate, or raising black wages and ending high profitability. 'I'm rather inclined to think that a political party should leave these things to negotiations within industries,' he wrote. Nor did he like the idea of including agricultural and domestic workers within a minimum wage. 'It's a tricky question from many points of view and I wonder whether it's necessary to go into these details.' His reservations were not surprising, given the large number of white South African farmers, most of whom employed domestic servants. The wages of both groups were abysmally low and some farm labourers were unpaid; they exchanged their labour for the right to occupy land as subsistence farmers. He also succeeded in softening the policy on unions, which he felt ought not to be recognised 'unless they can meet a proper standard'. Unskilled workers were to be under the guidance of the Department of Labour.

Oppenheimer wrote a minority report for the party's Molteno consitutional commission in which he argued for a Standard 6 level of schooling to be accepted as the minimum qualification for the right to vote. The majority at first wanted the lower Standard 4, but Oppenheimer's option was eventually adopted.[17]

Finally, the party was almost wholly dependent on his personal fortune. When the Progressives decided in 1964 to contest the four 'coloured' seats in the white parliament, Oppenheimer funded the whole operation with donations of up to 40,000 rand a year. The 1965 provincial council and the 1966 general election campaigns were funded by 50,000 rand on each occasion. By contrast, the regional party organisation contributed a mere 1,310 rand to central party funds between July 1964 and June 1965.

Oppenheimer did not hesitate to use this influence. When the party fell into disarray in the mid-1960s, under the onslaught of Nationalist legislation and fervour, he wrote to Harry Lawrence questioning the efficacy of an extended campaign:

> I have not committed myself whether to give or not to give further sums for the specific purpose of the general election. I shall have to make up my mind in the light of the circumstances at the time. I am however entirely clear in my mind that the idea of fighting fifty seats is entirely impractical. I certainly don't intend to finance such a plan.[18]

In the event, Oppenheimer gave another 50,000 rand and the party contested twenty-six seats.

The Progressives' dismal performance at the ballot box led to further exchanges. Future funding, Oppenheimer said, was contingent on a complete reorganisation of the party, a shake-up of its leadership and a closer orientation to business. Zach de Beer wrote a survival plan. While the party was attracting little support, he said, events in the long term would prove it right. He identified its supporters as the well-educated, the rich, the internationally orientated, the sophisticated, employers, Jews and Catholics rather than Protestants, and youth. It was not until 1974 that the Progressives managed to increase their seats from one to seven. But by that time, South Africa's black population was well on the way to taking its own opposition road.

5

From Sharpeville to Soweto

Harry Oppenheimer's public conflicts with the Nationalist government and his allegiance to an opposition party of one MP did nothing to diminish the steady march of Anglo through the South African, southern African and international economy. When Harry assumed control of the empire on his father's death in 1957 and retired from parliament, the group had amassed formidable resources. It controlled 40 per cent of South Africa's gold, 80 per cent of the world's diamonds, a sixth of the world's copper and it was the country's largest producer of coal. The family lived in the style to which they had always been accustomed. Installed at Brenthurst, the Oppenheimers indulged their private interests and tastes. Harry collected impressionist paintings to add to Ernest's old masters, and antique silver. He was fond of Louis XV furniture. The old formality and gentility were retained: even when alone they would dress for dinner. There were also grand parties in the gardens overlooking downtown Johannesburg.

In the family tradition, their two children were dispatched to English public schools, the strong-willed Mary to Heathfield, near Ascot, where she became head girl, and the more stolid, unassuming Nicholas to Harrow, where Harry's cousin Philip and his son Anthony had been. Nicholas was a most dutiful son; he always expected to join the business and one day step into his father's shoes.

Meanwhile, the parents became successful racehorse owners, winning many of the South African classics. Their personal scrapbooks, detailing each and every mention of them in the press, have as many cuttings about horses and form as politics and business. On Bridget's initiative, their stud at Mauritzfontein – including the pigsties – was painted pink. Later, to add to their ranch in Zimbabwe and their London flat in exclusive Belgravia, they had a holiday home built beside the sea on the Natal coast near Durban. Milkwood, a two-storey terracotta house with white shutters and sea-green tiles, could accommodate thirty guests. It had five luxury suites, ten bedrooms, fifteen bathrooms, a separate dormitory wing for children and a swimming-pool, half Olympic size. In the sitting-room Graham Sutherland's painting *The Angry Ram* hangs on a gold damask wall. Bridget's bathroom suite is of mother-of-pearl with gold taps.

Although he was out of parliament, Harry Oppenheimer continued to be a political power in the land. The ANC Treason Trial had not quelled black unrest and in 1959 a section of young militants in the ANC broke away to form the more radical, exclusively black, Pan-African Congress (PAC).

The business community took fright at these developments, not least because of the threat of the withdrawal of foreign capital, and set about trying to improve South Africa's image abroad. The result was the South African Foundation, which brought together English and Afrikaner business leaders for the first time in a concerted and sophisticated effort to soften the country's international image. Oppenheimer and a number of senior colleagues in the Anglo group joined the galaxy of bankers, industrialists, former diplomats and publishers. One of its first vice-chairmen was his friend and business collaborator, the American mining magnate and racehorse owner, Charles Engelhard.

Ironically, the Foundation attracted considerable venom from the Progressive Party, partly because it drew potential financial support away. But a policy directive also accused it of being 'in support of the futile attempt to maintain a fascist society in South Africa'. Oppenheimer did not appear to worry about the contradictions, as both positions served his purposes. The Foundation proved to be an invaluable asset for the Nationalist government. As the deputy president Dr H. J. van Eck, the powerful chairman of the Industrial Development Corporation, said some years later, the Foundation had won 'good friends and reliable supporters in key positions in the power structure of the world. When one looks back on the many vicious attacks that have been launched on South Africa in the past seven years, it must be obvious that without behind-the-scenes interventions on our behalf at crucial stages of these campaigns, we would never have won through to the position of international respect and domestic peace and prosperity which we enjoy today.'[1]

The test of the Foundation's strength came within weeks of its creation. In March 1960, the killing by the police of sixty-nine Africans who had been protesting against the Pass Laws at Sharpeville reverberated around the world, leading to a flight of foreign capital. During the year there was an outflow of £81 million. Oppenheimer revealed that the value of the quoted holdings in the group had fallen by 23 per cent. His contribution to the crisis was twofold.

First, Anglo companies joined the government and the large Afrikaner insurance companies in stemming the financial rupture. The 1961 annual report explained how it was done:

In June 1961 the authorities imposed stringent exchange control regulations which, inter alia, prevented the repatriation by non-residents of the proceeds of securities sold in South Africa and prohibited South African residents from remitting funds abroad for the purchase of South African or Rhodesian securities in other markets. These measures together with the raising abroad of a number of loans by private companies resulted in a severe curtailment in the net outflow of private capital.[2]

One of these private loans, of £30 million, was raised by Anglo's Rand Selection Corporation. During the 1960s, De Beers supported state loans and by 1968 had subscribed 40 million rand to government stocks.

Second, Oppenheimer adopted a strategy of on the one hand denigrating the black protest movement and on the other attacking the Pass Laws. In a statement published simultaneously in Johannesburg and London, he showed his masterly ability to balance on a rickety fence. Criticising Verwoerd's Pass Laws as unworkable, he said: 'In no fewer than four instances, large-scale projects have had to be put into cold storage for the time being, because our overseas associates are not willing to proceed until the political situation in the Union is clearer. In spite of all these difficulties our confidence in South Africa is unshaken.'[3] He then went on to endorse the government's crude view that agitators had been responsible for the troubles:

> There can be no doubt that there is deep discontent among the African population in the urban areas. That is why agitators have been so successful. Law and order have been restored, but only at the expense of far-reaching interference with the liberties of the population, black and white alike. Unless we can create conditions in which agitators are ineffective, not because of draconian legislation but because people do not want to listen to them, the future of South Africa will be a gloomy one.

One of his suggestions was a relaxation of the liquor laws for Africans.

In an interview a few days after Sharpeville, Oppenheimer was asked when he thought black South Africans would get political freedom. 'Eventually,' he conceded, 'there must be a large preponderance of non-white voters. When do I foresee that happening? I should not like to say, but not at least for twenty-five years.'[4]

His views were widely canvassed by the international media. He told the *US News and World Report*:

First of all, people disapprove of what is going on here, rightly or wrongly. They condemn it and think it immoral. That is one factor . . . the government's racial policy. After all, even investors have their feelings about the morality of such things, and that is, I would think, quite a serious factor.

Another factor is that people think – and I think this is a bit exaggerated – that what is going on here is going to be some sort of revolution. I think that thought arises largely from the third factor which, to my mind, causes this lack of confidence in South Africa, and that is an idea that this country is on exactly the same basis as tropical Africa. What the South African government was trying to do in separating the black and white races was not necessarily immoral as partition had proved the answer to problems in many parts of the world.

But I do think the economic integration of the races has gone much too far for there to be any successful separation. I therefore think that the South African government's policy cannot be maintained and the effect of trying to follow a policy that cannot be maintained is unfairness in the treatment of the African population.[5]

It was a speech with so many subtle caveats that it could have been made at any time over the next twenty-five years. Pressing on with his campaign, Oppenheimer told the Institute of Directors in London that South Africa was a good risk worth taking. Back home, he turned to the experience of black independence further north in the African continent: 'What the Congo does show is that primitive, uncivilised people cannot be trusted with the running of a modern state, and that independent democracy is only possible if the electorate has reasonable standards of education and civilisation.'[6]

Despite Oppenheimer's support for the South African state, and his ambivalent attitude towards reform, the size and influence of the Anglo group and its link with the

Progressives still attracted government censure and paranoia. In 1962, Prime Minister Hendrik Verwoerd spoke in
parliament about the power of 'certain business undertak-
ings such as the Oppenheimer group':

> The directors, when they meet, hold private discus-
> sions. In the case of such a powerful body there is also
> a central body which lays down basic policy. The
> influence of that central body, to say the least, must be
> great in our economic life. Nobody knows, however,
> what they discuss there. In the course of his speeches
> Mr Oppenheimer, the leader, makes political state-
> ments; he discusses political policy, he tries to exercise
> political influence. He even supports a political
> party . . . in other words he has political aims; he
> wants to steer things in a certain direction. . . . He can
> secretly cause a good many things to happen. In other
> words, he can pull strings. With all that monetary
> power and with this powerful machine which is spread
> over the whole country he can, if he so chooses,
> exercise an enormous influence against the Govern-
> ment and against the State.[7]

Verwoerd's strictures, which he repeated at his party's
annual congress, were similar to the attacks on Ernest
Oppenheimer thirty years earlier, and more sophisticated
commentators were quick to take up the point and reveal
their fundamental impotence. 'Don't worry, Mr Oppenheimer,' ran a leader in the Johannesburg *Sunday Times*:

> They cannot do without you. They know it and you
> know it. The National Party, at its congress this week,
> indulged in one of its periodic outbursts, this time led
> by the Prime Minister, against the figure they identify
> with 'big capitalism' and the mining industry.
>   Perhaps it was the heady influence of the party's
> jubilee, for there were distinct echoes of its earlier
> days, when the mining magnate and big money – *'die
> georganiseerde geldmag'* – were the enemy. The fact, of
> course, is that it is Mr Oppenheimer and men like him
> who make the wheels go round in South Africa, who

provide it with the sinews of war and enable it to
withstand the assaults of the world. Basically, it is they
who keep the Government in power – and the Government knows it.[8]

Nevertheless, Oppenheimer was not insensitive to the old
hostilities of Afrikaner business, which had for years
yearned for a stake in one of the seven gold-mining houses.
In an effort to engage Afrikaner business in transforming
the policies of the National Party (as it was called after
merging with the small Afrikaner Party in 1951), he opened
the golden door.

All the South African gold houses were in the English-
speaking camp and, of the four outside Anglo's control, the
group had a minority interest in three. In 1963, Oppenheimer agreed to help the Afrikaner finance house Federale
Mynbou to acquire control of the second largest mining
concern, General Mining and Finance Corporation, now
known as Gencor. Federale was part of the giant Afrikaner
finance conglomerate SANLAM (South African National
Life Assurance Company) and the deal, with Anglo taking a
substantial minority interest, cemented a long relationship
with Afrikaner capital. Tom Muller, Federale's managing
director, commented: 'The takeover would probably not
have come about but for the integrity and assistance of Mr
Oppenheimer. He has been extremely constructive about
the whole thing and has shown a genuine desire to assist in
creating an opening for the Afrikaans business world to
come into the world of mining and finance.'[9] For all this
cordiality, and an official endorsement of the deal from the
government, the extreme right wing of the National Party
still pursued its vendetta against Anglo and succeeded in
mounting a damaging investigation of Anglo's economic
power.

Dr Albert Hertzog, the leader of the hardline *verkrampte*
(conservative) group, commissioned an internal report from
Professor Hoek at the University of Pretoria. It was completed after the assassination of Hendrik Verwoerd in 1966.
The new Prime Minister, John Vorster, refused to publish

it, and when parts of the report were leaked in 1969 Hoek took out an injunction to suppress it, while at the same time denying his authorship. The report described Anglo as the largest private group in the economy, large enough to be able to frustrate government policies.[10] It claimed that Anglo paid a disproportionately low level of tax, which amounted to a loss of government revenues running into millions of rand. Hoek pointed out that, as an important supplier of key minerals to South Africa's defence industry, Anglo should be brought under much stricter government control. He suggested that its operational boundaries in South Africa be limited, and restrictions placed on its foreign-based companies such as Charter Consolidated in London.

Vorster knew better than to undermine the engine of South Africa's economy and one of its much-needed sources of foreign investment. He had recently thrown Hertzog out of the cabinet as he tentatively moved towards improving relations with the emerging independent black states. What was more, Anglo's transport company, Freight Services, was secretly shoring up the illegal Smith regime in Rhodesia – and indirectly protecting South Africa's north-eastern frontier – by helping the oil companies to evade British sanctions (see Chapter 10). Oppenheimer, in fact, was able to develop cordial relations with Vorster. Although, as Minister of Justice, Vorster had savagely put down the black unrest in the early 1960s, his imperialist designs on southern Africa happily coincided with Anglo's wish to expand economically to the north.

A similar incident occurred in the run-up to the 1970 election when the Minister of Mines and Planning, Carel de Wet, accused Oppenheimer of trying to use his industrial muscle to promote racial integration and to resist the government's policy of setting up industries near the black 'homelands'. He warned that all applications for govern-ment permits and concessions from Anglo would be refer-red to him for a personal decision. Oppenheimer was in Australia at the time and he told the *Melbourne Herald*: 'I realise I am living in a country which politically is a failure.

But somehow we are surviving. It is a nasty sort of survival and I often wonder what will happen in ten years' time. South Africa could be wiped out; its rulers are so damned bloodyminded.'[11]However, on his return to Johannesburg, he promised that his companies had no intention of refusing to comply with the laws and he denied sabotage of the apartheid labour policies. De Wet declared himself delighted with the reply, but his attack angered many even in the National Party, and there were calls for his removal. Vorster responded by depriving de Wet of his planning portfolio and then sending him off to be ambassador in London.

So the frictions and the mutual accommodations continued. In the year that Harry Oppenheimer accused the government of having taken 'a long step nearer towards being a police state' after sixteen black and white students were banned from the University of Cape Town (UCT), he was granted the freedom of the city of Kimberley. A year later, in 1974, as part of Vorster's détente diplomacy to encourage negotiations between Ian Smith and the black nationalists in Rhodesia, an Anglo jet was used to fly nationalist leaders to a conference in Lusaka. It was primarily Anglo's influence in Zambia that eased a temporary truce between Vorster and President Kaunda over the Rhodesian problem.

In successive annual statements, Oppenheimer argued that Blacks should be brought into the free-enterprise system and he warned of the perils of communism taking root if their lot was not improved. Little wonder, he said in 1976, that South African Blacks were looking towards revolutionary Angola and Mozambique for inspiration. It was the year of the Soweto uprising of black youth, and of the humiliating withdrawal of South Africa forces from Angola before the victorious MPLA and Cuban troops. The ranks closed. In a speech in Nelspruit, in the Eastern Transvaal, Oppenheimer said that the abandonment of separate development 'would strike at the roots of the National Party's power base and, therefore, in the short run anyhow, is not compatible with national unity'. Turning to Angola, he saw only doom:

After the events in Angola, it is not even plausible to suppose that the defeat of South Africa in a war of race would result in rule over the Whites by a black majority who were themselves free. All that can be said with certainty is that such a war would mean the extension of the African power vacuum in the richest and strategically most important part of the continent. And into that vacuum forces of one kind or another would certainly flow. And therefore South Africans of all races and colour have good reason to unite in support of the South African state. . . .

It is essential that we South Africans should be clear, not only about what we are fighting against but also what we are fighting for – and that is, in the first place, orderly government under the rule of law and an economic and political system which offers equal opportunity to all our people.

It is true that the conditions under which black South Africans live and work have over the last few years been improving. And the homelands policy, whatever some of us may think of it as an overall solution to our racial problems, has certainly thrown up leaders with the courage and ability to give effective representation to their people in the public life of the country.[12]

It was an extraordinary appeal from a man who had for years paid tens of thousands of black miners wages below the poverty line. And now he was suggesting that the Blacks had a reasonable voice through the homelands leaders, who were manifestly in thrall to the Pretoria government.

★   ★   ★   ★   ★

South African businessmen reacted to the 1976 Soweto uprising with a certain degree of fatalism. The anger and the frustrations that had erupted in that vast slum just a twenty-minute ride from the lawns and villas of Johannesburg came as a stunning blow. What was to be done to stave off wider unrest and, unspeakably, revolution?

Irene Menell decided to turn her social contacts to a more constructive purpose. As a Progressive Party activist whose husband Clive was the chairman of Anglo Transvaal Mines Consolidated (Anglo-Vaal), she encompassed within her circle both government ministers and South African corporate leaders. She thought of calling on them to form a social welfare organisation.

Clive [Menell] and I talked to Freddie van Wyk [director of the South African Institute of Race Relations] and George Palmer [editor of the *Financial Mail*] about it and they said, 'Great idea. There are little pockets of that sort of concern all round the country. Why don't you try and put them all together? Anglo American's got this big housing conference geared up for November, why don't you see if you can move it through that?' So we got hold of Nick Demont – Harry Oppenheimer was away in England; Nick was then his personal assistant – and sold him the idea of using that as a vehicle. Not hosted by Anglo American, but co-hosted by a kind of business power-house in South Africa and moved away from the strict housing thing into a broader urban problem framework. Nick was very excited by it and flew over to England and sold it to Harry and Zach [de Beer, the Anglo executive and ex-Progressive Federal Party MP]. Harry then contacted Anton Rupert [chairman of the Rembrandt Group], who was also overseas, and sold it to him. Then Clive and David de Villiers [former president of the South African Press Association] took letters that had been signed by Harry overseas, and delivered them and persuaded the other twelve co-hosts, or whatever it was, to participate in this exercise.[13]

The result was the Urban Foundation, founded in November 1976 at Anglo's Carlton Hotel in Johannesburg. It was to become a powerful arm of the Oppenheimer influence machine. Harry was elected its first chairman, and

Jan Steyn, a judge on special leave from the Cape Supreme Court, became executive director.

Its aim was to establish highly visible welfare projects in black urban areas which would, by example, help reshape government thinking. Modelled on the US organisations which sprang up after the riots in Watts and other cities, the Urban Foundation's philosophy was that reform, rather than repression, would do more to ensure South Africa's long-term future. 'As the arm and voice of the private sector,' Judge Steyn later wrote, 'the Urban Foundation is now applying its resources to help achieve the growth, prosperity, peace and stability that all South Africans seek.'[14] The *Financial Mail* took a more pointed view. The Foundation, it wrote in 1979, was set up to search for 'constructive ways and means of preserving an economy endangered by African revolt against conditions in the townships'.[15]

This logic appealed to the corporate community. Right from the start, the Foundation drew support from across the board: from English- and Afrikaans-speaking, South African- and foreign-based companies. It opened offices in London and New York. Its leadership was primarily corporate, with Anton Rupert as deputy chairman and Zach de Beer and Clive Menell among its twenty-three directors. Anglo, with six directors on the board of governors, in particular threw its financial weight behind the new organisation, with 10 million rand, half its budget, from associated companies in the first two years. E. Oppenheimer & Son put in 1 million rand.

Since then, the Foundation has considerably broadened its base of support. A total of 358 companies, institutions and individuals contributed 45 million rand to the Urban Foundation during its first five years. So successful were its fund-raising efforts that in 1980 Jan Steyn announced that its target of 25 million rand was far too low and would be hiked up to 50 million rand. The government pitched in, with the National Housing Commission paying for a new 80 million-rand housing project, and South African and international financial institutions supplying soft loans of 43.5 million rand in the first five years of the Foundation's existence.

By the time of its tenth anniversary, it had raised a staggering 490 million rand for infrastructure and housing projects, and another 83 million rand from nearly a thousand companies – all of which has helped support the Foundation's offices scattered throughout South Africa, its outposts in London and New York, and six housing utility companies.

Armed with capital of this magnitude, the Foundation has pursued its goals energetically. Many of its research documents on urbanisation and the abolition of influx control ended up on the desks of senior bureaucrats and politicians. In no small measure it spearheaded and defined the limited process of reform that P. W. Botha grudgingly endorsed in the early 1980s. The Foundation recognised that rural poverty forced people to seek work in the towns. It elevated the migrant worker, the backbone of its members' wealth for a century, into the 'cream of society'. They were 'the risk takers and innovators, the pioneers. They embody the very essence of the free-enterprise ethic.'[16]

Two kinds of projects were sponsored: community-based, low-cost schemes for the benefit of the general urban black population, and larger construction and education projects aimed at encouraging the formation of a skilled black middle class. The majority of these projects were locally based and included building schoolrooms and community centres, improving road drainage, upgrading homes and funding facilities for recreation, health and education. In an entirely different league are several large-scale and altogether more spectacular ventures.

One of the Urban Foundation's first actions was the negotiation with the Association of Building Societies of 99-year leasehold rights for a limited number of Africans in urban areas, making them eligible for mortgages for the first time. This gave the Foundation a reputation for challenging the restrictions of apartheid and was followed by others. Two notable examples are the electrification of Soweto, probably the biggest recipient of funds, and an 80 million-rand housing development, also in Soweto. During

1985 it successfully lobbied for the reintroduction of freehold rights in urban African townships and later argued for
the abolition of the Pass Laws.

So who benefited?

In the quest for stability, many of the Foundation's
projects were aimed at the relatively well off, who could
afford mortgages and small-business loans. Judge Steyn
wrote of the benefits of home ownership: it led to 'social
stability', 'capital formation by Blacks', 'private enterprise
values amongst Blacks', and 'the impetus toward the rapid
development of a stable [black] middle class'.[17] Harry
Oppenheimer, for once, was frank about the risks involved
in this strategy. Writing in his 1981 chairman's statement
about the dangers of half-hearted reform, he went on:

> Nor should the government or industrialists expect
> either gratitude or praise from black politicians or
> workers for the changes they are seeking to bring
> about. On the contrary such advances are likely to be
> met by new demands, heightened unrest and the open
> expression of hostility which in the past it was thought
> prudent to conceal.[18]

The urgent need to address the question of power-sharing
led the government and the Foundation to co-operate in the
formation of African 'community councils' as a substitute
for a national political voice for the urban Blacks. Judge
Steyn played a leading role in drafting the Black Local
Authorities Act, the legal basis for the councils. According
to black activists, the Foundation used its funds to encourage support for the councils. On the eve of the elections
in November 1984, the Foundation announced that it
intended to build 2,500 houses and 800 flats in Soweto with
the Rand Administration Board and the Soweto community
council. Tom Manthatha, the secretary of the Soweto Civic
Association, accused the Foundation of 'propping up apartheid' and trying to boost the credibility of the council,
which was to be based on a franchise limited to those 'legal'
residents with section 10 rights to live there. Thousands of
'illegal' residents who lived permanently in the townships

were excluded. The Foundation published a poll suggesting that at least 40 per cent of township residents would participate in the November 1983 elections. In the event, the poll was 21 per cent and in Soweto 10.7 per cent. Despite this massive rejection, Foundation support for the councils continued, with pressure on the government to recognise their umbrella organisation, the Urban Councils Association of South Africa. In the early 1985 uprising in black townships, the 'comrades', young radicals who rejected cosmetic reform, showed their more violent opposition when many African councillors and their supporters were attacked. Some were killed and their homes burned down. Over 150 resigned, one of them describing his decision as a move to place himself 'on the side of the people'.

Although the Foundation has called for the release from prison of black leaders, its hopes for a future South Africa are firmly based on the protection of white interests. At the 1985 annual meeting, Steyn urged the creation of a 'framework within which a legitimate negotiating process with Blacks as equal partners can take place on an open agenda'. But that open agenda would include 'the sharing of power at central government level' and 'the possibility of a federal component in the ultimate (probably unique) constitutional dispensation which is to emerge'. This is precisely the platform of the Progressive Federal Party (formerly the Progressive Party), which has rejected African demands for 'one person, one vote' in a unitary state. The Foundation has since joined the sanctions-circumvention industry by proposing new and ingenious ways for overseas companies to get their tax breaks and keep their South Africa stakes – a proposal which may solve the problem of the Foundation's corporate funding, 15 per cent of which has come from US companies, but will hardly enhance its reputation in the black community (see Chapter 12).

Education projects are less overtly political and less prone to criticism. This is where Anglo's own organisation for channelling spending in the direction of social projects – the AAC and De Beers' Chairman's Fund – is most active. This Fund is financed by annual grants of a fixed proportion of

De Beers and Anglo's profits amounting to about 0.5 per
cent – equal to several million rand a year. Before 1973 the
money was devoted to helping white private schools, but
thereafter a second branch was established for promoting
black education with an Anglo executive working on it full
time. Like the Urban Foundation, the Chairman's Fund
now operates from a strong sense of the importance of black
economic development to the future of the South African
economy as a whole. 'Why else would a company spend
millions of rand when it has no legal obligation to do so?'
Gavin Relly asked a symposium of managers in Switzerland. 'The case for doing something that brings in no
immediate financial return and which, anyway, you do not
have to do is that an investment in the future well-being of
your society and of your country must in the long run be of
benefit to your business.'[19]

The Fund's analysis of black deprivation was primarily
concerned with its effect on stability. 'Shortcomings in
education available to the black community strain South
Africa's social fabric more than any other factor.' They
retard economic growth and provide 'fertile ground for
social and political unrest'. It estimated that of the 6.2
million illiterate adults in the country, 5.8 million were
black. The task, therefore, was to improve the supply of
trained and educated black people to meet the demand for a
skilled and settled labour force. The case of the Mangosuthu Technikon showed how it was done.

In 1974, Oppenheimer met the KwaZulu leader
Mangosuthu Gatsha Buthelezi (after whom the college was
named) to discuss the need for black training in technical
skills. Inspired by the meeting, Oppenheimer commissioned a study from the South African Labour and Development Research Unit (SALDRU), another Chairman's
Fund project, at UCT. The research showed that only a
third of the technicians needed were being produced each
year. The Fund provided a total of 6.6 million rand for the
new college. Between 1977 and 1982 the Fund spent over
23 million rand on major education projects for black South
Africans, including the Soweto Teachers' Training College,

the Isidingo Technical College in Daveytown, and the Agriculture and Rural Development Research Institute at the University of Fort Hare. In 1986 the Fund's total commitments came to over 53 million rand. It contributed 4.6 million rand to the Mangosuthu Technikon, paid for a hostel for male students in Orlando, Soweto, and completed a college in the Transkei for 7.5 million rand, among other things. In honour of its 1988 centenary, De Beers is donating even more funds to education. Among its projects are a 750,000 rand endowment at the University of Stellenbosch for the Harry Oppenheimer Chair of Human Rights ('a subject which we believe to be of particular relevance to the future of our complex society,' says De Beers in its 1986 annual report) and 2 million rand towards a building to house the Harry Oppenheimer Institute for African Studies at Cape Town University.

Quite separately, the Ernest Oppenheimer Memorial Trust has provided support to bodies such as the Council for Education, Witwatersrand. As a result, Anglo has considerable influence in the liberal white universities, especially at Witwatersrand and Cape Town. Its executives sit on the Council of Witwatersrand University (and have done for decades). Oppenheimer himself is chancellor of the University of Cape Town, where yet another Chairman's Fund project, the Urban Problems Institute, is based. The story of Anglo's response to criticism from one group of white students illustrates its sensitivity and the limits of its tolerance to open inquiry.[20]

In 1971, students at Cape Town established a Wages and Economics Commission with the brief to investigate the wages and conditions of black workers. The Commission became part of the university's representative council and wrote a series of reports on conditions in different industries. After the shooting of miners at Anglo's Carletonville mine in 1973, UCT students called on Oppenheimer to resign as chancellor, in a demonstration that was deeply embarrassing to Anglo. At the end of the year, the Commission produced a survey of the gold mines, with Carletonville as its starting point. Later used as a UN publication, the report attacked the mining houses for their 'selfishness, callousness and inhumanity'. The report gained wider circulation in 1975, when parts were published in the *Times of Zambia*. A former Anglo executive turned MP, Dr Alex Boraine, wrote to Francis Wilson, an academic at UCT, expressing his concern over alleged inaccuracies. He asked Wilson, 'Would you know who the students are referred to in the article and whether or not they would appreciate a visit to Johannesburg, and especially to one of our mines?' Wilson, who later became head of SALDRU, passed on the invitation. An all-expenses-paid trip to Anglo head office in Johannesburg for Commission members was quickly arranged.

The itinerary of this two-day visit included a series of discussions with Anglo management. The second day was enlivened by a sumptuous lunch with most of the Anglo board, served by black waiters wearing white gloves and fez hats. The Commission's report of the visit was published in September 1976. There was little bite to it. A former Commission member told us: 'It was a shrewd move by the company. Anglo did not exactly tell the students to stop the research, but it disarmed them. The result was a report which was very toned down, but did not really get to grips with the gold mines' practices and wages and did not have much impact.' The report's preface, however, did include a caveat: 'We were unable to verify any of the information given to us because it was not possible to visit any of the corporation mines. We had, furthermore, no opportunity to discover the basis upon which data was computed. The material that has been presented should, therefore, be interpreted with extreme care.'

*   *   *   *   *

Oppenheimer's response to the Soweto uprising coincided with some new alignments on the national scene which at first sight appeared contradictory. With the break-up of the moribund United Party in 1977, the Progressive Party was renamed the Progressive Federal Party (PFP) and became the largest opposition party in the white parliament with 16.6 per cent of the votes and seventeen seats. Its new leader in 1979 was Frederik van Zyl Slabbert, a young Afrikaner professor of sociology, who established the new policy of a federal state with a universal franchise and, crucially, a minority right to veto legislation. Anglo maintained a strong presence in the party hierarchy, besides the continuing funding from Oppenheimer which had sustained Helen Suzman as its only MP from 1961 to 1974. Gordon Waddell, who was a Progressive MP between 1974 and 1979, remained on the PFP executive and was its national treasurer from 1978 to 1979. Zach de Beer also remained on the executive after resigning his seat in 1980 in order to concentrate on business as the chairman of the group's insurance, property and construction division. Alex Boraine, another Progressive MP and chairman of the party in 1985, was a former labour consultant to Anglo, while the present head of labour relations, Bobby Godsell, was a former chairman of the Young Progressives. There were changes, too, in the monolithic National Party, whose leader, John Vorster, foundered on the Muldergate crisis – the scandal within the Department of Information about its secret propaganda war.

The election of Defence Minister P. W. Botha as Prime Minister in 1978 signalled a profound shift in Nationalist ideology. Backed by the military and Afrikaner capital, Botha began the tortuous process of 'healthy power-sharing' which antagonised the right wing of his party, leading to the expulsion of sixteen MPs and the founding of the Conservative Party. While differences existed between the PFP and the Nationalists, there was an agreement on the need to abolish petty apartheid, to recognise trade unions and to make the economy more efficient with a better use of black labour. Botha called his plan the 'total strategy'. He had first enunciated it in a speech in 1977: 'Up to and including the beginning of the twentieth century the successful resolution of conflict was based purely on the victory of one army over another. The resolution of conflict in the times in which we now live demands interdependent and co-ordinated action in all fields – military, economic, psychological, political, sociological, cultural, etc.' The strategy had a two-pronged approach. The first was a programme of reform, co-opting members of the black community through the new trade unions, relaxing job reservation and softening some of the apartheid restrictions on the right of movement and residence for urban Blacks. The Urban Foundation was, in many areas, pushing at an open door. The other side of total strategy was an increasing militarisation of the state with the co-operation of the business community.

At the Carlton Centre in 1979 Botha met with business leaders, including Oppenheimer, to agree on the reform initiatives. 'I wanted to unite the business leaders behind the Defence Force . . . and I think I have succeeded,' Botha felt able to say a year later. He increased his own powers enormously by replacing the system of cabinet government with himself as state president and a state security council which has a strong military representation and which takes all the key decisions of government. South African Defence Force officers attended business seminars on labour relations and private businessmen served on the Defence Advisory Council and on secondment to the Armaments Corporation of South Africa (Armscor), the state's arms manufacturing and procurement agency. Legislation through the National Supplies Procurement Act and the National Key Points Act provided for the state to demand any essential supplies. It further required companies – over 600 of them – to set up their own security forces. At the same time industry was encouraged to increase South African control of key manufacturing plants.

On the regional front, 'total strategy' involved increasing South African penetration of dependent and independent African states, together with military destabilisation aimed at those giving succour to the African National Congress. Oppenheimer's fear of communist influences and the PFP's equally hard line on 'states harbouring terrorists' meant that there was little basic conflict with

Botha's objectives. Apart from his warning of half-hearted reform, Oppenheimer considered that Botha was courageously moving in the right direction.

It seemed, for a time, as if Oppenheimer's life-long ambitions were beginning to bear fruit. In 1982, at the age of 74, he retired from the chair of Anglo American and handed over the position to his right-hand man Gavin Relly while remaining as chairman of De Beers. On his last day in December, thousands of people from Anglo's ten buildings in Johannesburg's business district converged on Main Street to listen to his parting speech. The company had to get official permission for the gathering under the Riotous Assemblies Act. It was in some ways the end of an era; in others nothing seemed to change.

Relly had a reputation for being a tough, commercially minded man, but still very much in the Anglo mould. From his early days as an Oppenheimer personal assistant he had rapidly moved up the hierarchy, becoming a manager at the age of 32. He brought the Highveld Steel plant to fruition, negotiated the nationalisation of the Zambian copper mines, then headed Anglo's North American interests from Toronto, becoming a close friend of Charles Engelhard. At one of his first international conferences he complained that 'failure to redress black grievances in the industrial sphere, no less than in others, will make it vastly more difficult to persuade Blacks to participate constructively in a new dispensation for South Africa – and downright impossible to persuade them that the private-enterprise system and its wealth-creating function serve their interests as well as ours.'[21] But, against the advice of colleagues, he accepted the post of president of the South African Foundation, with its explicit support of the government. In 1980, he sat on Botha's Defence Advisory Council. While Harry Oppenheimer opposed the exclusion of Blacks from Botha's 1983 proposals for Indian and coloured parliaments, Relly supported the idea. In his 1984 annual statement, continuing with another Oppenheimer tradition, he wrote:

Mr P. W. Botha had chosen to set the country on a course of what might be called decentralised democratisation which, while it maintains a substructure of national co-operation, also appears to envisage a superstructure of national co-operation. Both the left and the right will advocate more conventional solutions to the problems posed by the complexity of our society; but if Mr Botha can maintain the thrust of his policy to embrace the urban black population and then move to some federal system to embrace the country as a whole, we may have reason to hope that these intiatives will evoke the vitality and optimism to bring about a new era, with profound implications for southern Africa as a whole.[22]

While Relly grew in confidence in his new role, Oppenheimer finally relinquished the chair of De Beers in 1984, declaring that the diamond industry was out of the rough. The successor here was just as predictable, with Oppenheimer's other protégé, Julian Ogilvie Thompson, the deputy chairman of both De Beers and Anglo, taking over the job.

As his father gradually withdrew from public control, Nicky Oppenheimer moved up to secure the dynasty. Deputy at AAC in 1982 and then at De Beers in 1984 at the age of 30, he finally took over the Central Selling Organisation (CSO) in 1986, after the retirement of the man who had forged the Russian connection, Sir Philip Oppenheimer. 'These days,' he ventured in a rare interview, 'it's not enough to have the Oppenheimer name. If you can't run with the ball, you're going to be dropped from the team.'[23] Nicky has perfected the Oppenheimer trait of diffidence to a fine art. Asked what he would like to be remembered for at the age of 75, he replied: 'Oh, not for any particular thing. Perhaps for having lived a worthwhile life, for not being boring. It would be nice to be remembered for having been polite to people all one's life.'[24]

Still, he does have more to say than this. At an investment

speech in Johannesburg in 1979 he showed that he had
mastered the Oppenheimer philosophy.

> We must draw everyone into a truly free-enterprise
> system. Capitalism is only attractive if one has the
> opportunity to enjoy its benefits. When I did my
> national service, because I had a degree, I was com-
> missioned immediately into basic training. Beforehand
> I had to fill in a long questionnaire at the end of which
> was the crunch question. Was I a communist? With
> little hesitation I was able to answer that I was a
> confirmed capitalist. This answer came very easily,
> because I and my family before me have been able to
> benefit from the capitalistic society that we have lived
> in. . . . But had I been black, would the answer have
> come quite so easily? Would capitalism have appeared
> quite so attractive or would I have mistakenly thought
> that it was capitalism that was preventing me from
> earning the same as the next (white) man, from
> owning my own house or from living in the suburb of
> my own choice? To have a true partnership between
> free enterprise and government it is important that the
> answer to that question should come more and more
> easily. This will be the case once the renewed partner-
> ship has so changed South Africa that investment
> flows in proportion to the benefits offered the investor,
> and the benefits that in turn flow from investment are
> enjoyed by all South Africans. Then and only then will
> South Africa be politically acceptable.[25]

There spoke the chip off the old block.

Harry Oppenheimer's retreat from formal control of the
group did not, however, diminish his influence or his
readiness to intervene in public life. Gavin Relly and
Ogilvie Thompson regularly seek his advice for what Relly
once called the 'sensible understandings' which are the
imprint of the continuing management style. In fact
Oppenheimer regards the business as very much a personal
responsibility – as much for his family as for anything else.
He still travels, almost as much as before. In November

1986 he turned up for a four-day 'holiday' in Hong Kong. Financial commentators were sceptical, given Anglo's large steel and coal exports to Hong Kong and the clandestine re-export of steel to China. He would have been sure to get a welcome from his friends at the Blue Train Club, an informal luncheon club of South African businessmen. Six weeks before his visit the club played host to Pik Botha, the South African foreign minister, who was touring Asia to diversify sanctions-threatened South African trade. And what better place than the entrepot port of Hong Kong where politics has no part in trade.

In Johannesburg he can retreat into the multi-million-pound Brenthurst Library which was opened in 1984 on the family estate. His private circular study, overlooking a calm lily pond, contains his collection of Romantic Poets and first editions. The spacious building, with a vaulted dome and American-ash shelves for the 10,000 volumes of Africana, has a technical system of humidity control, dust filters and lights with ultraviolet filters that is equalled only by the new wing of the Library of Congress in Washington. The collection includes most of the works of the nineteenth-century art historian Thomas Baines, letters of Livingstone, Winston Churchill's hand-written account of being taken prisoner in the Boer War and a number of splendid natural-history folios. There is a volume of François Le Vaillant's *Histoire Naturelle des Oiseaux d'Afrique*, published in 1799, and two sets of Redoute's *Les Liliacées*, published in Paris in 1905. The library has a full-time restorer, and a press publishes limited editions. A deluxe volume with only 125 copies is bound in half red Algerian goatskin and hand-marbled paper and tooled in gold. The average price is 300 rand. Visitors – not more than two at a time and carefully vetted – can examine the big bound volumes of press cuttings relating to the family. One year's volume is as thick as a *Shorter Oxford Dictionary*. Anglo's public relations people have been extraordinarily vigilant. There are also cuttings from the racing pages, showing every time an Oppenheimer horse ran or won. The librarian, Marcelle Weiner, is currently engaged on an even more rigorous job sorting out thirty years of Bridget Oppenheimer's menus, meticulously written out so that guests did not get the same meal twice running. From Brenthurst, higher up the estate, you may not be able to see the smoke rising from Soweto beyond the skyscrapers of downtown Johannesburg, but the image of Nero sitting atop the Tower of Maecenas is irresistible.

6

Bringing in the Yankee Dollar

Anglo's industrial expansion in South Africa in the early
1960s, financed by profits from the Orange Free State gold
mines, coincided with an ambition to become a truly
international mining house. In the light of the group's
unprecedented resources and the small domestic economy,
the logic for future growth was to prospect and invest
beyond the African continent. The chosen target was first of
all Canada, and the catalyst was an extraordinary American
whose unqualified support for the apartheid regime gave it a
valuable respectability in the United States right up to the
White House.

   Charles Engelhard, a rotund, diminutive man, was the
son of a German émigré who had built up a precious metals
refining business after his arrival in the States in the 1890s.
Engelhard Metals and Minerals Corporation was to become
a giant among US companies. Engelhard first visited South
Africa in the late 1940s to buy gold. However, South Africa
prohibited the direct export of gold bars, while allowing the
export of jewellery. Engelhard got round the restrictions by
manufacturing gold jewellery which was shipped to Hong
Kong for melting down. The idea had come from Engelhard's London financiers, Robert Fleming and Company, a
family firm owned by a former naval officer by the name of
Ian Fleming. Much later Fleming, the novelist and creator
of James Bond, was to use Engelhard as a model for the

eponymous character in *Goldfinger*. Engelhard liked South
Africa. He made substantial investments in gold and platinum mines and settled in the country a few years later.

He was a man of considerable influence. A supporter of
the Democratic Party in the United States, he was a friend
of both Presidents Kennedy and Johnson. At the independence ceremonies of Algeria, Zambia and Gabon,
Engelhard was the official representative of the US administration. In 1963, he was the American presence at the
coronation of the Pope. In South Africa, he became a close
friend of Harry Oppenheimer and through linking investments sat on Anglo's board as an executive director. Like
Oppenheimer, he loved racehorses and at one time owned
250 around the world including Nijinsky, the winner of the
English Triple Crown. He even shared his famous stallion
Ribofilio with the Oppenheimer stud.

Engelhard threw himself wholeheartedly into the South
African mining world. He was on the boards of the
Witwatersrand Native Labour Association and the Native
Recruiting Corporation, through which the Chamber of
Mines hired labourers from Mozambique and Rhodesia. In
1958, anxious to attract American capital at a time of
international unease about the Nationalists' policies, he set
up the American South African Investment Company,
which took minority holdings in nine gold mines, including
a 10 per cent stake in the enormously rich Doornfontein
mine. His interests finally gave him the chair of Rand
Mines, part of the third largest gold group, Central Mining.
Just before the shock of Sharpeville and the flight of foreign
capital, he was a founder with Oppenheimer of the South
African Foundation and became its vice-chairman.

His high-profile public support for South Africa, which
included the raising of $30 million from American investors
in 1963, encouraged other US-dominated institutions to
follow suit, not least the International Monetary Fund and
the World Bank. 'If you find somebody who doesn't like
living in South Africa, he hasn't been paid enough,' was one
of his more cynical remarks.[1] In the year after Sharpeville,
$150 million of official loans flowed across the Atlantic.

Although US policy was to distance itself from direct associations with apartheid – hence the support for the voluntary United Nations arms embargo in 1963 – the administration preferred friendly co-operation and mild persuasion. Returns for American investors, both direct and indirect, were twice as high as anywhere else in the world. For the Pentagon, South Africa was a crucial pivot in the strategic alliance against communism in the South Atlantic and the Indian Ocean. Naval co-operation remained close, and the US military gained valuable information from the three tracking stations set up in South Africa in the late 1950s by the National Aeronautics and Space Administration (NASA). Little wonder, then, that President Johnson personally received Harry Oppenheimer in 1964, after being briefed by his officials on Oppenheimer's 'humane policies towards his African workers'.[2] Two years later, when Vorster succeeded Verwoerd, Engelhard remarked: 'The policy of South Africa as expressed by the new Prime Minister is as much in the interests of South Africa as anything I can think of or suggest. I am not a South African but there is nothing I would do better or differently.'[3]

Engelhard's first contribution to Oppenheimer's expansion overseas came in 1958, when they formed a consortium to take over Central Mining and thwart a counter-bid from Gold Fields of South Africa (GFSA), Anglo's main rival at the time. Central Mining, with eight gold mines (compared with Anglo's twelve and GFSA's eleven), also had an important stake in the Canadian oil and gas industry.

Anglo was no stranger to the great mineral deposits in the Canadian frozen north. Consolidated Mines Selection (CMS), the group's original parent company based in London, had a controlling stake in the rich Baffinland Iron Mines in British Columbia, as well as an interest in Canada's largest mining investment company, McIntyre Porcupine Mines Selection. De Beers, which supplied drills to the Canadian mining industry, was actively looking for diamond pipes. Another Anglo-controlled company, Rhodes' old British South Africa Company (BSAC), had also invested in Canada with its profits from the Zambian copperbelt. The stage was set for a major advance.

The first move, with help from Engelhard, came with Anglo's $20 million purchase of a 14.5 per cent stake in the Canadian mining company Hudson Bay Mining and Smelting. Raising the finance had not been easy, because of currency-exchange restrictions designed to prevent the outflow of domestic capital from South Africa. In the end, the whole amount was raised in New York. These constraints persuaded Harry Oppenheimer of the need to establish an overseas finance house. The by now familiar Oppenheimer tactic was used, whereby the new company would appear separate and independent, yet was firmly in Anglo's control. An added advantage was the ability to distance overseas investments from the taint of apartheid.

The creation of Charter Consolidated in London in 1965 was brought about by a merger between the BSAC, Central Mining and Anglo's original parent, Consolidated Mines Selection. BSAC, which had controlled mining rights in Northern Rhodesia, brought with it $4 million compensation from the first independent government of Zambia in 1964. Charter quickly became a holding company for operations in the USA, Britain, Canada, France, Australia, Malaysia and Mauritania. In its first three years, Charter more than doubled in value to £324 million, almost rivalling the market value of the Anglo American Corporation. One of its first objectives, which set a pattern for future Anglo operations abroad, was to raise each investment to a minimum of 10 per cent in order to qualify for double tax relief in the UK.

Before his death in 1971, Charles Engelhard provided Oppenheimer with a more important entrée into the North American market. His personal holding in the Engelhard business was through a private company, Engelhard Hanovia, which held a controlling interest. In the late 1960s, he sold more and more Hanovia shares to E. Oppenheimer and Son until the South African interest reached 70 per cent. Oppenheimer then secured control of the parent by exchanging his Hanovia shares for 10 per cent of Engelhard and three men on the board. The arrangement was ideal for both groups. Engelhard Minerals had assured access to South African minerals, especially platinum in the new platinum catalyst business for auto exhausts, and Anglo had at last secured a considerable foothold in the United States. The relationship, at an appropriate arm's length, is explained in the small print of the Engelhard annual report: 'The company, in the ordinary course of business, purchases raw materials from entities in which it is informed Anglo American Corporation of South Africa has a material interest. Anglo American holds indirectly a significant minority interest in the common stock of the company.' Engelhard's purchases from Anglo in 1983 were worth $198 million.

That holding was eventually deposited with Anglo's second international company, which became in 1981 the largest foreign investor in the United States of America. Minerals and Resources Corporation (Minorco) had its origins in the Zambian copper mines that Sir Ernest had exploited in the early days of the group. The lineage began as far back as 1928, when Rhoanglo was formed in London to finance the expansion on the copperbelt. It moved to Zambia in 1954, and ten years later was renamed Zambian Anglo American (Zamanglo) when the country acquired its independence. In 1970, when the new government took 51 per cent of the company, it was transferred to the tax haven of Bermuda to receive the compensation monies in the form of dividends from government bonds. Four years later, it was renamed Minorco and was soon to overtake Charter as the group's overseas flagship. By 1988 it had over $3 billion invested, nearly half of it in the United States. Of its 170 million shares, nearly 12 million, worth £82 million, were owned by members of the Oppenheimer family.

As the launch-pad for Anglo's penetration into America, Minorco's African history is a telling commentary on the actual practice, as opposed to the rhetoric, of the Anglo empire. Sir Ernest's much-vaunted claim that Anglo's objective was to benefit the communities in which it operated, as well as the shareholders, proved to be rather threadbare when the state of Zambia at independence is examined. Although copper alone made Zambia one of the richest countries with the fastest growth rates in sub-Saharan Africa, its level of development was dramatically uneven. At independence in 1964, there were no more than 100 graduates and 1,000 children with secondary-school certificates out of a population of 4 million. The two big copper mining companies, Anglo and the US firm American Metal Climax (AMAX), had sent £260 million out of the country in dividends, interest and royalty payments during the previous ten years. The British South Africa Company had received £82 million net for its mineral royalties from 1923 to 1964. Over the same period, the British treasury received £40 million in taxes, in part because the mining companies were based in London until the 1950s.

Even after Zambia's independence the two companies sent out about three-quarters of their profits in dividends. When President Kaunda declared in 1968 that the companies must retain half their profits in the country, both Anglo and the Americans increased their capital and adjusted their accounting policies in order to maintain dividend payments without going above the 50 per cent profit limit. When the government finally took over 51 per cent of the mines, the companies were granted generous tax concessions, freedom from exchange controls and, until 1974, the management contracts. Yet they resisted the process of 'Zambianisation' of their staff, preferring to bring in expatriate managers, and they repatriated as much profit as they could. Kaunda complained: 'Our experience in the last three and a half years has been that they have taken out of Zambia every ngwee that was due to them. A major part of the capital for the expansion programmes of both companies has been obtained from external borrowing and not from retained profits.'[4] Anglo's compensation had been £73 million, with a further £22 million for the loss of the management contract. This was Minorco's start-up capital, bled from a former British colony in Africa and deposited, nicely sanitised, in a British colonial tax haven in the Caribbean. Other assets were transferred into Minorco, including the hugely profitable 29 per cent stake in Engelhard. By 1981 Minorco's assets stood at £2 billion, compared with Anglo American's $2.5 billion. The group as a whole held over three-quarters of Minorco's shares.

Cash-rich Minorco proceeded on an acquisitions binge. One in New York and another in London aroused considerable controversy. The remarkable raid on Consolidated Gold Fields in London, which teetered on the borders of legality, is explained in Chapter 8. The American coup involved once again the Engelhard business.

In 1981, the reorganised Engelhard Corporation sold off its commodity-trading arm, Philipp Brothers, known as Phibro. This was the world's biggest publicly owned marketer of raw materials, with 1980 pre-tax profits (mainly from oil that year) of $589.6 million on a turnover of $24 billion. Before the year was out, Phibro had successfully negotiated an extraordinary merger bid which allied it to American's largest private investment bank and the world's largest bond-trading firm, Salomon Brothers. Wall Street gasped as much at the audacity of the deal as at the way in which it was engineered. In the new business of Phibro-Salomon, the Oppenheimers had a 27 per cent stake.

The deal was widely regarded as a cheap buy, but the reason it was acceptable to Salomon was primarily because a small group of people became immensely rich. Salomon Brothers was a private company, whose sixty-two partners were entitled to a share of the profits which were frozen in the capital fund. They were thus millionaires who could not spend their money. Phibro's proposal was temptingly ingenious: the partners would be able to have their $254 million while Phibro would buy the then empty company for $300 million and recapitalise it. At a mandatory meeting, held on 31 July 1981 at the Terrytown Conference Center near New York City, the partners took a day and a half before every one of them had signed the agreement to sell. General managers were thereby enabled to take out an average of $2.7 million, tax-free; in addition they were each given an average of $3.2 in bonds. Members of the seven-man executive committee

were entitled to about $11 million apiece. Ira Harris, one of
the partners who negotiated the deal, picked up $16 million
on bonds alone, not counting his capital and share of the
1981 profits. The managing partner, John Gutfreund, who
was accorded a standing ovation at the end of the weekend,
received a total payout of $32 million. 'Any time someone
wants to stick me in a room and give me millions of dollars,'
said one partner afterwards, 'please, don't throw me out
into the briar patch.'[5]

Reporting the merger, the *Financial Times* commented:

> It will create what observers say will be the most
> formidable trading house in the world, combining
> skills in virtually all commodities, financial and physi-
> cal, with a client list that includes governments and
> most of the biggest corporate names around the
> globe.[5]

The honeymoon, however, was soon over. The Oppenheimer interest attracted public concern about the company's connections with apartheid, and senior executives of
Phibro-Salomon had to insist that the Anglo group was a
passive partner. Yet when the Phibro arm turned in a poor
performance in 1983, and an internal row was predicted
between Gutfreund, who had stayed on at Salomon, and
Phibro's head, David Tendler, *Fortune* magazine suggested
that Harry Oppenheimer as the major shareholder would
have an important role in settling it. He was no stranger to
the company's two chief executives, who had flown to
Johannesburg to meet him and Anglo officials. Gutfreund,
a regular visitor to Manhattan society gossip columns for his
extravagant parties and his young air-hostess wife,
described the trip as a pleasant, English-country-house
kind of weekend. As usual, the talk of passive investments
was a piece of fiction. The board set up an ad hoc committee
of four people to resolve the crisis when Tendler made a
move to buy out the commodity business and go it alone. It
included Henry R. 'Hank' Slack in his capacity as a
Minorco director and Harry Oppenheimer's American
hatchet-man. Tendler eventually resigned.

Although over the next two years Minorco reduced its interest in Phibro-Salomon by half, its remaining investment was valued at $907 million, nearly 40 per cent of Minorco's assets. Besides Engelhard, the other holdings were a 38 per cent stake in Charter, 29 per cent of Consolidated Gold Fields (Consgold), 50 per cent of Zambia Copper Investments (ZCI) and 60 per cent of its wholly reorganised North American interests, including Hudson Bay, under the name of Inspiration Resources. Inspiration's interests in copper and other base metals, at a time of declining world prices, meant that the company was making a loss up until 1985. But its value to Anglo lay elsewhere. The merger that resulted in Inspiration in 1983 created a company listed as the 357th largest industrial concern in the Fortune 500. It had a New York Stock Exchange listing – Anglo's first – and subsequently it expanded and consolidated its oil and gas interests into a major new oil company with drills in North America, Paraguay, Indonesia and the North Sea.

Like other American majors, Inspiration has a history of careful patronage. The Federal Electoral Commission for 1984 showed that its copper company in Arizona contributed $1,000 each to Republican Representative Eldon Rudd and Democrat Senator Dennis DeConcini, both of the state of Arizona, in 1982. A further $100 went to the political coffers of Representative James D. Santini of Nevada, who was the chairman of the minerals and mines subcommittee of the Committee of the Interior.[7]

The holding in Consgold brought Anglo indirect involvement with an old American friend. Consgold had acquired a 26 per cent interest in the giant US natural resources combine, Newmont Mining, which helped to put up some of the capital for the formation of Anglo in 1971. Newmont held 10 per cent of Anglo's Highveld Steel and Vanadium, and both groups had interests in the big copper, lead and silver Tsumeb Corporation in Namibia. In addition, Newmont's third-owned Sherritt Gordon mines in Alberta and Manitoba were a major supplier of zinc and copper concentrates to Inspiration Resources. Newmont was the largest

US employer of labour in southern Africa. In 1984 it resisted a shareholder resolution calling for no further expansion in South Africa on the basis that its investments provided jobs and raised living standards for all races. It justified its refusal to sign the US Sullivan Principles on minimum wages and conditions on the ground that they did not apply to mining operations in remote areas with a migrant work force.

The directors who sit on Minorco's board and those of its major investments illustrate how, as in South Africa, the group is held together by a skein of personal relations and mutual self-interest. Minorco's chairman is the ubiquitous Ogilvie Thompson of De Beers and the president is Hank Slack. Their colleagues include such luminaries as Ernest Oppenheimer's old friend, Sidney Spiro, of the prestigious Hambro merchant bank; Sir Michael Edwardes, the South African-born former chairman of British Leyland; Cedric E. Ritchie, chairman of the Bank of Nova Scotia; Neil Clarke of Charter and Johnson Matthey; and Gavin Relly, Reuben F. Richards, the former head of Citibank's European division, manages to combine being chief executive officer of Inspiration Resources with directorships on Minorco, Engelhard and Phibro-Salomon.

But perhaps the most influential man on the Minorco board until he stepped down in November 1986 was Felix G. Rohatyn, a senior partner in Lazard Frères since 1947 who has a reputation as one of the most powerful investment bankers. His connections with Anglo go back to 1971, when he began a ten-year tenure as a director of Engelhard. Renowned as the man who saved New York from bankruptcy in the 1970s, Rohatyn was tipped as a potential high-flyer in the next US Democratic administration, possibly as Secretary of the Treasury. In the early 1980s he was one of the foremost spokesmen for the concept of an 'industrial policy', drawing together leaders from business, the unions and government to tackle the problems of the US economy. An ad hoc committee to examine the idea, based on his Municipal Assistance Corporation in New York, included Lane Kirkland, the head of the US union body AFL-CIO, Senator Edward Kennedy and Irving S. Shapiro, the former chairman of DuPont. Rohatyn counts among his friends Henry Kissinger, François Mitterand and the Agnellis of Fiat. When asked why he had agreed to join Minorco, Rohatyn replied: 'I think Harry is a very unusual and courageous man. Companies that consider associating with Anglo are worried about the possible impact on their business. I think that Harry Oppenheimer wanted to bring in outside directors who would be sensitive to these problems and also provide broader views on investments.'[8] Given the international perception of Anglo American as a liberal and reforming employer, Rohatyn's concern about reluctant partners was initially ill-founded. The US disinvestment campaign had still to find its teeth. After Rohatyn's retirement from the board he still acted as an occasional financial adviser and the Lazard Frères connection was maintained with a succession of two other partners on the board.

Anglo's penetration of the US market in the late 1970s did not go unremarked by the American authorities. A US Department of Commerce report on publicly available information about direct foreign investment between 1979 and 1982 identified 'Harry Oppenheimer and Family' as owning nearly $1,000 million dollars in eighteen American companies. Yet Gavin Relly, after he became chairman of Anglo American in 1982, was able to say that his company 'has absolutely no business in America'.[9]

It is remarks like this that have obscured the real character of the Anglo group in its wide-ranging international operations. On a narrow interpretation, Relly was correct. For even the 60 per cent holding in Inspiration Resources included only 46 per cent of voting shares. As in South Africa, however, the question of control becomes largely irrelevant when a substantial minority stake is combined with intimate trading relations, sympathetic and entrenched management, cross-shareholding, and political and financial friends.

Nevertheless, Anglo remains vulnerable, cautious and secretive when it ventures beyond South Africa. Sometimes its manoeuvres are carried to absurd lengths.

When, in 1983, Charter Consolidated made a bid to take over the leading Scottish coal-mining equipment firm of Anderson Strathclyde, the board maintained that its relationship with Anglo was 'largely historical'. Charter claimed that no single shareholder had a controlling interest in it. Anderson Strathclyde punctured that claim in one of the most robust rejection documents issued in the City of London. It pointed out that Charter was 35.6 per cent owned and effectively controlled by Minorco, and continued:

> Six of the fifteen directors of Charter are directors of Anglo, two others are directors of Anglo companies and one other is an alternative director of Anglo. The Anglo presence constitutes a clear majority.[10]

A year later, Charter had to eat its words. Gavin Relly launched a pruning exercise. He decided to shut down Charter's company in Ashford, which provided services in the UK to De Beers, Anglo, Minorco and about fifty other Anglo group companies. 'The decision was not taken by us,' a Charter spokesman commented lamely. 'It has been a profitable business as far as our company is concerned. The ruling has come from Johannesburg. They say there will be very big economies in handing the work over to outsiders.'[11]

Anglo has always disliked and discouraged, in the politest possible way, any investigation of its broader activities. Its critics are met with aloof disdain or, alternatively, with a handsome invitation to correct their 'misunderstanding' about South Africa's 'complex' society. The group's sensitivities about its South African base and its grip on the mineral resources of the West are palpable. Diamond analysts have long remarked and complained about the paucity of information emanating from the secretive De Beers. Successive Anglo American reports have reduced the amount of information given about its true exposure in black Africa. The 1986 report was the slimmest for many years. America is portrayed as just a remote investment. The British connections go to risible lengths to distance themselves from their Johannesburg masters. For example, Charter is obliged to disclose – albeit only in one obscure paragraph – in its 1987 annual report:

On 10 June 1987 Minerals and Resources Corporation held 37,860,075 shares of 2p each representing 36.0 per cent of the share capital of the company. Anglo American Corporation of South Africa Limited and De Beers Consolidated Mines Limited were deemed under section 203(2)(b) of the Companies Act 1985 to be interested in that shareholding.[12]

        ★   ★   ★   ★   ★

A long-held secret of Minorco was punctured in the most bizarre fashion in 1986 from a most unlikely source. A group of young squatters discovered that the dividends from Minorco's multi-million-dollar investments were being shunted half-way round the world and back again in an enormous tax avoidance scheme. The story is worth telling in some detail.[13]

The chosen site for this subterfuge was the tranquil city of Amsterdam, in one of the elegant terraced houses on a cobbled canal street. Here was the wealth of the Dutch East India Company, which opened its refreshment station at the Cape of Good Hope in 1652 and then encouraged the slave-owning settlers to provide supplies from the land they stole from the indigenous Khoisans.

It was in one of those streets that we met 'David' and 'Pieter', on their ancient upright bicycles. These are not their real names, of course. It is not only what they have done to Anglo that necessitates this anonymity. In the squatter circles of Amsterdam, few use their full names except when they disappear to another part of the city to adopt their official personas. This keeps them safe from eviction, since the landlord would need their full names in order to secure an eviction order. So your address book would list squatters under K for *Kraker*: John K, Pieter K, Annete K and so on. But David and Pieter do not use their true Christian names, or give you their phone number, or even tell you when next to expect them. They need extra security, because what they have done is regarded in some circles as highly reprehensible as well as illegal.

It was the mass dismissal of 17,400 Anglo mine workers in April 1985 that first sparked the Amsterdam squatters' special interest in the Anglo American Corporation. Their movement had reached its peak in the late 1970s and early 1980s, culminating in mass battles to stop the Amsterdam police from clearing major squats. A large group of radical activists emerged from this essentially anarchist-orientated movement, and from that in turn smaller groups developed which concentrated their attention on taking 'direct action' on more specific and difficult subjects. One, for instance, invaded the Ministry of Economic Affairs and came out with papers exposing the nuclear power lobby. These documents were sufficiently damning almost to cause the downfall of the minister responsible.

When Anglo's mass dismissals sparked headlines around the world, the group of which David and Pieter were a part was already concentrating on the fight against apartheid. They began to research Anglo, using public sources. They soon found that AAC group had some companies in the Netherlands, and they set to tracing their structures, activities and locations. As usual with Anglo, that was difficult enough in itself, given the many and varied forms of those interests. As well as AAC and De Beers themselves, companies such as Charter, Engelhard, Johnson Matthey and Consgold all have interests registered in Holland. But what the *aktiegroep* Splijt Apartheid soon discovered was that Anglo had one small office in Amsterdam whose sole function seemed to be to act as a Dutch channel for the group's international holdings. What is more, inspection of the company records at the local Chamber of Commerce revealed that the assets involved were very substantial. Here Splijt Apartheid were fortunate in that under new rulings some of the companies had for the first time had to provide more comprehensive information in their annual reports.

Those days, every multinational of any substance has a

multiplicity of non-trading subsidiaries scattered around the globe. Usually these companies have no staff whatso-ever, and are simply based and run out of a convenient lawyer's, accountant's or bank's office. Their *raison d'être* is generally some complex scheme for tax avoidance (which is legal), if not tax evasion (which is illegal). The boundary is often difficult to distinguish even for the tax authorities. There can also be other reasons for such artificial corporate structuring. One is to service transfer pricing, whereby profits can be spirited away as goods cross national borders to pass between separate subsidiaries. Another is to provide a secure ownership base for international investments.

Anglo certainly did not need its Amsterdam operations to provide a secure European base. It already has just that across the Channel in London, primarily in the Charter Consolidated/De Beers/CSO complex at Holborn Circus. While the group could well be heavily involved in transfer pricing in order to move funds out of the rigid confines of South Africa's exchange control, Amsterdam is far too upright a city in which to base such activities. Better to use the more easygoing havens, such as Liberia, Bermuda, the Netherlands Antilles, Liechtenstein or even Luxemburg, where Anglo's resoures will impress the tax inspectors far more.

Splijt Apartheid's researchers did not know the details, but it was clear that the small Amsterdam office played an important role in minimising the group's tax liabilities. It was also apparent that the only way to unravel the details of the web of holdings was to obtain information from within the office, and their research had convinced them that Anglo was a justifiable target. They decided to take direct action against Anglo, with the three main objectives typical of their political philosophy:

First, we wanted to take away all the company's administration material. Then you frustrate them in their work.

Second, we hoped that when we have all their secret things we could bring into the open their activities and provoke a reaction by the public authorities. By bringing it to the public attention you hope to make them close down. You hope to make a scandal.

Third, by producing a report on the company and these activities you hope to increase the knowledge of the people in Holland as to what happens and get them to take action.

Prinsengracht is the name of the third canal you cross moving west from the centre of Amsterdam. It is a pleasant, historic street, which begins at the Zee close to the station and curves round to the south-east. The top end is quiet and gradually becoming sought after, its most famous building being Anne Frank's house. Towards the middle stands the central courthouse, a vast monumental stone edifice once noted for its graffiti – a problem that has been overcome, in typical Dutch fashion, not by heavy-handed policing but by applying a special paint so that the most insulting graffiti can be washed off.

Located at the bottom end of Prinsengracht, close to Amsterdam's rich business centre, is No 783, a handsome, wide, six-storey former merchant's building, complete with gable, beam and pulley hook, though it has now been thoroughly modernised to provide self-contained offices on each floor. In mid-1986, the nameplate for the first-floor offices read 'Plain Holdings'; a few months earlier it read 'Erabus SA (Branch Office)', but the same people go through the plate-glass front doors, and the same desks and files stand on the same luxurious carpets. This is Anglo's Amsterdam office, though the files are now somewhat depleted.

Both David and Pieter are tall and thin. They dress in dark, loose and well-worn clothes, the scruffiness of their attire matched by the even layer of stubble on their chins. But when they made their move on Saturday, 7 June 1986, over a year after the squatters had started to investigate Anglo, they were clean-shaven and smartly attired as high-powered young executives. By then, they knew a great deal about the office, having 'cased the joint' very thoroughly. The office was cleaned by a Dutch couple on Saturday

mornings, and the plan was to trick them into leaving
David and Pieter in the office when they finished their
work.

Carrying briefcases, the two young men presented themselves at the door as Van Asperen and Van den Berg,
employees of Anglo's Dutch merchant bank Pierson Heldring & Pierson, part of the Amsterdam–Rotterdam Bank
NV group. They claimed to have been engaged in pressing
discussions in Luxemburg the previous day, and to have
driven over for an emergency meeting at half-past two that
afternoon with the head of the Amsterdam office, Mr
Wiersum. They had arrived a bit early, and would like to
wait in the office. The cleaners let them in, and they settled
down, opening up briefcases to extract Dunhill cigarettes
and the *Financial Times*. No, they would not like coffee
(that would slow the cleaners down). However, the cleaners
were not ready to leave as early as usual. The executives
were becoming more worried by the minute, but eventually
the cleaners went. The operation was just beginning when
one of the cleaners returned.

'We thought that we should telephone Mr Wiersum just
to make sure that it is all right to leave you in the office. You
don't mind, do you?'

'Of course not, but he will almost certainly be on his way
to the office by now.'

They had to watch, their stomachs in knots, as the
number was dialled; but, as predicted, there was no answer.
The cleaner left, though the danger remained that one of
them would try phoning again when they got home.

The group did not choose us because of our knowledge
of Anglo, but because we fitted the parts the best. We
already knew that the office was quite small, so that we
could take everything out. So when the cleaner left, we
just grabbed everything and got out. I don't even
know how long it took, I have no idea, just as fast as
possible. It was two rooms together. We just took all
the paperwork, no sorting at all. We left all the desks
and filing-cabinets almost empty. We only left the

annual reports of AAC and De Beers and the other group companies.

It was quite terrifying for us, but there are worse ways to do it. For example the South African library was raided by a large group of people during opening hours; they terrified the people there, took what they wanted and threw other material into the canal. So at least the way we did it was less confrontation, less risk for ourselves and less unpleasantness for the staff.

David and Pieter walked out of 'Plain Holdings' with large travel bags full of documents, most of them covering the period from when the office was first named 'Erabus SA (Branch Office)' in 1981. This material and that already gathered on Anglo was quickly compiled into a full report on the group and its Amsterdam-based tax-avoidance activities, complete with numerous illustrations from the 'liberated' documents. It was published in the squatters' magazine *Bluf!* in August 1986, causing an immediate sensation, with the government forced to promise a full investigation of Anglo's Dutch interests.

Splijt Apartheid's raid on 783 Prinsengracht produced a remarkable set of documentation. It is rare for substantial quantities of papers to escape from any multinational's office, rarer still to have a full set of papers, and practically unheard of that they should be taken in a country such as Holland. In some ways, the information the Amsterdam documents provide is limited. This is, after all, a local office geared entirely to the mechanics of tax avoidance, and so there is little connection to the real mining, commercial and industrial enterprises that underpin Anglo. This function also means that much of the material was prepared for semi-public view, in that its authors knew that the tax authorities could demand to see the various companies' books at any time. As a result, these are somewhat sanitised papers, fit for the tax inspector's gaze. Therefore trying to draw the line between corporate fact and fiscal fiction in these papers feels a little like entering the underworld.

What was immediately evident was that Anglo had gone

to great lengths to avoid tax, using an expensive network of companies, offices and financial and legal advisers. The impression lingers that perhaps the group is better informed on such affairs than it is on the investment realities they are meant to support. Perhaps this partly explains the many international investment disasters that have afflicted Anglo in recent years. While hundreds of millions of dollars have gone up in smoke in US copper mines, oil-rig yards and even oil wells, in bad loans to fund rotten trade with Nigeria and in developing doomed African mines, Anglo's international offices such as that in Amsterdam have been scurrying around dealing with the minutiae of saving often quite small sums by tax avoidance.

The papers also show an astounding tolerance by Western states of blatant, wholesale and entirely artificial tax avoidance. The principal states involved are not credit-card duchies such as Monaco or Liechtenstein, but the United States of America, Great Britain and the Netherlands. This role represented the core of the Amsterdam office, because by far the largest part of Anglo's international investments, held via Minorco, is based in the USA and Britain. Salomon, Engelhard, Inspiration Resources, Charter and Consgold together provided $47 million or ninety per cent of Minorco's dividend income in 1983–4; without the tax avoidance, this would have been reduced by almost $8 million in that year alone. On top of this, large capital gains embedded in some of the investments were also secured against capital taxes by this route, potentially an even more valuable saving, as was illustrated when Minorco took huge profits by selling Phibro-Salomon shares in later years.

Until 1981, the documents reveal, the basic routing for the dividends was quite simple. Both the US and UK shares were technically held in companies in Holland called Plain Holdings and Erabus rather than in Bermuda, and current bilateral tax agreements between the countries allowed the tax to be reclaimed by Dutch shareholders when, as in this case, the shareholdings were over 25 per cent. The holdings – and dividends – were then channelled to Bermuda via companies in the Netherlands Antilles, which had a similiar agreement with Holland. This routing would have been quite obvious to any tax inspector who cared to look or ask, since companies such as Charter and Engelhard were obliged to reveal Minorco's holding in their annual report. Despite the scale of avoidance, neither the US nor British authorities attempted to halt this bleeding of their treasury at source. Instead, they attempted to do so by renegotiating the relevant tax treaties, a minefield of special-interest group pressures which is invariably made ineffective because full advance warning is given.

The result is shown by events after a new UK–Netherlands tax treaty was announced in 1981, which required the Dutch investor to be a quoted company to earn the tax relief. This threatened to prevent Anglo from reclaiming Advanced Corporation Tax (ACT) from the British tax authorities on the dividends from Charter and Consgold. Large sums were at stake; a successful scheme could increase the cash value of the dividends by as much as 43 per cent, depending on the effective ACT rate, to over £20 million a year.

Two options soon emerged, and were put to legal and financial advisers in Amsterdam and Luxemburg. The first was to use a Minorco subsidiary with 10 per cent or less of its shares floated on the Amsterdam Stock Exchange, which would then be eligible for the refunds under the new tax treaty. This would, however, be very demanding and expensive in terms of meeting the Stock Exchange's requirements and selling shares to the public. The second option, which was eventually adopted, was to create a convoluted structure that changed nothing but won back eligibility for the ACT refund. The Dutch company originally 'owning' the shares, Erabus BV, would set up a new subsidiary in Luxemburg, Erabus SA, which would not trade actively in Luxemburg but would open an office to do business in Amsterdam by placing a new nameplate – Erabus SA (Branch Office) – on the front of the Prinsengracht offices. The 'Branch Office' would buy the UK shareholdings from Erabus BV: ownership would be transferred from one file to another within the office, in other words.

It was certainly an elegant solution. The UK–
Luxemburg tax treaty had not been renegotiated and still
allowed ACT to be reclaimed by Luxemburg companies
on investments of this sort. The beauty of the scheme was
that the British could be made to believe that the shares
were owned in Luxemburg, while the Luxemburg authorities saw them as being owned in Holland and did not
charge tax as a result. From the Dutch point of view it did
not matter, since these were foreign shares owned by a
foreign company via Curaçao (in the Netherlands Antilles), and hence only negligible tax was payable under the
Dutch–Antilles agreement. The crazy part was that the
British tax office fell for it, to the point that Minorco was
not even asked to wait for its ACT refund. The sensitivity
of the Curaçao connection was revealed in a letter to
Wiersum from Charter's P. M. Odd writing from Luxemburg. He suggested 'that in the future you do not make
similar references to the Curaçao companies as you have
done this time. As you know, we do not want it to be seen
that such companies are administered and controlled from
the Netherlands and whilst this work is being done here, it
might be dangerous to suggest that a Netherlands-based
employee is the person doing the work in Luxemburg.'
To Anglo it was all routine, as the reports from its
advisers and inter-office memos make clear:

New company Erabus SA to be founded in Luxemburg on March 31st as a subsidiary of Erabus BV.
    Erabus SA to have a branch office in Amsterdam
(using premises and personnel (in whole or in part)
presently used by Erabus). The shareholdings in
Charter Consolidated and Consolidated Gold Fields
to be transferred from Erabus BV to Erabus SA
Branch Office before April 30th when Consolidated
Gold Fields interim dividend is paid, and Erabus SA
in Luxembourg can claim ACT refund. The shares
are regarded as being held by the A'dam branch of
Erabus SA and therefore no capital tax would be
applicable.

P. M. Odd, one of Minorco's senior European managers, spells out one big advantage of the scheme over the proposal for a flotation: the 'structure can be tested and collapsed at minimal cost if found unworkable'. In other words, if the British did not fall for it, they could go back to square one and try another scheme.

So a little paperwork, some relatively small expense, and shuffling the UK shareholdings folder from one file to another in the same desk was enough to frustrate a main intent of the hard-won UK–Netherlands tax treaty before it had even entered the statute books. Anglo's Amsterdam office staff could get back to their usual routine of dealing with the myriad of smaller tax-avoidance schemes that Anglo has running through the office at any one time. These did not always go as smoothly as planned. Schemes visible from the Amsterdam office involved: De Beers' holding in the Belgian-quoted company Sibekka; AAC's and Charter's French holdings; Canadian investments linked to Hudson Bay Mining and Smelting and Minorco Canada; some of AAC's shareholdings in South African gold mines; AAC's and Minorco's Zambian, Zimbabwean and Latin American investments; Charter's Irish shares; and royalty deals for AECI and De Beers. Further up the pyramid, the tax havens used included Liberia, Panama, Liechtenstein and Bermuda, as well as the Netherlands Antilles.

To keep tabs on their corporate charges, the Amsterdam staff had to maintain a closely handwritten chart, pasted over two sides of an A4-size piece of cardboard, listing their details. The lower layers of the board revealed that it sometimes had to be rewritten twice a year. Yet they only had to deal with a small part of the whole. As organigrams for some of their companies show, control often meanders across continents and through tax havens in a seemingly senseless fashion. Yet these greatly over-simplify the relationships between the group companies, because they omit the large inter-company loans which can completely distort the structure. No wonder that senior management too gets confused at times, and the local staff have to clear up the mess with accountants, financial advisers and, ultimately, the tax inspector.

At the same time, a constant corporate twisting and turning goes on with the object of keeping a few loopholes ahead of the tax authorities, both in specific cases and over the general rules. By late 1983, it became apparent that further legislation was on the way to block the main tax route from the USA and Great Britain. The idea of an Amsterdam Stock Exchange flotation was resurrected, and a full-blooded eleven-strong meeting was arranged with financial advisers Pierson Heldring & Pierson and accountants Price Waterhouse on 16 December 1983. David Fisher, the secretary and treasurer of Minorco, summarised the conclusions:

> Minorco presently receives ACT credits amounting to approximately US$4 million per annum on its UK investments through the Erabus SA structure which are expected to be terminated in 1984 under the provisions of a protocol to the Luxembourg/UK tax treaty which is due to come into effect shortly. The reductions in US withholding tax on the present level of investment income being obtained by Minorco through its present Netherlands company structure amount to approximately US$3.8 million per annum. By arranging an appropriate Netherlands quotation for a Minorco subsidiary it is hoped to preserve the tax benefits of approximately US$7.8 million . . . under the existing threatened arrangements.

In the event, the UK–Luxemburg protocol was postponed, and the flotation, complete with eminent Dutch supervisory board member, was judged too unwieldy and constraining. A new possibility, of a withholding tax from the Netherlands to Minorco's Antilles company, Pampas Holdings, meant that Anglo had to keep open the option of getting the main shareholdings out of Holland altogether. When considering the flotation, Price Waterhouse had pointed out the dangers of pushing large deals through that route:

> We have previously obtained Antilles opinions confirming this treatment [i.e. tax-exempt capital gain] in other cases. Nevertheless, in view of the sums involved we recommend that an opinion (or possibly a tax ruling from the inspector) be obtained to confirm the position on the Pampas/Plain/Erabus facts.
>
> The ruling procedure in the Antilles is very much a matter of individual negotiation.

With this in mind, Minorco set about reorganising the upper tier of its holding company, clarifying the tax position of Pampas Holdings in the process:

> On April 16, 1984 a tax ruling was negotiated by the PMB with the Curaçao tax inspector whereby for the financial year ended June 30, 1984, Pampas would pay minimum/maximum amount of Curaçao tax of US$250,000. . . . The inspector has stipulated that the amount of tax presently owed by Ladycliff (US$750,000) should be settled by the end of May 1984.

With $1 million spent, they could push what they wanted through Curaçao.

All the while, though, the Amsterdam loopholes seemed to be getting tighter. The first sign that the rot was really setting in came in March 1984. Price Waterhouse informed Anglo that the Amsterdam tax inspector was going to ask the Netherlands Government Accounting Department to conduct a full inspection of the records and books of Anglo American Services (Netherlands) BV. This meant that at some point in the future the government inspector would be going through that company's files in the Amsterdam office. Worse, there would be nothing to prevent him asking to see the records of all the other companies as well.

Then, on 1 November 1985, the Amsterdam Inspector of Corporation Taxes wrote to Price Waterhouse, pulling half

of the Amsterdam office's house down: the previous ruling
allowing the Branch Office holdings in Consolidated Gold
Fields and Charter Consolidated to go untaxed would be
rescinded from 1 January 1986. On this date also, the new
UK–Luxemburg protocol would begin to operate, and a 5
per cent witholding tax would be charged on dividends
from Holland to the Antilles. Then, on 16 January, Price
Waterhouse revealed that all existing tax rulings were being
reviewed.

One month later, on 10 February 1986, Mr Schweers of
the Netherlands Government Accounting Department
arrived to investigate the books and records of Anglo's
Dutch companies. By then, the bird had flown. According
to the records, the Consgold and Charter shareholdings
had been sold to Minorco Luxembourg on 18 December
1985, and the Erabus SA Branch Office had been closed
down on 30 December 1985, with all its assets naturally
reverting to its Luxemburg parent. On 31 December 1985,
Plain Holdings had sold its shares in Phibro-Salomon and
Inspiration Resources to Pampas Holdings in the Antilles.
The proceeds of the sales of these assets had also been
effectively spirited out of the country on that day, by the
cancelling of loans and the payment of huge dividends to
the Antilles.

The Amsterdam office continued to operate in 1986, but
under its new name of Plain Holdings. Certainly there was
plenty of work to be done in clearing up previous years'
accounts and answering the investigator's queries. In 1987
Minorco extradited itself from the embarrassment and
announced that it was moving from Bermuda to Luxemburg, where it would seek a quotation on the Luxemburg
stock exchange. Ogilvie Thompson said the reason was to
help with the company's new strategy: to move away from
passive investments and towards ownership and direct
participation in resource-based assets.

The year saw some radical changes in Minorco's portfolio
which signalled a significant emphasis on strengthening its
international base. On the personnel scene, Tony Bloom of
Premier announced that he was moving with his family to

Britain to develop Premier's overseas interests. Paradoxically, the most important move was the selling of Minorco's remaining 14 per cent in Salomon Inc., the new name for Phibro-Salomon. For some years Salomon's earnings had been decreasing, particularly with the drop in the American Treasury's bond market and the company's own accelerating growth in the deregulated world financial markets. The actual sale in September 1987 took place at the height of a co-ordinated Anglo defence of Newmont Mining in the face of a hostile bid which gave an unprecedented insight into the internal workings of the whole group (see Chapter 8). But the word that Minorco wanted to divest itself of Salomon had been quietly put about among American investors some months earlier, after Salomon could not find a friendly buyer. The news reached Ronald Perelman, a corporate raider (who later became chairman of the Revlon Group), through the Anglo grapevine: Felix Rohatyn put out the first feelers and Perelman heard of the opportunity through First Boston, the financial advisers to Consolidated Golds Fields. Salomon's chairman, still John Gutfreund, did not want Perelman as a large shareholder and at the last minute Gutfreund bought his own shares and promptly sold them to the billionaire investor Warren Buffett.

The disposal of Salomon was not the only shift in Minorco's profile. It sold its investments in Anglo American Investment Trust to De Beers for $159 million, which was exported out of South Africa in financial rands. This was therefore an expensive operation for De Beers, but it served two valuable purposes. Because of Anamint's substantial holding in De Beers and some of its diamond trading companies, De Beers was in effect buying a stronger interest in itself. On the other hand, Minorco had shed one of its South African connections and gained extra cash for investment elsewhere. Much of its new money is still, however, being kept within the United States, in the development of Newmont's and Consgold's American gold interests and in the expansion of Inspiration and Adobe. Australia, too, going through the biggest gold rush for a century, has become a target for the group's investments. Production has doubled every year since 1980. Despite the world-wide share crash in October 1987, gold stocks were still the best investment of the year, showing a 68 per cent increase. Newmont operates Australia's largest gold mine at Telfer in Western Australia and both Newmont and Consgold's Rension are developing the newcomer to the big gold producers – Indonesia, where production is expected to be about 50 tons a year. This international as well as domestic strength makes Anglo the least vulnerable of all the great South African corporations to political revolution. Yet it also has the most to lose. Gavin Relly has seen the writing on the wall; his opening up of a dialogue with the banned African National Congress, in 1985 in Zambia, was the first shot in a campaign to impress upon black leaders that the group, in some form, is indispensable to the future economic growth of South Africa (see Chapter 11).

If Anglo can survive and flourish in Zimbabwe, mine diamonds in Angola and come to terms with Zambia over copper, it can feel moderately assured of an accommodation within a future black-governed South Africa. But if the worst comes to the worst, there is always Europe, Brazil or North America. It may, indeed, be no coincidence that Mary Oppenheimer and Hank Slack recently bought a multi-million-dollar mansion in Far Hills, New Jersey, Charles Engelhard's old town, where they can be neighbours of Jacqueline Onassis, the king of Morocco and the man who owns Johnson's Baby Powder. In South African slang it is called joining the 'chicken run', a decision already taken by Gordon Waddell. His decision to leave the country in January 1987 at the age of 49 came as a shock to his colleagues. For, although he had recently endorsed majority rule as the only way of ending the violence, his robust reputation never smacked of defeatism. However, Waddell's concern for the future of South Africa was more intimately linked with his pessimism about the future of private enterprise. 'I am concerned that business people here don't realise how clearly private capitalism is perceived to go hand in hand with apartheid by the majority of people in this country. And I do not think we are regaining ground in the perception of the majority of people.'[14]A black trade unionist took a more pointed view: 'It's all very well for Waddell to talk, but he's no different from the others. Where are JCI's black directors? Where are its black managers? There aren't any.'[15] Indeed, of the 100 directors in the six mining houses, only two were black.

7

The Diamond Conspiracy

In November 1980, two very different men arrived in Moscow on official business. Samora Machel, Mozambique's ex-guerrilla leader and one of the Soviet Union's most important African allies, was on a state visit. He was given the red-carpet treatment, which included a private meeting with President Brezhnev. The Soviet media were at the time particularly busy denouncing apartheid and vilifying the West's ties with Pretoria.

One evening the BBC's Moscow correspondent, John Osman, went to a performance of the opera *Boris Godunov* at the Bolshoi Theatre.[1] In the bar during the interval, and much to his surprise, Osman recognised Gordon Waddell. Waddell was with an Anglo man and two Soviet officials. He was reticent. 'Out of natural journalistic curiosity,' says Osman, 'I asked what he was doing there and he said, well, there's no story, he was just passing through. But of course it's a pretty unusual thing to see in Moscow. In fact, unprecedented to see in Moscow anybody with this kind of South African connection.'

Osman pursued the matter the next day. 'I tried his hotel, the Metropole. He was no longer there. I tried the Soviet Foreign Ministry, Soviet Foreign Trade Ministry, the State Bank, various other contacts, commercial contacts, diplomatic contacts and nobody knew anything or said they knew nothing.' If Waddell was trying to defect, the Soviets did not seem anxious to claim him.

In theory, of course, a top South African businessman like Waddell – he had taken out South African citizenship – could not possibly have been in Moscow. A white South African, with no exceptional family connections like those of Tony Bloom, would never be granted a visa. The USSR had called for a world trade boycott of apartheid in 1963 and maintains no official diplomatic, trade or economic links with Pretoria. Such theories, however, do not apply when it comes to the business of earning foreign exchange. The self-styled champion of black African nationalism has been trading and dealing with South Africa for years through price-fixing 'understandings' on gold and platinum, and the sale of Russian diamonds by De Beers.

On that occasion Waddell was in fact accompanied by Sir Albert Robinson, a senior Anglo executive and then in his last year as chairman of Johannesburg Consolidated Investment (JCI). They were en route to a platinum conference in Tokyo[2] and were no doubt renewing their regular contacts with the gentlemen from the Soviet Diamond and Platinum Trading Organisation whom they meet every May at the annual 'platinum dinner' held at London's Savoy Hotel. In the autumn of 1980 there was a particular urgency for the meeting. The signs were that the diamond market was heading for a major slump, with De Beers having to finance an ever-growing stockpile from its cash resources as the demand for gems weakened. Antwerp dealers were reporting an unexpected sale of polished Russian stones at low prices outside the De Beers system. The Russians, it was said, needed the hard currency to use for importing grain and supporting their intervention in Afghanistan. They would have to be spoken to.

South Africa's association with the Soviet Union began in 1957 when Harry Oppenheimer's cousin Philip was sent to Moscow to bid for the growing quantity of Russian diamonds that had been discovered in Siberia. He was told to offer a price above the open-market level for the Soviet's entire production. Despite having just severed diplomatic relations with South Africa, the Russians could not refuse. After the Sharpeville massacre of 1960, however, the deal became a political embarrassment. It was repudiated by Moscow. Harry Oppenheimer announced in 1963 that the arrangement was finished. Other ways had to be found to have it secretly reinstated. One of the principal routes is believed to be through the London merchant bank Hambros and its subsidiary Consolidated Gems. De Beers now buys a substantial part of Soviet production, estimated at 12–20 million carats a year, of which 2.5 million are gems. This accounts for nearly a third of world output.

One of De Beers' regular buyers, breaking the unwritten code of discretion, has revealed:

> One always found a certain amount of rough [uncut] which is of Russian origin. You can tell its origins by its characteristics. So a manufacturer is able to say, this kind of rough came from South Africa. One knows that they are marketing Russian rough.[3]

For several years the British Department of Trade published figures of Russian diamond imports but the practice was stopped in 1980, at which time diamonds accounted for £367 million out of a total import value of £786 million. The present figure is likely to be nearer £500 million.

This convenient relationship has regular upsets. In 1984 large quantities of low-priced Soviet gems were again dumped on the Antwerp cutting market. A furious De Beers advised the Russians to get back into line. By the end of the year, Harry Oppenheimer remarked: 'The Russians are acting responsibly. They do not want to disrupt the market.'[4]

From its creation on the South African diamond fields in the 1870s by Cecil Rhodes, De Beers has grown to dominate the world diamond business with a cartel that knows no equal. It was quick to organise the chaos of the Kimberley diamond rush into an orderly monopoly of production and sales. As mines were discovered in other countries, the company moved in to control the supply of diamonds reaching the market. De Beers now owns only about a third of the world's mines, but its marketing arm, the Central Selling Organisation (CSO), in London distributes 80–85 per cent of all rough stones. Integrated into every aspect of the trade, the company excludes competitors, punishes defectors and governs supply with such determination that prices never fluctuate. They just keep rising.

Understanding De Beers' accounts is not meant to be simple. The cartel has always been notoriously secretive. One London broker has described the experience as 'like being in a Kafka novel'. De Beers' slim annual report raises more questions than it answers. It uses section 15a of the South African Companies Act to avoid disclosing income from subsidiaries. Another schedule withholds group turnover. Details of individual mines are masked by consolidation and the figures are given as an aggregate. The 1986 accounts show a profit before tax of 1.5 billion rand. The bulk of the capital is tied up in huge diamond stocks that grew to unprecedented proportions during the depression of the early 1980s and that the company uniquely values itself. The stockpile in the CSO's four-storey vaults in Charterhouse Street in London was only slightly down from the 1984 all-time record $1.9 billion. Unless De Beers are anxious to pay tax and interest, this figure is likely to be a conservative estimate. No one, however, is in a position to challenge it.

The Johannesburg stockbrokers Davis Borkum Hare commented in their 1983 report on De Beers: 'It is submitted with respect that both the balance sheet and income statement depend largely on the positioning of diamond stocks within the various companies in the De Beers group and also on policies that are implemented on consolidated.' That is financial marketspeak for 'these figures are practically meaningless'. The way in which ownership of one of the companies in the CSO, the Diamond Purchasing and Trading Corporation (DPTC), is split between De Beers, AAC and JCI is typical – it does not have to be accounted as a subsidiary of any of them.

De Beers' role as the arch-manipulator and sustainer of the diamond market makes secrecy essential. Above all, the group has to be able to hide the true size of its diamond stocks, particularly when times are hard. De Beers' customers, the major diamond dealers, are all well aware of how the system works. They know that to keep prices steady De Beers has to buy up surplus supplies of diamonds when the market slumps during a recession. They also know that the worse the slump, the faster the CSO's stocks build up. While many of its diamonds, such as those that have been in stock for a long time or those from De Beers' own CDM mines in Namibia, may have cost the group far below their valuation, nevertheless buying up enough diamonds from other producers to maintain stability can be extremely expensive when the market is weak. At such times, even Anglo's extensive resources may be severely tested, and the biggest danger then facing De Beers is that the diamond dealers should decide that the company will be unable to find the resources to maintain its hold.

It is only the secrecy over the diamond stocks that prevents the dealers from knowing whether any particular crisis is liable to spell the death-knell for the CSO, and it is probably only that secrecy that has allowed De Beers to keep the CSO intact for so long. It is like a game of poker, with the stiff-faced Oppenheimers playing banker against relatively poorer partners, the difference being that in the diamond game the CSO never has to show its hand. So as long as Anglo can and is prepared to raise enough money to keep the CSO intact, it will be able to maintain the cartel.

As well as the profits to be made from the diamond mines, and the huge stock profits from the cartel when times are good, Anglo has another good reason for risking large sums of money on De Beers. This is De Beers' unique position, in that its large and relatively liquid stocks of diamonds and funds in London and elsewhere outside South Africa provide what probably amounts to the largest 'free' foreign currency reserve of any South African corporation. The company does, of course, have to obey South African exchange-control regulations like any other business based in that country, but the regulations were not drawn up to control the financial activities of an organisation such as De Beers. It is the only organisation trading internationally in a commodity that only it can value, and the South African government depends on that organisation for practically all its revenues from diamonds; it is apparent that the tail wags the dog. The South African government may make the foreign-exchange regulations, but it can do little more than trust De Beers to adhere to them in its fashion. From Anglo's point of view, with an eye to the unstable political future facing its South African base, this gives the diamond business a very special appeal, and it is fiercely protected.

When the British Inland Revenue investigated the possibility of taxing the main diamond profits in London rather than in South Africa, the CSO threatened to move its operations to Switzerland. Only recently have some of the inner workings of the CSO been revealed – and, as we shall see, they show that the bulk of the diamonds are conduited through paper companies registered in Bermuda to minimise taxes.

But first let us examine the nature of the jewel. Diamonds occur the world over, but the most significant deposits are in southern Africa, the Soviet Union and Australia. The industry has created one of the wonders of the modern industrial world, the Big Hole at Kimberley. De Beers owns the Kimberley, Finsch, Premier and Namaqualand mines in South Africa, the CDM mine in Namibia and, jointly with the government, the Orapa, Letlhakane and Jwaneng mines in Botswana. Together these mines produced 23,945,041 carats in 1986. Through a management company, Management and Technical Services, it also runs the diamond mines in Angola where, despite implacable political differences, De Beers has a 1.5 per cent stake in the government diamond concern, Diamang. Synthetic industrial diamonds are manufactured at De Beers' factories in South Africa, Ireland and Sweden. The group's other interests, which in 1985 account for 23 per cent of the company's profits, are in many of Anglo's South African and international investment companies.

Diamonds consist of pure carbon that has been subjected to intense heat and pressure. They are usually found in 'pipes' of kimberlite ore, the roots of ancient volcanoes up to two kilometres in diameter and extending deep underground. They are also found on river-bed courses and at the mouths of rivers that have swept the diamonds, known as alluvials, down from unknown pipes to the sea. Every diamond is different and its value depends on its size, shape, colour and the clarity of the crystal. Most mined diamonds are of insufficient size or quality to be turned into jewellery and are classified as 'industrial'. Because of their extremely hard quality they are used in tooling and electronics, or are crushed into abrasive pastes. Increasingly, 'synthetic' industrial grades are being manufactured by a laboratory process. Their trading is more akin to other industrial commodites and De Beers' control in this area is less heavy-handed.

It is the remaining stones, the gems, which account for about one-sixth of world output (89 million carats in 1986 – a carat is 0.2 of a gram), that De Beers has made so valuable. A white diamond is considered to be the most valuable, though they come in many shades, including orange, pink, red, green, blue and black. Cut properly, the stones have a brilliance achieved by the high reflective and refractive qualities that can produce the separate colours of the spectrum. Every gem must be sorted and graded – a highly specialised skill in which De Beers claims to have an unparalleled superiority. When there are 2,000 categories and the difference between one and the next may be $30 a carat in value, it is little wonder that De Beer's profit figures are essentially meaningless.

The company's secrecy ensures that no producer can know the price that dealers are prepared to pay for their output. And the select 250 or so dealers who are invited to buy from the CSO at the five-weekly 'sights' in London have to accept the company evaluation. There is no bargaining, and those who complain or refuse to buy the selection of gems offered in a box may not be invited again.

At Oranjemund on the Namibian coast, De Beers' wholly owned subsidiary, Consolidated Diamond Mines (CDM), presides over the largest civil-engineering project in the southern hemisphere. It is also the world's richest source of gem diamonds. The diamonds, carried out to sea by the Orange River from inland pipes, have been deposited along the beach on a series of marine terraces. Abraded by their long journey, the larger stones are the only ones that remain. High-quality gems make up 95 per cent of CDM's output. In 1985 the mine contributed 13 per cent to De Beers' net diamond profits of 779 million rand. Security is especially intense. The town of Oranjemund, built by De Beers in the middle of the desert, exists only to serve the mine and to house some 8,000 employees. The mine itself lies in a *Sperregebiet* or forbidden zone – 200 miles of desert controlled exclusively by CDM and enclosed by a barbed-wire fence. The beaches are patrolled by helicopter and Alsatian dogs. There is only one way in and, to prevent temptation, no vehicle or piece of equipment ever leaves. Instead it is left to rot in an enormous scrap yard. Visitors and employees are surveyed by a central computer and high-technology X-ray units as they pass through the mine's 'Personnel Control Centre'.

De Beers is stripping the entire beach at Oranjemund. A sand dam 45 feet high and up to 60 feet thick holding back the sea has to be replenished by a fleet of lorries working round the clock. The exposed area behind the dam extends up to 200 yards offshore and must be continuously pumped out. Three hundred earth-moving vehicles and a $4.2 million caterpillar-tracked excavator the size of a football pitch shift 60 million tons of sand and gravel every year. The result is one million carats of diamonds worth more than 200 million rand. Working alongside these machines are black migrant labourers who sweep the exposed bed-rock by hand to recover remaining gems.

The irony of such great investment and hard labour is that the value of diamonds rests on a number of assiduously cultivated myths. The first is that diamonds are special. Industrial diamonds are manufactured in laboratories throughout the world. De Beers was not the first to patent the process, and it had to fight a long legal battle with the United States' General Electric Company (GE) for the licence to produce synthetics in South Africa and market them in Europe. GE remains the world's largest producer. In 1970, GE announced that it had perfected a process to make synthetic gem diamonds of more than one carat in unlimited quantities. It decided not to proceed. As one GE executive explains: 'We would be destroyed by the success of our own invention. The more diamonds we made, the cheaper they would become. Then the mystique would be gone and the price would drop to next to nothing.' The USSR, a big producer of synthetic industrials, has from time to time, been suspected of manufacturing gems. In 1983 the *Sunday Times* of London carried a story suggesting that the CSO was in fact purchasing such gems from the Soviet Union, a suggestion that did not go down well with De Beers. Once the brilliant illusion is shattered like so much cut glass, the whole edifice could come crashing down.

The second myth is that diamonds are scarce. Quite apart from the spectre of unlimited synthetic gems, the world markets are already glutted. De Beers' number one problem is a situation of chronic over-supply which is stretching even its vast resources. By 1981, in the face of a worldwide recession, De Beers was stockpiling up to 60 per cent of its production, and output in South Africa was cut back. In an unprecedented move, the De Beers dividend was cut for the first time since 1944. From being bankers to the Oppenheimer empire with its huge cash reserves (1.38 billion rand in 1978, falling to 127 million 1982), the company had to borrow 200.6 million rand from Anglo. Profits, once twice as much as Anglo's, were down to 754 million rand, compared with Anglo's 982 million rand. Servicing and maintaining this stock requires huge resources, and Harry Oppenheimer admitted that it was the worst recession in the business since the 1930s, when all South African diamond production had to be suspended. Despite record jewellery sales in the two big markets of America and Japan, the stockpile in 1984 remained the same, and only began to drop in 1986 when the gem market began to pick up. The scarcity value had been tenuously preserved, but the myth has suffered.

The price of diamonds to the dealers and cutters has also

been maintained – the central tenet of the cartel. But the idea that a diamond is for ever, that it maintains and increases its value, has taken a severe battering. Before the high US interest rates of the 1980s' recession, diamonds looked a good hedge against inflation. Gem stocks outside of De Beers' control flooded the market. In 1980, the price of the rare and beautiful 1-carat D flawless stood at $63,000. Two years later, it had collapsed to $15,000, and by 1985 the market for larger gems was still sluggish.

'Diamonds are as precious and unique today as they were when worn by princes and kings,' according to De Beers' promotion. To believe this requires a certain amount of mental agility, since there are now an estimated 500 million carats of gems in the hands of the public. This accumulated stock – the 'overhang' – is equivalent to about fifty times annual gem production. It must at all costs be prevented from becoming supply and interfering with the delicately crafted market. Since the mark-up between wholesale and retail is about 50 per cent, a piece of diamond jewellery will have to be held for a long time before it can be resold at even the price for which it was bought, as Elizabeth Taylor found to her cost. In 1969 she and her then husband Richard Burton paid $1.1 million for the world's fifty-sixth biggest stone, a pear-shaped pendant weighing 69.42 carats. A few days earlier, it had been sold within a minute at public auction to Cartier of New York for $1.05 million. Ten years later, Elizabeth Taylor put it up for sale with a $4 million price-tag. There were no takers. She finally sold it in 1980 for $2 million, thereby sustaining, with inflation and insurance payments, an enormous loss. Jewellers are extremely reluctant to buy secondhand pieces, and the prices they offer bear no comparison with the original selling price. One of the largest buyers is Empire Diamonds in New York City, which gives no more than 60 per cent of the wholesale price.

The diamond myths for public consumption are sustained by a $90 million[5] worldwide advertising budget that has created one of the most potent double-sided images of modern times. One is safe and the other is sexy, dividing women into the patriarchal categories of wife and whore. The two most familiar catchphrases perfectly capture the idea. 'Diamonds are forever', the official De Beers slogan, was invented in 1948 by its New York advertising agency N. W. Ayer to promote the engagement ring as a symbol of enduring love. But when in the 1950s Marilyn Monroe immortalised the song 'Diamonds are a girl's best friend' in *Gentlemen Prefer Blondes*, sparklers became the price of a mistress or a sugar-daddy's way of paying the rental. The Ayer campaign was initiated by Harry Oppenheimer in 1938 to restore public interest in diamonds after the Depression. 'There was no direct sale to be made,' one Ayer executive said. 'There was no brand name to be impressed on the public mind. There was simply an idea – the eternal, emotional value surrounding the diamond.'[6]

Even the British Royal Family were drawn into the act as part of the Ayer plan. On a royal visit to South Africa in 1947, 3-year-old Mary Oppenheimer presented a 6-carat brilliant to Princess Elizabeth and a 4½-carat gem to Princess Margaret. Three days later, on Princess Elizabeth's twenty-first birthday, General Smuts presented her with eighty-seven flawless diamonds which had been matched for a necklace.

The campaign has had a phenomenal success, first in America and then around the world. For the post-war generation in Europe and America, a diamond engagement ring was considered to be a necessity. During the 1960s the campaign received an extra fillip with the invention of the 'eternity ring' for married women. This was a wholly artificial idea, designed to soak up the huge number of small Soviet diamonds that De Beers had agreed to buy. Instead of emphasising the size of a diamond, the campaign switched to promoting cut, colour and clarity. In 1968, 5 per cent of Japanese couples bought a diamond ring; now 70 per cent have succumbed to the romance. Jewellery sales in the United States in 1984 reached a record level, while advertising reached new heights of fantasy: 'The diamond has been the traditional symbol of love since the Middle Ages. The very word "diamond" comes from the Greek "adamas" meaning the eternity of love.' A more recent campaign has created another need: the anniversary ring, 'a band of diamonds that says you'd marry her all over again'.

Sustaining the myths has been easier than maintaining the cartel, which has been periodically threatened by independent producers, Israeli cutters, African governments and smugglers, and most persistently by the United States Justice Department. Over four decades, the anti-trust division of this department launched a series of investigations and indictments against the De Beers cartel, effectively keeping Harry Oppenheimer out of the country for several years.

The group's uneasy relations with the United States government began at the start of the Second World War, when Washington was anxious to build up a strategic stockpile of industrial stones. Documents released under the US Freedom of Information Act, some passages heavily censored, reveal an extraordinary tale of pressures and threats and political manoeuvring on both sides. De Beers survived it all.

A Justice Department memo sets the scene:

> On July 15, 1940, Sir Ernest Oppenheimer met in Washington with representatives of the British Embassy, the National Defense Council . . . with a view to assisting the United States government in its rearmament program.[7]

Sir Ernest offered a deal. He would sell the government $3 millions' worth of selected industrial diamonds if the anti-trust division allowed him to open a 'New York Corporation, [the] diamond Syndicate'. Although tempted, Justice officials decided that the proposal was plainly illegal. Instead, the American government decided to put pressure on the British, then in receipt of US war materials. In 1941, after the supplies were formalised under the Lend-Lease Act, the department unofficially told the British government that there would be no more warplanes without the diamonds. A Justice official, writing to assistant attorney-general Thurmond Arnold, complained that the stockpile was only 14 per cent completed: 'The diamond syndicate will not sell us a stockpile because it will not tolerate large stocks outside its monopoly control.' He stressed the importance of the matter in adding that 'Hitler's war machine would have collapsed had he not had diamonds from a stockpile started as soon as he came to power'. Pressure on Britain, however, was not proving very successful: 'The diamond section of the government and the syndicate seem to be the same.'

By 1944, an agreement was worked out whereby De Beers would supply diamonds from its own stockpile in Canada. Even then the Americans were unhappy. Assistant attorney-general Wendell Berge, writing in January of that year, remarked that the cartel was hoarding the better stones and driving prices up. What was more, 'it is now moving to secure control of South American [diamond deposits] to forestall increased production there'. Berge recommended legal action 'to split up the combine and to prevent the carrying out of restrictive covenants'. The action was filed in New York in 1945, but it fell for lack of jurisdiction over a foreign company, although De Beers formally agreed to refrain from operating in the USA.

The Justice Department returned to the offensive in 1957 (the year in which Sir Ernest died and Harry took over), when the Federal Bureau of Investigation's director J. Edgar Hoover was asked to investigate anti-trust violations of the diamond grinding-wheel and tool industry. The FBI looked at three companies that bought plentiful supplies of diamonds from De Beers during a time of a worldwide shortage. It took three years before the FBI decided that the US companies were victims rather than conspirators: 'The facts are that the syndicate has an absolute monopoly. . . . [The US companies] are offered diamonds on a take-it-or-leave-it basis.'

Harry Oppenheimer, meanwhile, had not been idle. An intriguing 1974 FBI memo refers to a Maurice Templesman, one of Jacqueline Kennedy's escorts after the assassination of her husband. It said:

Templesman was the man who arranged the meeting for Harry Oppenheimer with John Kennedy when Kennedy was President-elect [between November 1959 and January 1960]. The meeting was held at the Carlisle Hotel. [Unnamed informant] had informed us several months ago that the De Beers organization is a large contributor to both political parties and that should this investigation get to a stage where cases were actually filed that we would probably receive much political pressure.

These new investigations had begun in 1972, when the anti-trust division began separately to examine the diamond abrasive and diamond drill business. A grand jury was empanelled and in late 1974 an indictment was filed against De Beers and two US abrasive companies for conspiracy to fix prices and allocate customers. The two companies had combined diamond grit sales of $14 million out of total De Beers sales worldwide of $47 million. In April 1975, the companies pleaded no contest and were fined $50,000. De Beers, however, failed to appear or plead, and Justice officials recommended seeking a contempt judgment with a running fine. In the event, it proved unnecessary, for the action was transferred from De Beers to its Irish marketing subsidiary, which agreed not to enter into arrangements that amounted to a restraint of trade. The attack on the diamond drill monopoly never reached the courts, although it had a major impact on Anglo's future relations with the USA.

The two companies concerned were Boart and Hard Metals Products, wholly owned by AAC, and its 50 per cent owned subsidiary, Christensen Diamond Products. In 1973, both companies agreed to sever their joint stock interests in order to comply with anti-trust legislation. Their decision was prompted by a Justice Department subpoena to yet another Anglo company, the Engelhard Corporation, which made diamond abrasive wheels and was already under investigation as the leading United States user of Anglo's huge platinum exports. Unlike De Beers,

AAC had felt it safe at least to have an office in New York. But news of the subpoena, according to a Justice Department memo, forced Anglo to close this office down and hurriedly move to Toronto. Engelhard was thrown into disarray. A 1974 Justice Department memo records:

> At the last meeting of Engelhard Minerals & Chemical, Blake, chairman of Engelhard, told the board of directors that the Engelhard directors who were also members of Anglo American Corporation were not at the meeting because of our investigations. The general counsel for Engelhard had a fit when Blake said this and spent the rest of the meeting explaining that Blake didn't really mean what he said. In any case, the next meeting of the board of directors is going to be held in London so that the Anglo American directors who could not attend the last meeting will be able to attend and also so that Oppenheimer can attend.

Unable to mount a case against Engelhard, the Justice Department finally admitted defeat and in October 1976, the year of Soweto, Oppenheimer visited the United States. Before that, he admitted, 'I was just a little afraid they might throw me into a dungeon.' There was no longer any fear of that. In November 1977 he was back addressing the Foreign Policy Association in New York. The South African Department of Information, then at the height of its covert and open propaganda war, took out a large advertisement in the *New York Times* to publicise his speech. It was headed: 'One man, one vote in South Africa. It's not the answer – Harry Oppenheimer.'

In other parts of the world, attempts to secure the De Beers monopoly were pursued with rather more ruthlessness which, at one time, did not stop short of murder and hired mercenaries. In the early 1950s, Ernest Oppenheimer believed that up to 20 per cent of diamonds reaching the cutting centres were smuggled from Central and West Africa. One major route was from Sierra Leone, where the stones were easily found on river banks, to the Lebanese traders in Monrovia, the capital of Liberia. Tens of thousands of peasants were involved in the diggings. To stem the flow, Ernest Oppenheimer hired Sir Percy Sillitoe, the retired head of Britain's counter-espionage agency, MI5, to lead his newly formed International Diamond Security Organisation.[8] In Sierra Leone, Sillitoe hired a group of mercenaries to ambush the diamond caravans. According to one account: 'Many of the ambushes were bloody affairs. A caravan of a dozen or so tribesmen would emerge from the jungle and head for the bridge across the Mao River into Liberia. Suddenly mines and flares would be detonated around them. Then the mercenaries would open fire with hunting rifles.'[9] Within three years the traffic had ceased and De Beers' agents were set up in small corrugated-iron huts to buy the stones direct from the diggers.

In the diamond boom of the late 1970s, De Beers was able to crack the whip with equal effectiveness. The company found that some of its clients were reselling their boxes to cutters in Tel Aviv for double the price. The Israeli stockpile, financed by huge bank loans, began to match that of the CSO. There was the possibility of either an Israeli panic and a flooded market or even a rival selling organisation. Forty clients who had been selling their stocks were denied further consignments. The CSO insisted that all clients must cut and polish their stones. The buyers got the message.

In June 1981, frustrated by De Beers' low prices and its 20 per cent sales and sorting commission, the government of Zaïre, the world's largest producer of industrial diamonds, announced that it was pulling out of the cartel and refused to renegotiate its contract with the CSO. Middlemen, it said, would be done away with and the diamonds would go straight to the market. This was a challenge that De Beers could not ignore. The profits from Zaïre's modest 'boart' grade industrials were not so important; it was the possibility of other, more damaging defections that was worrying. At first Zaïre's prospects looked good. Three dealers in London and Antwerp agreed to buy the entire production for five years at prices higher than those offered by De Beers. The dealers planned to set up a cutting business in Kinshasa, and the Zaïre government hoped to attract foreign investment to modernise its fifty-year-old and largest mine at Miba.

Two years later, a humbled President Mobutu was signing a two-year exclusive contract with the CSO. It did not pay to buck the monopoly. De Beers' strategy had been a simple piece of muscle-flexing, together with clever exploitation of Zaïre's endemic smuggling. De Beers flooded the market with industrials, dramatically reducing Zaïre's exports, and placed several dealers across the border in Brazzaville in the Congo to buy the 50 per cent of smuggled small gem production at higher prices. Harry Oppenheimer was indiscreetly blunt about putting Zaïre on the rack: 'I can't pretend we are pleased that anybody breaks away. It's a bad example. I think you will find that over the period ahead people who looked at the thing carefully may come to the conclusion that the Zaïre experience should be looked upon as a warning rather than as an example.'[10]

Zaïre's return to the fold was also influenced by another serious threat to the De Beers monopoly, the opening of the world's largest and richest diamond mine at Argyle in Western Australia in 1983. In its first year Argyle yielded 6.2 million carats and after 1986 was expected to produce between 25–30 million carats a year. (In that first full year of production the expectations were more than met with an output of 29.2 million, three times South Africa's output.) The quality of the stones, however, was poor, with industrials making up 60 per cent. But its ore grade of seven carats per tonne was five times the world average. De Beers had made its pitch long before the mine came onstream, but the political climate was distinctly unfavourable. Both the federal government and the Australian Labour Party, in opposition, resisted De Beers' approaches. In 1981, the Australian Prime Minister, Malcolm Fraser, said he could see no advantages in 'arrangements in which Australian diamond discoveries only serve to strengthen a South African monopoly'.[11] There was talk of Australia going it alone, and the Indian government's Metals and Minerals Trading Corporation offered to outbid the CSO for 20 million carats each year for its small gem-cutting industry.

De Beers meanwhile launched a high-profile publicity campaign that included a three-week, all-expenses-paid trip to South Africa for Australian journalists and a resident public-relations officer in Melbourne. Whatever the impact of this, by February 1982 the Deputy Prime Minister Doug Anthony was proclaiming that the CSO was the only organisation capable of marketing Argyle's large deposits. Even the Labour Party, then in government, seemed to agree. Their treasurer, who had warned previously that Australia's diamonds were to be 'raped by the South Africans', conceded: 'Given the central role of the CSO in marketing . . . there is no real commercial alternative.' On 8 February, it was announced that a basis for marketing arrangements with De Beers had been agreed. The CSO was to take 75 per cent of Argyle's industrial output and 95 per cent of its gems.

The De Beers Australian coup can be explained not simply in terms of the group's overwhelming power and expertise in the market. Not all the Argyle owners were happy with the deal. The mine is controlled by three companies through Ashton Joint Venture (AJV). Ashton Mining has 38.2 per cent, CRA owns 56.8 per cent and 5 per cent is held by Northern Mining. In 1980, AJV had commissioned a marketing study, which recommended that negotiations be immediately opened with the CSO. Only the minority company, Northern Mining, disagreed. It leaked an internal report which expressed concern that 'it was clear at the time that the marketing group more or less confined its enquiries to the CSO'. Only on Northern Mining's insistence were other buyers approached.

An examination of the share interest helps to explain the disagreement. Northern Mining is an Australian company owned by the Western Australian government. CRA is a subsidiary of the London-based Rio Tinto Zinc (RTZ), in which Anglo had a 4 per cent stake through Charter, and Anglo's Sidney Spiro, as director of De Beers, was on the

board of RTZ. Ashton Mining's parent company is Malay-
sian Mining, in which Charter had a substantial minority
interest. With this web of stock ownership and boardroom
ties, De Beers was not short on influence or friends. As the
diamond market picked up in 1986 and 1987, Argyle's gems
were given the full De Beers marketing treatment. The
pinks have become the mine's hallmarks and the yellows
and browns are being sold as 'champagne' and 'cognac'.

Even on home ground, attempts to investigate the De
Beers organisation have come up against a patrician wall of
silence. In 1982, a commission of inquiry was set up in
Namibia under Judge Pieter Thirion of the Natal Supreme
Court, to investigate allegations of corruption and official
incompetence in the Namibian administration. To De
Beers' dismay, the inquiry turned in 1984 to examine the
state controls exercised over the mining industry, and in
particular the methods by which tax from mining companies was assessed. Thirion approached the subject with
high principles. 'A country's mineral wealth,' he declared,
'is the heritage of the people and the investor or exploiter of
the minerals is entitled to no more than a reasonable return
on his investment.'[12] Unlike South Africa, mineral rights in
Namibia (Thirion throughout refers to the country as South
West Africa – SWA) are vested in the state, and Thirion
spelt out the state's duty to the people of the country to see
to it that those rights to the minerals are dealt with in the
best interests of the people'.[13] He went further: 'The state
also has an interest in the benefication [sic] of the minerals
before export so as to create job opportunities. At present
by far the largest proportion of the minerals mined in SWA
is exported without any benefication.'[14] Allegations were
made that De Beers had over-mined the richer and easier
deposits in the boom 1970s, shortening their life by fifteen
years, and had indulged in transfer pricing to avoid tax
payments. If this was proven, the inquiry threatened to
drive a coach and horses through Anglo's proudest claim,
enunciated by Ernest Oppenheimer and constantly
repeated since: the aim of the company, he said, was 'to
earn profits for its shareholders, but to do so in such a way

as to make a real and lasting contribution to the welfare of the people of the countries in which it operates'. Or, to quote Harry Oppenheimer in successive De Beers annual reports, the CSO monopoly 'protects not only the shareholders of diamond companies, but also the miners they employ and the communities that are dependent on their operations'.

Diamonds are Namibia's second largest export-earner after uranium, so the impact on the economy of tax avoidance would be considerable. De Beers denied the allegations, and agreed to let its senior management give evidence before the commission but only if it was heard in private. Thirion rejected this. He described a document presented to the inquiry by Doug Hoffe, CDM's chief executive, as 'an insult to even the lowliest form of intelligence'. As the evidence mounted over the following months, De Beers was reduced to sniping from the sidelines through press releases claiming their aggrieved innocence. Thirion's eight-volume report, published in March 1986, told a story of plunder. De Beers, he concluded, had been operating uninhibited by the law for over twenty years. He found the allegations of over-mining and tax evasion proven and he accused the company of deliberately doctoring reports to state officials who were, in any event, incompetent. In one of many caustic remarks he said:

> The protestations of multi-national companies that their activities result in bringing prosperity to the host country reminds one of the cynical observations of Jeremy Bentham. 'I am a selfish man, as selfish as any man can be. But in me somehow or other, so it happens, selfishness has taken the form of benevolence.' The overriding object of multi-national companies is to make a profit and all other considerations are subordinate to this one.[15]

Thirion based his inquiries on the 1923 Halbschied Agreement, which laid down conditions for mining in clause 3: 'The CDM when working any area pegged under this agreement shall conduct operations as thoroughly and economically as it does its other mining fields and shall carry on mining satisfactorily to the Administration and not with a view to exhausting the superficial and more valuable deposits to the detriment of the low-grade deposits.' In theory, CDM's operations were overseen by the Diamond Board of South West Africa, which advises the South African-appointed Administrator General. However, he discovered that the board never had physical possession of the diamonds. All inspections and supervisions were done on its behalf by CDM employees, who parcelled up the diamonds and dispatched them to the Diamond Producers' Association in Kimberley, where they were valued by De Beers' officials. Four of the seven members of the Association work for De Beers. More extraordinarily, the man who calculated the tax owing to Namibia, Stanley Jackson, the secretary of the Diamond Board, was also the company secretary of CDM. In castigating the Diamond Board and the Mines Inspectorate, Thirion said:

> Despite the trappings and façade of state control, all aspects of the mining and marketing of South West Africa diamonds remains firmly in De Beers' hands. . . . This naïvety and inability to conceive that a multinational corporation could stoop to any impropriety pervades the approach of the State representatives on the Board and is not conducive to the proper discharge of the watchdog functions which they have to perform. The pretence of the multinational corporation that it is incapable of abusing its power, convinces the unwary that there is no need for control.[16]

The commission was presented with a mass of documents by Gordon Brown, a former CDM senior production planner, who worked for the company from 1968 to 1983. They showed that over-mining of the richer grades began in 1963 and reached a peak in the late 1970s. He alleged that a decision was taken in about 1970 to operate a scorched-earth policy on the mine, to get as much out of the ground as possible before the country came to independence.[17] (Only in late 1984 did the South West Africa People's

Organisation (SWAPO), the internationally recognised representative of the Namibian people, intimate that CDM might be allowed to stay if it agreed on favourable terms with the state.) An independent Namibia, when it comes, may not have many diamonds left, however. Brown calculated that the life of the mine had been reduced by about fifteen years, with no future beyond 1992. A 'life of mine' review by the production manager in 1981 warned: 'Unless we have a conscious change in strategy effective some time in the future, we will power the mine into the ground and we will be unable to conduct reclamation and clean-up operations which could extend the life of the mine by three or four years. What is required is a stable production platform from which costs, both direct and indirect, and infrastructure can be critically managed.'[18] From the documents it appeared to Thirion that CDM was deliberately misleading the state about over-mining. A report by the assistant general manager in 1968 spoke of the 'excessive' depletion of large stones due to over-mining. In a company report in 1982 the same sentence is used without the word excessive.[19]

CDM's operating figures supported the thesis which Thirion accepted. At 1986 prices, the company's profits rose from 262 million rand in the 1960s to 434 million in the 1970s when the demand for gems was booming. The tonnage of ore treated, round the clock for six days a week, rose from 8.5 million tons in 1976 to 16.9 million in 1980. Carat production, almost all in gem stones, jumped from 1.2 million to 2.1 million in 1977. The contribution to De Beers' coffers was huge. Although CDM's output represented only 14 per cent of carat production, it formed 50 per cent of declared profits. From 1980, with the diamond slump and reduced production, CDM experienced a decline in declared average stone size and lower ore grades.

Thirion was also critical of the network of internal CDM companies designed to reduce the taxable income. CDM leased the mine – 3 million hectares of the *Sperregebeit* – under the Imperial Mining Ordinance of 1905 drawn up for the original German mining companies. The rent was 800 rand a year and it had never changed. De Beers, however, had created a number of subsidiaries that held its mining and prospecting rights, and the fees paid to them were set against tax. One subsidiary, the Marine Diamond Corporation (MDC), leased to CDM several prospecting and mining areas along the Atlantic coast. The agreement stipulated that CDM should pay a rental of 500,000 rand or the equivalent of the annual net profit, whichever was the greater. But the administration's receiver of revenue was unable to say what CDM's income was from the areas. Since diamond mines attracted income tax of 55 per cent and MDC only paid the ordinary company tax of 44 per cent, Thirion concluded that the deal was made to save De Beers paying tax. A further tax saving was made because the actual prospecting was carried out by another group company, De Beers Marine, which also was taxed at the ordinary rate. Correspondence from De Beers to the administration merely noted that 'it is a longstanding principle of taxation in most mineral producing countries that prospecting expenditure is allowed against mining income'. Thirion pointed out that some countries were limiting those concessions because of widespread company abuse, and concluded: 'It seems obvious that the real motive behind the scheme is the self-interest of De Beers. . . . The drive to find new diamond deposits in SWA is inspired, not so much by a desire to serve the interest of SWA, as by the necessity to maintain the production of its affiliated companies at a high level so as to enable it to keep its monopolistic position as a "swing producer".'[20]

The commission heard more disturbing evidence from one of its investigators about the way in which the diamonds are marketed. Martin Grote calculated that the export price of CDM stones was 215 rand a carat lower than the 1981 American import price. It emerged that diamonds were conduited through another daisy chain of CSO subsidiaries, which each took a cut of the profits. Two of them are registered in Bermuda. The surprise was the scale of the Bermuda operations, which had been kept secret for twenty years. The commission learned that in the first six months of 1983 diamonds worth US$717 million were channelled through the tax-haven island. At the end of the day, CDM received only 86 per cent of the selling price.

Another practice of mining companies, including CDM, was the export of mineral 'samples'. The Mining Commissioner who issued special permits for these consignments was never told of their content or value. Sometimes the quantities were huge: one small company exported over 420,000 tonnes of samples between 1978 and 1983. Large quantities of rare mineral samples were exported from the uniquely rich and diverse Tsumeb mine, part of the Consgold–Newmont group. Many of these samples ended up in the Smithsonian Institution in Washington, DC, which boasted 1,147 Tsumeb specimens. CDM and another De Beers company, Tidal Diamonds, both applied for permits for the removal of samples, without indicating the mass or what was in them.

De Beers' response to the report infuriated Thirion. The company suggested that it could satisfy any 'impartial' inquiry that the allegations against it were false. It wrongly claimed (and this was later written into the De Beers annual report) that the commission's findings had been made without CDM 'having given evidence or been called upon to do so'. Not surprisingly, given the lack of state control, it was able to argue that the administration in Namibia had never suggested that CDM was not mining in a satisfactory manner. At one point its rebuttal admitted that the rate of production rose to meet market demand. But it rested its case on the assertion that 'by the introduction of innovative and cost-effective techniques CDM has rendered hitherto unpayable ground payable, and thus progressively extended the life of the mine'.[21] The available and persuasive evidence may point in quite the opposite direction, but who in South Africa is going to challenge the mighty De Beers?

An interesting side light was thrown on the distribution of the Thirion report in Johannesburg. Several months after its publication, it was nowhere to be found. The Johannesburg public library had no trace of it. It was not to be had at Anglo American's sumptuous library in Marshall Street, or at Harry Oppenheimer's private library at Brenthurst. The Standard Bank, which maintains a prestigious business library, had tried unsuccessfully to acquire a copy for its many enquirers. Academics interested in the mining industry at Witwatersrand University could not lay their hands on it. Finally, De Beers has a library in Johannesburg. The librarian said it was not in stock: 'It's not very important, you know. It's just a very legal document.'

The Nambian administration finally responded to the Thirion report in November 1987 with a white paper which completely exonerated CDM of both over-mining and transfer pricing. It said that the company had always tried to improve its techniques to extract more and more lower-grade ore at a profit. And it suggested that Martin Grote, lacking experience in international metal marketing, had adopted a simplistic approach to the question of transfer pricing. The company agreed, however, to a government request for the diamonds to be sorted in Windhoek with a government-appointed valuator to take over the function of the Diamond Producers Association. Referring to allegations against other mining companies, the paper said: 'it appears from these replies (by companies accused of transfer pricing) as if the Thirion Commission investigators did not make adequate allowance for the complexities of international metal markets.' The implication was that the companies know best. Thirion was reportedly unimpressed.

In July 1986, Julian Ogilvie Thompson gave the address at the World Diamond Congress in Tel Aviv with a cheerful report about how the diamond market was beginning to come out of the recession, thanks to the steadfast work of the CSO. The Israeli Prime Minister was guest of honour. Another guest, still keenly overseeing the business, was the director of De Beers, Harry F. Oppenheimer.

8

The Golden Arc

The news from the Chicago International Monetary Market reverberated around the financial centres of the world on 21 January 1980. One ounce of gold, for the first time in the history of the metal, had broken through the $1,000 mark. A consignment for delivery in late 1981 was sold at $1,031. It was the peak of an extraordinary, latter-day gold rush; only this time the prospectors were speculators in the Middle and Far East, playing the round-the-world, round-the-clock gold markets of New York, London, Zurich and Hong Kong. At the other end of the scale, hundreds of people dug out their heirlooms for ready cash and in London's Hatton Garden, the historic centre of the business, the fences had a field day in the knowledge that the bullion houses would immediately melt down their pieces and no questions asked.

As the Nobel economist Paul Samuelson had remarked a decade earlier: 'Gold is of interest only to French hoarders, Middle East oil sheikhs and underworld gangsters.' He might have added South African mining magnates. For the Oppenheimer empire, the rise in the gold price from $234 at the beginning of 1979 to a London high of $850 in January 1980 meant a huge windfall. AAC's profits more than doubled to 866 million rand, allowing a cash investment programme that was to shake up the City of London and Wall Street.

South Africa's gold lies in a 300-mile arc from Evander, east of Johannesburg, down through Carletonville and Klerksdorp to Welkom in the Orange Free State. It is the richest vein of real estate in the world. Through the administered mines of AAC, Johannesburg Consolidated Investment (JCI) and Gold Fields of South Africa (GFSA), Anglo controls over 60 per cent of South African production, which itself contributes over 50 per cent of new gold outside the Soviet Union. It has the world's biggest gold mine complex in Freegold in the Orange Free State with over 100,000 workers and 1986 production of 109 tons worth US$1,384 million; the world's deepest at Western Deep Levels, where shafts plunge 3.7 kilometres into the sweltering rock; and controls the world's richest gold mines, Kloof and the Driefonteins, which yield up to 15.5 grams of gold for each ton of rock milled and are the largest tax contributors to the South African government as a result.

Although gold contributes only 10 per cent of the country's gross domestic product, the metal brings in around half of all the foreign exchange. It also contributes considerably to economic activity indirectly through the industry's large purchases from other industries such as steel, electricity and engineering. In addition, the state's share of profits and taxes on the gold mines amounted in 1986 to 3.4 billion rand out of a total working profit for the industry of 7.7 billion rand. As gold is priced internationally in US dollars, the depreciation of the rand against the strong dollar in the mid-1980s has meant that rand receipts have been even higher than during the gold rush of 1980. In that year an ounce was fixed at 478 rand; in 1986, with an average of $363 an ounce, the rand price was 756.

In keeping with its decentralised structure and its concern to avoid allegations of monopoly, Anglo's grip on gold is clad with a velvet glove. It relies on a number of factors.

First, it has an effective control over production in companies where it is a minority shareholder. This is especially true of the second largest mining house, GFSA, which was locked into Anglo's sphere of influence after the

raid in 1980 on Cecil Rhodes' old company, Consolidated
Gold Fields (Consgold), based in London. This also gives
Anglo a decisive influence over the policy of the Chamber of
Mines which supposedly regulates the industry.

Secondly, the group has access to intelligence by having a
stake in two of the world's leading precious metals refiners,
Johnson Matthey in London and Engelhard Minerals in
New York. Both have extensive networks of plants and
offices stretching right around the globe, putting them in
direct contact with all the leading trade users of the metal.

Thirdly, through both of these companies and Salomon
Brothers, Anglo has close contacts with the international
gold markets. The two refiners are the sole UK suppliers of
the standard 'good delivery' bars of bullion, approved by
the London gold market. Each weighs 12.5 kg and is worth
around US$150,000 apiece. All three companies are asso-
ciate members of the London gold market: Salomon in
particular is a large trader in London, possibly more
important in fixing the international benchmark price of
gold twice a day than the official members such as N. M.
Rothschild.

Fourthly, it has discreet contacts with the Russians, the
main gold production competitor, which ensures that the
erratic market for the metal does not spiral completely out
of control.

All this, added to Anglo's local economic dominance,
means that within South Africa the group's position in gold
mining and marketing is unassailable. Outside South
Africa, however, the gold market still has a life of its own,
neurotically susceptible to any rumours on the political and
economic world scene.

Gold is a most peculiar commodity, as Harry Oppenheimer recognises: 'My philosophy has always been that
people buy diamonds out of vanity and gold out of stupidity, because man has proved incapable of coming up with a
monetary system based on anything else. To be quite frank
I had to make a choice between stupidity and vanity; it was
an easy decision.'[1] To suggest that the Oppenheimer
empire is based on ostentatious folly may not be too far

from the truth. In Greek mythology it was Eris, the
personification of unrest, who threw the golden apple of
discord among the gods, who squabbled for its inscription:
'For the Fairest.'

The metal does have some remarkable properties. It is
malleable, ductile and does not corrode. An ounce can be
stretched into a wire 50 miles long, or even finer thread. It
is used in space as a thermal reflector and in electronics as a
highly efficient conductor of electricity. But its real value as
a dense and beautiful rare metal is as the only universally
accepted commodity of exchange. Harry Oppenheimer
would probably not quarrel with an earlier analysis from an
old enemy:

> The discovery of America was due to the thirst for
> gold which had previously driven the Portuguese to
> Africa, because the enormously extended European
> industry of the fourteenth and fifteenth centuries and
> the trade corresponding to it demanded more means of
> exchange than Germany, the great silver country from
> 1450 to 1550, could provide.[2]

That was Karl Marx, who anticipated the impact of gold on
the South African economy with his remarks about the
nineteenth-century gold rushes:

> As a result of the Californian and Australian gold rain,
> and other circumstances, an unprecedented expansion
> of world trade relations and business boom set in – it
> was a matter of seizing the opportunity and making
> sure of one's share.[3]

The development of the South African goldfields can be
described no better.

Although the world came off the gold standard in the
1930s and the price was allowed to find its own level in the
markets, the metal has remained a monetary standard for
governments, central banks and rich individuals. President
Roosevelt took America off the gold standard in 1933, but it
was not until 1971 that the final link between gold and the
dollar was severed, when President Nixon withdrew the

right of foreign governments to exchange their dollar reserves for gold. Like oil, it is seen as an economic salvation. Latin American countries pay their debts with it; the Soviet Union balances its trade account with increased sales; banks speculate on the futures market; and the princes and entrepreneurs of Saudi Arabia and the Gulf States hedge their monumental fortunes with gold bars. Only the French and the Indians have a taste for petty hoarding.

The primary impulse behind the rise in gold prices during the 1970s was uncertainty. The timing of the final take-off can be put precisely. When the United States froze Iran's assets, including gold, after the fall of the Shah in November 1979, a handful of wealthy Arabs decided to diversify their dollar holdings abroad into gold held at home. On a broader front, distrust of paper money and fear of inflation contributed to the rise, just as the high interest rates and a strong dollar in the early 1980s brought the price down. The unstable fuel in this combustible mix is the state of the world, or, more precisely, the headlines that flicker into the gold-dealing rooms on Reuters' monitors. Dealers in gold are notoriously fickle creatures. The slightest rumour of crisis can dramatically affect the price. The worse the news, the higher the price goes. The Russian invasion of Afghanistan in late 1979, after the trauma of Iran, helped it to soar. In the heady days of January 1980, rumours of the Shah's arrest in Panama and reports of Tito's death sent it haywire. Reports on 28 January that Russia was pulling out of Afghanistan sliced $40 off at a stroke. In the Hong Kong Gold and Silver Exchange during that month dealers took to assaulting their rivals with Kung Fu kicks from their rubber plimsolls.

Although New York does more trading in gold as a futures commodity, and although Zurich probably handles more of the physical metal, the centre of the world gold market is still London, and a bar with the Johnson Matthey assay mark is the favoured form of bullion from Bahrein to Bangalore.

The London Fix, which sets a twice-daily price, is an

arcane and yet sophisticated operation. Every morning, five men gather in a pale wood-panelled office of the Rothschild bank in St Swithin's Lane in the City, surrounded by portraits of European nineteenth-century royalty who turned to Nathan Mayer Rothschild for their loans. Besides the Rothschild's chairman, the other men represent the bullion dealers Mocatta & Goldsmidt, Samuel Montagu, Sharps, Pixley and Johnson Matthey Bankers (JMB). Each man is connected by telephone to his trading room, which in turn is in contact with bullion dealers and banks around the world. On each desk is a small Union Jack; when it is up, it signifies that the dealer is discussing the supply and demand with his trading room and the meeting goes into suspension. The price is fixed when there are enough sellers to satisfy the buyers. At 10.30 a.m. or thereabouts, the price for the day is announced to the world. At 3 p.m. the process is repeated.

South Africa's connections with Johnson Matthey go back a long way. It was Johnson Matthey that assayed the first big gold find on the Witwatersrand in 1884. The company refined much of South Africa's gold in the following decades, so it was not surprising that Anglo decided to take a financial interest in it through the group's London associate, Charter Consolidated. The collapse of JMB in October 1984, after a series of bad loans, some involving the illegal export of money from Nigeria, allowed Charter to raise its holding from 27 per cent to 35 per cent. The collapse caused a major political scandal in Britain, with the Bank of England being accused of incompetence in failing to spot the danger facing JMB before it was too late, and for having committed large sums from the public purse to its rescue. The Bank's response was that the rescue had been essential to protect the London gold market: if JMB collapsed, the market and its large foreign-exchange earnings would go with it.

It is now clear that the Bank of England did not play its cards too well when the crisis broke. Normally the City of London is deserted on a Sunday, but that day 200 bankers and bullion dealers gathered together with Neil Clarke from

Charter Consolidated and executives from Johnson Matthey and the Bank of England. The danger was that JMB would collapse with huge losses, pulling down both the parent Johnson Matthey and possibly the gold market as well, though no-one could be certain. Neil Clarke generously proffered Charter's help as the largest shareholder in Johnson Matthey: Charter would pump lots of money into Johnson Matthey (increasing its shareholding very cheaply in the process), providing the Bank of England and the City banks took JMB off their hands with a fixed contribution from its parent.

The Bank fell for it, and Anglo walked away with greatly increased control over the parts of Johnson Matthey that were vital to it. Neil Clarke, an Anglo executive director, soon took over as chairman of Johnson Matthey, and set about appointing a completely new executive. The only part that went wrong was when other shareholders in Johnson Matthey heard about the deal Anglo had carved out for itself – the institutions demanded that they too should get a share of the action, and Anglo's embarrassment at the coup was such that it conceded.

From Anglo's point of view the beauty of it was that it had persuaded someone else to pay for its blunders. As by far the largest shareholder, Charter's job was to keep tabs on Johnson Matthey, though this had to be done discreetly to avoid US charges against Anglo's platinum monopoly. It had failed to do so, and let Johnson Matthey's management lose a pile of money through a supposedly exceptionally profitable banking operation. When the crash came, it needed a conjuring trick to get out of the banking operations while losing as little money as possible and keeping the rest of the business. There was no possibility of Anglo giving up Johnson Matthey as a whole unless the situation was absolutely desperate: its role in Anglo's international precious metals business is simply too important. Above all, Anglo certainly would have paid a great deal of money to keep it. Neil Clarke pulled the Bank of England like a rabbit out of a hat, and at very little cost.

The scandal of the banking operations, with evidence of

extensive fraud and mismanagement, has obscured Johnson Matthey's real position in the precious metals world. Its bullion operations accounted for only 15 per cent of the London gold market. More importantly, however, it has the world's largest platinum refinery at Royston in England and is the leading manufacturer of platinum catalysts, which are used in cars to control pollution. The company supplies half the catalyst needs of General Motors and Ford and is the sole supplier to Chrysler and American Motors. Out of a total profit of £50.5 million in 1987, just under a third came from the catalyst business. About 80 per cent of the West's platinum comes from South Africa and the biggest mine, Rustenburg, is controlled by none other than JCI. Anglo as a group has a majority shareholding in Rustenburg, Johnson Matthey is Rustenburg's sole international selling agent, and the two companies jointly own the Royston and Rustenburg refineries, the latter handling the mine's entire output.

The market for platinum is very different from that for gold. Although both metals are virtually indestructible, and consequently every ounce mined permanently increases total holdings, platinum has been mined in any volume only in recent years, and then largely for industrial use. The gold market is overhung by stocks of bullion and jewellery equivalent to over seventy-five years' Western mine output, and in consequence is fundamentally unstable, entirely at the mercy of any move towards mass hoarding or dishoarding. The market for platinum by contrast, with stocks far more closely matched to output, is to a considerable extent in the hands for the producers.

Anglo's control of the world's most important precious metals refiners and fabricators puts it in an ideal position in both markets. In gold, Johnson Matthey and Engelhard must together have better contacts with the buyers of newly refined gold than anyone else in the world – they, after all, provided much of it. That is important information to have when you are either trying to expand a market or, even more crucially, avoid sanctions. The information is valuable for platinum as well, but here investment in the two companies also allows Anglo to exploit to the hilt its monopoly over production, without doing so overtly. Anglo has extended its platinum mining monopoly into an even wider platinum-refining and fabrication monopoly, whether for producing medallions and auto catalysts or key components and materials for petrochemicals and space weapons. The group makes profits all the way to the final consumer, not just in digging the metal: it can even make good profits on platinum from other people's mines. Together, then, Engelhard and Johnson Matthey comprise a unique and powerful marketing arm for South Africa's key mining giant; it is small wonder that much discretion must be employed to ensure they always appear far apart.

Anglo has been equally discreet – and successful – in creating a near-monopoly in South African gold production. The group's greatest coup was the 1980 raid on Consgold, the London mining house with a 48 per cent stake in GFSA. It was a clandestine operation which was kept a secret even from some of the senior members of Anglo's executive committee. Zach de Beer, for example, Harry Oppenheimer's old friend and a member of the committee for six years, heard of the planning stages only by rumour.[4] In acquiring a quarter of the company's shares, Anglo misled Consgold's management, manipulated the London Stock Exchange and flouted the British Companies Act, which subsequently had to be amended. The mechanics of the deal, pieced together from interviews, internal Anglo correspondence and a British government report, provide a rare glimpse into the workings of the Anglo phenomenon.[5]

During the whole of 1979 Anglo's stockbrokers in Johannesburg, Davis Borkum Hare, had been monitoring Consgold's shares through the group's London brokers, Rowe & Pitman. There had been rumours around the City of London since early 1978 of a take-over bid and they recurred in the autumn of 1979 when the British government lifted exchange controls on 24 October. Before this, people and companies not resident in the UK were prohibited from buying sterling securities if they were likely to gain more than 10 per cent of the voting rights. On 26 October Max Borkum, a senior partner in Davis Borkum Hare, telephoned Rowe & Pitman's senior partner, Peter Wilmot-Sitwell, and instructed him secretly to start buying into Consgold. The jobbers for all the transactions were Ackroyd and Smithers, who were told to leave the share transfer forms blank and not to deliver them to Consgold's share register. Wilmot-Sitwell was surprised; he had never received such an instruction before. But at 3.30 p.m. more than one million shares were bought up out of the issued stock of 149 million. By 12 February, the day on which Harry Oppenheimer personally launched a lightning raid on the London Stock Exchange, Anglo had acquired a quarter of the company.

His elaborate scheme was worked out by a handful of his closest executives – principally Ogilvie Thompson of De Beers, Neil Clarke of Charter and Gavin Relly of Anglo – and used Oppenheimer's private company, E. Oppenheimer and Son, as one of the central conduits. The shape of the plan was as follows: De Beers' banking and investment arm, De Beers Holdings (Debhold), put up 59 million rand for five group companies to buy the shares, which would then be divided equally between De Beers and Anglo American. Care had to be taken, during the secret part of the operation, to avoid any one company buying more than 5 per cent, since the Companies Act required any purchases above that to be declared. Wilmot-Sitwell personally told Gavin Relly on 15 November about the dangers of exceeding the limit. Relly assured him that the group was acting within the Act. In fact Relly and Oppenheimer knew that in practice their total secret holding would go way beyond that – it actually reached 14.7 per cent. Even De Beers' subsidiaries, Debhold and the Central Selling Organisation which made the first purchases, went above 5 per cent to 6.3 per cent.

When the affair later became public, De Beers claimed that the excess was a regrettable accident. A Department of Trade investigation showed up discrepancies in the amount held by De Beers, who then admitted that a sixth company had been involved. Brent Limited had an exotic pedigree. Registered in the West African state of Liberia, it had originally been set up by Charter and then sold to two Luxemburg subsidiaries of Anglo American and Debhold. With money from another Anglo-Liberian company, it bought nearly two million shares using foreign currency rather than rand. De Beers claimed that this was a temporary expedient because of difficulties in raising enough rand on the market. This transaction was authorised, like all the others, by Anglo's dealing department, but De Beers said it was not told until later. The Department of Trade inspectors called it 'a fortuitous failure of communication'.

On Monday, 11 February, the Consgold management was getting desperately anxious about the mounting evidence of a take-over because of the number of unregistered shares. It formally requested an investigation by the Department of Trade. Over the weekend, Ogilvie Thompson had discussed with Wilmot-Sitwell the possibility of raising the share price in order to attract enough buyers for the final, public bidding. At 8.30 a.m. the next day, Wilmot-Sitwell got his starting orders from Neil Clarke. Just after 9.10 a.m. Harry Oppenheimer picked up the telephone and called Consgold's managing director, David Lloyd-Jacob. He informed a stunned Lloyd-Jacob that De Beers had been the secret buyer and it was his intention to raise his stake to 25 per cent that day. Within the hour, as thirty Rowe & Pitman staff rang around up to 200 clients, 16.5 million shares were bought at 616p each. The market price was an average of 535p. When it was all over, Oppenheimer called Lloyd-Jacob to say that the raid had been completed.

Some months later, the Department inspectors concluded that 'De Beers formulated its scheme with the express intention of avoiding the disclosure provisions of the Companies Act'. They suggested that opinion be sought on whether an offence had been committed. There was no prosecution but the new Companies Act of 1985 covered the points.

Both Anglo and Consgold were adamant that the new

relationship between the two was at arm's length and that
Consgold was still a wholly independent company. It was a
somewhat tired argument, given the record of Anglo's
expertise in these matters. Anglo's stake was eventually
transferred to its Bermuda investment company, Minorco,
and increased to 28 per cent. In addition, the group's direct
investment in GFSA reached 21 per cent by 1984. Rudolf
Agnew, Consgold's chairman, joined Anglo American's
main board and Ogilvie Thompson became a non-executive
director of Consgold. At the very least Anglo has made sure
that no one else can control Consgold and GFSA. On the
other hand, it has full access to and considerable influence
over Consgold's financial strategies.

As Nicky Oppenheimer said afterwards: 'Our purchase
arose from a fear that a foreign company, for example an
American oil major, might gain control of Consgold, and
through it GFSA . . . we did not want a maverick loose in
the Chamber of Mines.'[6] He was almost certainly being
diplomatic. It was not American oil majors that worried the
Oppenheimers, but home-grown South African life assurance companies. By the beginning of the 1980s the two
largest already constituted the only real competition for
Anglo within South Africa. The biggest, Old Mutual,
controlled Barlow Rand, technically South Africa's largest
industrial company since Anglo's interests are not counted
properly. Barlow's Rand Mines is the smallest of the mining
houses. The second largest assurer, Afrikaner-based South
African National Life Assurance Co. (SANLAM), controlled the Federale Mynbou/General Mining and Finance
Corporation (Gencor) industrial, commercial and mining
group which includes the third largest mining house. If
either of these groups had won control of either Consgold or
GFSA alone, they would immediately have been catapulted
into a position quite threatening to the Oppenheimers.
Anglo's unique structure means that the Oppenheimers
must ensure that AAC is constantly successful in order to be
sure their hold on the group is secure. They can do so only
as long as they have no real competition within South
Africa.

In an interview with the authors, Zach de Beer made an illuminating comment on Anglo's use of its minority holding in Consolidated Gold Fields. Referring to the epic take-over battle for the Union Corporation gold company in 1974 (won by General Mining), he said: 'When Union Corporation became available we held 10 per cent and we thought that was enough to give us a veto power over what anyone else was doing.'[7] They have made sure they have enough with Consolidated Gold Fields.

Until 1987 the relationship between Consgold and Anglo remained, beneath the surface, mistrustful and wary, with each circling the other like rutting stags. Occasionally one lunges and draws blood. In January 1987 Ogilvie Thompson and Clarke of Charter, the two Anglo directors on the Consgold board, expressed astonishment that GFSA and its gold company Driefontein had secretly acquired a 7.8 per cent stake in Consgold. In 1983 GFSA had made an equally secret first acquisition of 3.9 per cent. But the company only told Consgold and Minorco about that after the event and it was agreed by everyone not to announce the change.

GFSA's deputy chairman, Dru Gnodde, claimed that he and two other directors had devised the new increase without even telling his own chairman, Robin Plumbridge, Agnew at Consgold or Anglo's Peter Gush who sat on both the GFSA and Driefontein boards. Having been caught at its own game, Anglo (through Minorco) asked for an investigation by the Department of Trade inspectors, who were already inquiring into an earlier secret but smaller raid on Consgold by the American Barrick gold company. These machinations caused considerable speculation in the London and Johannesburg gold markets. A consensus emerged which recognised the underlying hostilities between the two groups: GFSA was simply acting as a surrogate for Consgold's paranoia about being taken over and the only predator in sight was Anglo American.

A similar interpretation can be put on Consgold's further weakening of Anglo's gold ambitions in South Africa in July by selling 10 per cent of GFSA to the Afrikaner group Rembrandt, a fierce business rival of Anglo's despite the political friendship between Oppenheimer and Rembrandt's Anton Rupert.

But the binding South African influence on Consgold and, in turn, its American minority interests, was perfectly demonstrated when T. Boone Pickens, a 'corporate raider' from Amarillo, Texas, decided to make a bid for Newmont Mining in August 1987. Pickens had a notorious reputation for swooping on undervalued companies, making a large investment in them and taking off with the profits when the target company's shares were boosted by a rescue operation from other interested parties. He is credited with reshaping the US oil industry, making more than US$300 million on the way. Among his targets were Phillips Petroleum, Unocal, the twelfth largest US oil company, Boeing and Singer.

When Pickens announced that he had secretly acquired a holding of 8.7 per cent in Newmont there was consternation in the boardrooms of Newmont, Consgold and Anglo. Newmont, 26 per cent owned by Consgold, contributed one-third of Consgold's earnings and was set to become the largest gold producer in the United States. As such, it was a hugely valuable asset which fitted into Consgold's strategy – and that of Anglo – of diversifying away from South Africa. But the Consgold management did not want to commit large sums of money for a rescue bid; nor did it want to sell out to Pickens. That would have left the company with more cash than it could readily invest and with increased vulnerability to other predators.

The dilemma was acute. Three linked but apparently independent companies had to find common cause to beat off the unwelcome intruder from Amarillo. During the course of Pickens's manoeuvring, the arms-length relationship between the disparate companies collapsed into a joint defensive action. An extraordinary series of boardroom minutes from Consgold and Newmont were filed in the Delaware Supreme Court, revealing the intimate connections that everyone assumed but no one had been able to prove.

The Pickens investment was the only topic of conversation at the Consgold board meeting in London on 21 August 1987. Newmont's chairman, Gordon R. Parker, a Consgold

South African appointee, was there as a member of the group management, as well as Anglo's Ogilvie Thompson, a Consgold non-executive director. 'Must not take Pickens lightly, not to be overawed though,' the minutes said. While there was much debate about possible options, Newmont 'management need to feel independent, not our lackies'. It was only after Parker had withdrawn from the meeting that Consgold's chairman, Rudolf Agnew, remarked: 'How certain can we be that we get sensible financial policy out of Newmont?' An offer to help from Ogilvie Thompson was followed up with a meeting in London on 31 August with Minorco representatives. An idea was canvassed for Minorco to enter into a three-way partnership with Consgold and Newmont. But on the same day Pickens made his next move, offering to negotiate for Newmont shares at $95 each.

In New York the following day, the Newmont board were getting restless about Consgold's hesitations. 'Persuade CGF [Consolidated Gold Fields] to get off their duffs and protect their position,' the Newmont notes recorded. Agnew had flown over to be present but not all the Newmont people were happy with a Minorco involvement. When Agnew left the room for fifteen minutes with Robin Plumbridge of GFSA, one of them thought that the South Africans were no better than Pickens. But Parker's revealing response was: 'If Minorco [are] not invited in now, they'll end up being here via CGF in a few years from now.'

Back in London the next morning, a special Consgold board meeting was getting impatient with Newmont's advisers, Goldman, Sachs and Kidder, Peabody. 'Goldman useless, Kidder trying,' the note said. '[Newmont] is close to panic,' Agnew reported after another trans-Atlantic dash. The option of a Minorco partnership was causing some problems. The company's financial advisers, First Boston Corporation, had suggested that it would be prudent to avoid the South African connection. 'Inclusion of Minorco seen by our advisers as sort of mistake Pickens looking for – he could present himself as battling against Oppenheim [sic],' the note said; 'Would be boon to Pickens to involve SA.' But some directors were unconvinced, Questions at the meeting included: 'Is Minorco ready to buy [Newmont shares] at dollars 100?' And: 'Are CGF sellers [of Newmont shares] at dollars 100 – Harry [Oppenheimer] asked?' Then there was the question of whether the US Federal Trade Commission (FTC) would object to a Minorco stake in Newmont. The professional advice was that the Commission would probably not object because 'their [FTC] budget reduced, having manning problems, have 30 breaches waiting to go to court . . . partnership would sail through.' But, in a significant aside, the note goes on to pinpoint one of Consgold's perennial fears: a Minorco partnership 'weakens our argument that we in no way [are] involved with Minorco'. As Ogilvie Thompson was absent, Agnew was able to vent a little spleen at the ambitions of the Oppenheimers, who had marched uninvited into his company six years earlier. 'Harry is one of the niggers in the woodpile – wants dynasty for grandchildren – vehicle outside SA.' Another director highlighted the prickly relationship: 'We must do nothing that weakens us vis-à-vis Anglo – distrusts them.'

In the end both Consgold and Newmont rejected the Minorco alternative. Pickens was seen off with a massive injection of Consgold money and with Anglo standing in the wings as the ultimate guarantor. On 20 September 1987, Newmont announced a special dividend of $33 to all shareholders, including Pickens, in order to reduce the company's borrowing power. Consgold raised $1.6 billion from its American subsidiary and First Boston to buy 15.8 billion Newmont shares, taking its holding to 49.7 per cent.

While Pickens unsuccessfully challenged Consgold's purchases in the courts, the financial commentators were quick to make underwriting connections with another momentous shift in the Anglo camp. On 28 September Minorco announced the sale of its remaining 14 per cent holding in Salomon Inc. The price of $808 million just topped the First Boston loan.

With or without Minorco, the South African dimension was not lost on the American press, which unreservedly called Consgold a 'British company ultimately controlled by South African interests'. The *Washington Post* reported: 'The fight for the control of Newmont Mining Corp. has raised concern among anti-apartheid activists both in and out of Congress about the extent of South African investment in the United States.'[8]

A measure of the extent emerged in the early days of the Pickens bid. In order to boost the company's value, exploration plans were brought forward, the estimate of reserves was upped from 14 million ounces to 20 and production targets were raised 50 per cent. Newmont was to become the largest gold producer in North America and the first, boasted Gordon Parker, to yield 1 million ounces a year.

9

Working for Anglo

'We think that collective bargaining is a good alternative to street fighting and revolutions,'[1] said Bobby Godsell, Anglo's head of industrial relations in 1984. He was speaking at the end of a year which had seen ten black workers killed by the police and at least five hundred injured at Anglo mines during a strike over a pay claim. A month before, the Johannesburg *Star* had reported on the tactics of the police:

> In the Welkom area yesterday police were called in and used rubber bullets, tear gas and dogs to disperse crowds of angry mine workers at Anglo American's Western Holdings Division, Welkom Division and President Brand mine. At Welkom Division three armoured troop carriers, a sneeze machine and about ten police vehicles headed for the mine shortly after 2 pm . . . More than 250 people had been admitted to the Ernest Oppenheimer Memorial Hospital by early this morning.[2]

The *Star* found that the injuries 'included ruptured spleens and livers, several fractured skulls and the loss of an eye in two cases'.

Anglo's annual report for 1985 described the 'protracted and difficult' negotiations in two terse sentences which managed to omit any references to the deaths: 'They included the staging of a legal strike. Though shortlived, the industrial action was characterised by intimidation and violence which resulted in injuries to a number of employees.'[3] The writer of the *Star* story was Caroline Dempster, the paper's labour correspondent and the only journalist to venture out into the gold fields to report the strike. On one of Anglo's gold mines, she and her photographer were detained by armed security officials and accused of trespassing. They were taken to see the mine manager and held for two hours for questioning. The photographer's film was confiscated. There was more to follow. After visiting Anglo's hospital, she was told by the administrator that he had been threatened with the sack for talking to the press about the injuries.

Ms Dempster remarked later: 'So many people had been hurt that I wondered, if that is the price of Anglo American's industrial relations, is it worth it?' In her two years of reporting labour disputes, she was struck by two aspects of Anglo's personnel. First, the mine managers, many of them Afrikaans-speaking, found it difficult to implement the reforms emanating from head office and, secondly, the security officials 'were just raring to beat the hell out of the Blacks'.[4]

Her perceptions collided with the honeyed tones of Anglo executives. When the strike was resolved with an improved pay offer, the head of Anglo's gold divisions, E. P. Gush, was in a congratulatory mood:

> It was a victory to the union and the mining industry that the settlement could be reached at so late a stage despite the logistics. At noon on Sunday and with only a few hours in hand, details of the negotiated offer had to be conveyed and clarified to some 75,000 workers at 23 different shafts and in 22 separate hostels hundreds of kilometres apart.[5]

The 1984 miners' strike was the first legal stoppage in the industry and came only two years after the formal recognition of the fledgling National Union of Miners (NUM). It presented Anglo with a dilemma that went to the heart of the group's labour relations policy. How could it contain industrial unrest and worker militancy that struck at the jugular vein of the group and the country while maintaining its reputation as a reforming and liberal employer? Self-preservation also dictated that black workers had to be allowed to develop skills, if the business and the economy were to expand. Compared with other more conservative mining houses, AAC has been marginally more progressive in its labour policies, even though most of the changes have been wrought as a response to black militancy. It has initiated improved wages and conditions on the mines; it has called for the abolition of discriminatory job practices. Yet its enormous profits from gold and diamonds have demonstrably depended on the apartheid labour system with its Pass Laws, influx control and homelands policy. In times of crisis, Anglo has had no hesitation in falling back on the full panoply of coercion and force.

The authors have had access to a series of internal reports, prepared by the Chamber of Mines and Anglo American's industrial relations office over the past ten years. Together with interviews conducted between 1984 and 1986 with black miners, these show a remarkable consistency in workers' complaints about poor hostel accommodation and food, inadequate pay, corrupt personnel staff, racist and aggressive white supervisors, homosexual abuse and unnecessarily dangerous underground work. The contrast with the claims of caring progress from Anglo's executives cannot be more stark.

The key to reconciling these contradictions lies not so much in accusations of hypocrisy against Oppenheimer as in understanding his position as a major capitalist in a warped colonial state. For nearly forty years he has used every platform at his disposal to argue that 'in the long run a country which will not allow the majority of its population to make the best use of their capabilities, cannot hope for progress or prosperity'. An essential prerequisite was 'in building up and rapidly expanding a class of educated westernised Africans and co-operating with them'. For, as he saw it: 'Progress is a European conception and the traditional African society and way of life cannot be reconciled with it.'[6]

As early as 1961, after the massacre at Sharpeville, he was saying: 'Anglo American will seek ways of giving adequate recognition to higher skills and improving efficiences among our native workers. . . . If we are to achieve higher levels of productivity, greater attention must be given to the abilities, personal needs, inclinations and aspirations of individual Africans.' Ten years later he remarked that the economy had expanded to a point where the white population was not capable of manning it in terms of the traditional colour-bar system. By 1974 he was complaining that 'managements are more and more feeling the grave disadvantages of there being no effective [black] leaders with whom to negotiate in times of difficulty or conflict'.[7] In the same speech he said he did not believe 'that the Blacks will ever be brought to accept that an organisation of labour which is right and necessary for white workers . . . is not suitable for them. Black workers, like white workers, should be organised in trade unions.'

Zach de Beer developed the theme more politically. 'If the aim is to preserve the free enterprise system in South Africa because it is beneficial both to management and to workers, then surely joint institutions must be created which will enable the two parties to become aware of their common purpose, to make the enterprise successful and to give each the satisfaction of achievement.'[8] The strategy was becoming clearer. A stable, reforming South Africa must be maintained in order to ensure the continuing prosperity of the group and its shareholders. Humanitarian principles, which Oppenheimer had worn on his sleeve for international consumption, were bound to economic imperatives. He was not alone in fearing the consequences of failure. Charles Barlow, the head of one of Anglo's main competitors, put it distinctly: 'It is of equal importance that a black middle class is created if South Africa is to succeed in promoting a free capitalist society by all sections of the population in contrast to the leftist regimes of the countries surrounding South Africa with all their well-known inefficiences.'[9]

Traditionally the mine labour force has been drawn from other countries. In 1973, only 21 per cent of black miners came from South Africa. The rest were from Lesotho, Botswana, Malawi, Swaziland and Mozambique. In the past decade the mining companies have made efforts to reduce their dependence on foreign migrant labour. The supply became more precarious with the independence of Mozambique in 1974 and with political unrest in Lesotho. Higher wages and a black unemployment rate of 25 per cent did attract more local recruits who now make up 45 per cent of the workforce. The vast majority are employed on one-year contracts. When the contracts expire, the men have to return to their countries or – in the case of the South Africans – to their homelands in order to re-register as unemployed. While guaranteeing a regular supply of cheap labour, the system also prevents the growth of a settled black proletariat. The threat of dismissal was and remains a powerful disincentive to industrial action.

The migrant labour system, as it is practised today, has provided the economic underpinning of white supremacy for over a century. Cecil Rhodes defended it most succinctly after the passing of his infamous Glen Grey Act of 1894, which created native reserves and imposed a labour tax on landless male Blacks who had no regular employment. When the Act was criticised as a device to provide cheap labour for the white farmers and mine-owners, Rhodes told the Cape parliament that it 'removed Natives from that life of sloth and laziness, taught them the dignity of labour and made them contribute to the prosperity of the state. It made them give some return for our wise and good government.'[10] In fact it was the beginning of the impoverishment of several nations. After the reserves were formalised into the homelands of apartheid, the economic pressures on black families who were forced to live in small, barren enclaves guaranteed the labour supply. The injustice was openly recognised and officially suppressed. A South African Institute of Race Relations study of the Ciskei in the late 1940s reported: 'Productivity is generally so low that the population is wholly unable to support itself from activities within the district . . . without the earnings of the emigrants the population of the district would starve.'[11] In 1955 the Tomlinson Commission into homeland policy estimated that if the Transkei were fully developed agriculturally it could provide a living for only 47 per cent of the population. The Commission's recommendations for white capital to build industries in the homelands were ignored.

The system has caused incalculable social disruption and poverty. 'Tens of thousands of husband-fathers, with families to care for, suffer embarrassment and shame when they must return to see their wives and children malnourished, clothed in tatters, living in shacks. Yet there is nothing they can do, nowhere else they can turn for work.'[12] For the women who remain behind, though, the realities are even harsher.

> There is no escape from the grinding round of misery. Those lucky enough to have family plots struggle to till the hard red soil with hand hoes. They have no money to hire tractors or buy fertilisers. In the last four or five years, with little rain, few have produced more than a bag of maize from the exhausted soils. They must search for wild greens which provide the families' only condiments. Yet if they leave their family plots fallow for more than a year, the bantustan authorities will confiscate them and give them to landless familes.[13]

And for the children, tuberculosis brought back by their fathers is a major killer.

Life for southern Africa's black miners has long been notorious. In 1900 G. J. Christian, a delegate at the First Pan-African Conference in London, spoke out in a widely reported speech against the treatment meted out to Africans on the mines, 'where they had to work for months at the absolute mercy of a company. The payment was in things for which they had no use, and they returned to their homes after months of labour with nothing in return for their work' (*The Times*, 26 July 1900). Ten years after Harry Oppenheimer assumed control of Anglo, in the mid-1960s,

the continuing grim conditions on the gold mines were
graphically described by the South African photographer,
Ernest Cole, in the course of an assignment for *Drum*
magazine:

> I resolved to learn more about the mines and in the
> years that followed I made my way to ten or more big
> mine compounds in the Rand. Sometimes I made
> friends with an African guard at the gate who would
> let me in. Sometimes I showed up so often the guards
> assumed I worked there. Once in, I was rarely inter-
> fered with. To the white guards, as to the mine
> official, I was just another Kaffir and they paid no
> attention to me. As a result, I had considerable
> freedom to see what I wanted to see.
>
> The living conditions of the men who work the
> mines are miserable almost beyond imagining – worse
> even than in the worst slums of Johannesburg. The
> miners are quartered in long, brick-walled structures
> with corrugated iron roofs. They live twenty to a room
> that measures eighteen by twenty-five feet. Each man
> has a concrete cubicle, the slab floor of which is his
> bed. What little furniture the common room contains
> – a few wooden tables and benches – is made by the
> occupants. Threadbare tunics and trousers hang
> about; it is a jungle of clothes. The most privacy a man
> can get is to hang a blanket in front of his bunk.
>
> Plumbing is not only ancient but inadequate.
> Shower rooms are crowded with men trying to bathe
> while others do their meagre laundry.
>
> Food? Ask a man what the food is like and he says,
> 'like pigs' food.' At mealtime the men line up to have
> their ration ladled out by a kitchen employee who uses
> a shovel to slop the porridge on to their plates. Each
> man must show a job ticket; only those who have
> worked may eat.
>
> Breakfast is at 5 a.m. and consists of sour porridge
> and coffee. Lunch, after the first work shift ends
> between 1 and 3 p.m., is nyula, a stew of cabbage,

carrots and other vegetables, and sometimes meat. The men crowd into their stuffy rooms to eat or squat outdoors. There is no dining hall, although there is a bar serving beer and hard liquor. Whenever possible the men go outside the compound to buy extra food – corn meal, for instance – which they cook themselves.

Sunday is the miners' day off, but boredom makes this almost the worst day of all. Separated from their families, with recreation facilities almost nonexistent, the men mostly sit outside their rooms, doing nothing. Some sleep. Others take a walk or sew new patches on their ragged clothing.

To relieve the tedium, a number of men participate in programmes of tribal dances – the so-called 'mine dances' – which are a big tourist attraction for Whites visiting Johannesburg. . . . No admission is charged, but this is no more than fair considering that the performers do not get paid and that the audience is told, by signs on the walls, not even to toss a few coins into the arena as a tip.

Technically the workers are free to visit the nearby townships on their day off, but few do. They often are simple, inexperienced fellows and impressed by the florid company lectures on the perils of the city, with its rough tsotsi gangs and diseased women.

Thus their blank and indistinguishable days, their circumscribed existence, their cramped and inward-turning lives. With women unavailable, homosexuality is widespread. There is even a word in minetalk for sleeping with another man: matamyola. The mine officials condone and encourage this and raw jokes about matamyola are frequent.[14]

As we shall see, in some respects little had changed by the 1980s.

Recruitment to the mines is arranged through the South African Chamber of Mines' Employment Bureau of Africa (TEBA), the largest agency of its kind in the world. Through its 150 offices in ten countries, employing 6,500 people, it hires and processes up to 500,000 black migrant workers a year, mainly for the gold and platinum mines. The chamber describes itself as 'a bastion of free enterprise, representative of the South African mining industry as a whole, the flywheel of the country's economic machine'.[15] Ever since its foundation in 1889, its principal role has been to recruit cheap black labour. In these terms it has been a phenomenal success. In the sixty years up to 1970, the real earnings of black miners actually fell, while white earnings rose by 70 per cent.[16] Despite the rises since then, black wages as a percentage of white wages have advanced at such a slow rate that the International Labour Office in Geneva estimates that the gap will take a hundred years to close. The Chamber's other services to the industry include research, public and labour relations, and making representations to government.

Anglo's domination of the gold mining industry allows it to dominate the Chamber as well. On paper the Chamber has a wide membership. There are 109 representatives from fourteen finance houses which administer mines; 43 from gold mines; 38 from coal; and 14 from producers of diamonds, asbestos, copper, lead manganese and platinum. Within this, the gold and coal producers form the two main committees. However, the main decisions are taken in two small groups: the executive committee and the council, which is composed of 'heads of houses' and senior executives. Anglo has around thirty seats in the Chamber and its executives have regularly taken their turn as president.

Industrial unrest among Blacks in all sectors of the economy began to take on a more acute political edge in the early 1970s. In September 1973 the miners at Anglo's Western Deep near Carletonville protested about pay increases given to a small group of machine minders, as well as about the general level of pay. Faced with 7,000 angry miners in the hostel compound, the mine management called in the police, who opened fire after a baton charge had failed to disperse the crowd. Within 12 seconds, eleven miners were dead and twenty-six seriously injured. The international outcry was immediate. Harry Oppenheimer made a public apology and commissioned an internal inquiry. A new industrial relations department was set up at AAC's headquarters, and from 1974 the complex system of pay grades was streamlined and the general level of pay dramatically increased. AAC's old tribal system of liaising with 'boss boys' in the huge hostels attached to the mines was scrapped in favour of a two-way flow of information. A management briefing system was introduced down the line to the workers, which was prepared with the help of the Industrial Society of London. Works committees were established to channel complaints upwards.

These reforms built on other efforts to improve conditions and to create a more stable workforce. Sports facilities were provided and a big investment in hostel buildings was begun. Reliable migrant workers were given valid re-engagement certificates and bonuses if they returned promptly from their homelands when their contracts expired. During the 1970s the average length of service on Anglo's mines rose from three to six years. Secretly, at the same time, security was tightened up and plans were laid to install a tear-gas system into the kitchens and the liquor store at Western Deep, which had been looted during the dispute.

The improvements turned out to be spectacularly inadequate. They failed to stop the unrest and strikes spilling into 1975, and finally the government set up an inquiry into the 'riots on mines'. Its report was kept secret for two years. The Minister of Labour explained to parliament that the contents were 'in some respects of a sensitive nature'. In 1978 a copy was leaked to *Workers' Unity*, the newspaper of the South African Congress of Trade Unions (SACTU), which revealed just how sensitive it was.[17]

At the centre of its analysis was the conclusion that the migratory labour system, one of the bastions of apartheid, was the main cause of the riots. But it went on to say that 'it is a system which had been in existence for at least 75 years and, at this juncture, there does not appear to be any practical alternative.' Drawing on evidence from the mining houses, the police and selected academics, the report perfectly reflected the racist paranoia of the state. While recognising the need for improved conditions, a uniform pay structure and better communications, the report was principally concerned with security and with preventing the growth of an unstable workforce:

> Our investigations produced no direct proof that the riots were politically inspired or organised by agents of other states or foreign organisations, but, as already mentioned, the black worker is aware of what is going on around him, and of events elsewhere in Africa and the world. He is subject to many influences such as for example the political thoughts of the OAU (Organisation of African Unity) and allied states, radio propaganda from everywhere including certain African states and the Communist countries. . . . He is becoming more and more aware of himself and the important part he plays in the mining industry. He is aware of the enhanced gold price and that the industry is dependent on him and is very vulnerable – seen from the labour view point. We constantly must bear in mind that the black worker himself is very susceptible to communistic influences and that everything possible has to be done to protect him from those influences.[18]

Then, in a warning of rare prescience, it went on:

> We must reasonably expect that as propaganda is stepped up, the black workers, having their own problems, ideals and aspirations, will co-operate to an increasing degree to realise their political aspirations.[19]

Nowhere did the committee suggest the formation of trade unions to channel and control these developments. It was, in any event, assumed that the closed compounds and migrant labour system made union organising impossible. Indeed, the report maintained that the migrant workers were so backward and riven by tribal rivalries that they were not even 'ripe' for worker or liaison committees through which to air their grievances. It argued that thirty-three of the fifty-four incidents it examined were the result of 'ethnic differences' and 'faction fighting'. In the case of the Bantu, said the report, tribalism 'has its origin in fear or a feeling of insecurity which leads to violence. Despite the influence of the white man's civilisation, religion and Western standards, the tendency to become violent where tribal differences are involved is practically spontaneous.' Quoting a 'Bantu expert', the report claimed that the southern Bantu tribes 'even regard fighting as a form of recreation'.

Another expert was enlisted to suggest that 'the crux of the problem is tribal man's belief in insidious forces of evil. For however God-fearing he may be, or however assiduous his belief in the perpetuity of life, he can never really find peace of mind while he also persists in believing that much of his destiny is in the hands of diabolical influences poised to destroy him.'

(By contrast, a study of unrest in the mines in the 1970s by the South African Labour and Development Research Unit concluded: 'It seems likely that sources of the conflicts are to be found in such factors as differential treatment of workers, different lengths of contract and differential access to jobs.'[20] In nearly every incident that the unit examined, the unrest originated from grievances about either pay or conditions; in two of Anglo's gold mines the spark was the inadequacy of the hostel canteen meat rations.)

But the prime concern of the government committee was security and the problem of dealing with 'agitators'. The mining houses needed little encouragement to endorse and implement – where they had not done so already – the recommendation for a security unit at each mine, 'equipped with tear gas, dogs and where possible an armoured vehicle'. It recommended that each unit should train with the South African police and liaise with recruiting agents to screen potential troublemakers. In its own report on the disturbances, Anglo even identified one, though with a sinister sting in his tail. Anglo management said it was 'concerned about the role during the riots of a certain Daniel Ramotsetjoa, alias Mokimel, alias Kimberley – Reference Book No. 3522492. . . . He is understood to be a

Msotho/Xhosa, born in Herschel and employed on the farm Bloukrans, the property of a certain Mr Schutte. The mine concerned was Vaal Reefs. Mine management had good reason to believe that the person was definitely concerned with the riot in one of its compounds while apparently being employed by the state as an informer. He was seemingly protected.' Kimberley, a shebeen-owner and supplier of prostitutes, was more than just an informer, part of Pretoria's bid to destabilise the Lesotho government, which was taking an increasingly anti-apartheid line. According to a report by the Vaal Reefs South manager, a Mr Steyn of BOSS had approached his security officer at the beginning of December 1974 to allow Kimberley into the hostel to organise the Basotho workers into the Lesotho opposition party, the Basutoland Congress Party. The request was refused, 'as the mining company cannot cooperate with criminals which is morally wrong, and in the long term can only lead to major trouble'.[21] Despite this evidence of *agents provocateurs*, the report blandly went on: 'We accept that the South African police and the Bureau of State Security (BOSS) are well informed as to the role of this particular person.'

The committee, however, welcomed the use of the secret police, for it expected that 'with the passage of time (if it is not already happening), agitators (communistic or otherwise) and terrorists from outside the country will attempt to be absorbed as part of the migrant labour force taken up by the mines'. As an additional precaution, the committee said, it would be a good idea for a central bureau to be set up 'so as to keep an effective blacklist'. Four years later, it was revealed that a black miner had been banned indefinitely from all mines after taking part in the strike at Buffelsfontein, one of Anglo's main investment gold mines. The Chamber of Mines admitted that its labour bureau did 'keep track of employees who failed to comply with their conditions of service or who broke their agreement of service for unacceptable reasons'.[22]

Harry Oppenheimer's concern for the welfare of his miners was also translated into an official version that had as much to do with security and discipline as with humane treatment. There should be better compounds – but so planned that 'in the event of riots the task of the rioters should be rendered difficult while that of the suppressors (compound management, security officers and the SA police) be simplified'. More married quarters for key personnel and rooms for visiting wives should be built to prevent recourse to prostitutes. The committee was concerned about the provision of more recreational facilities to provide for 'the beneficial use of wages'. It was hoped that the black miner would spend less on strong drink. 'Modern buying centres (shops, outfitters, coffee bars, restaurants, cinemas etc.) are essential in order that the worker may spend his increased earnings more positively (also on Sundays) instead of wasting it on shebeens at the cost of his own welfare, health and public order.' The Bantu with his 'inborn gift' for singing should be encouraged to take it up as a group activity. On the other hand, after five days down the mine, the black worker could always keep on working. The committee singled out for praise one mine where hundreds of Malawians were 'fetched every weekend' to work as gardeners for Whites all over the East Rand.

In the month that the report was leaked, a meat ration riot broke out at President Steyn gold mine. More than 1,000 miners burned down three dining-rooms, a liquor store and three changing-rooms. Fourteen miners were injured and twenty-three arrested when the police moved in with tear gas and dogs. Damage to the buildings and equipment, described as the most modern in the country, was put at 1 million rand. When the morning shift refused to go down the next day, the management told the miners either to go back to work or else return to their homelands. Out of 7,000 miners at No. 4 shift hostel, 640 cancelled their contracts and did go home. Despite Anglo's vaunted communications system, the cause of the riot apparently left the chairman of the Anglo Gold Division puzzled. 'They didn't attack the administration buildings or the hostels,' said Mr Dennis Etheredge. 'The violence was restricted to the kitchen and the changing-rooms. This is odd – President Steyn is one of the few mines which provides changing facilities of this sort and the rioters were in effect destroying their own clothes.'[23]

Anglo's own inquiries into the riots of the mid-1970s depicted a grim picture which showed that little had changed. One account begins with a migrant worker from the mountains of Lesotho seeking work on the mines.[24] His children are hungry and his wife is impatient with his inability to earn enough. Attracted by the stories of rising wages on the mines, he leaves his family in the care of his parents and walks to the recruiting station at Maseru run by the Chamber of Mines. He arrives in tattered clothing with little money, only to be told that the Free State mines do not take on novices. He is told to wait for possible vacancies, so he sleeps in the streets or the caves above Maseru, fearful of the local police. If one of the clerks at the recruiting office is a relative or a 'home-boy' from his village, his chances of a job will be considerably better. When he signs on, he is taken to a dormitory with eighty others, young and old, and told to strip naked for a medical examination. For a Basotho this is his first humiliating experience. Circumcised men, by custom, are never naked before uncircumcised boys. The doctor perfunctorily examines each man's heart beat. They could have just removed their shirts. A young theology student, working on a vacation project, remarked: 'The process seems to be unnecessary, except as a way of initiating the miners into a subculture which is deprived of any values about human dignity.' The dormitory is furnished with iron bedsteads without mattresses. The room is infected with lice, bugs and fleas. The food, one recruit said, was 'no better than for dogs'. The student summed up: 'These people are altogether not regarded as human beings, they are treated no better than animals because they are being insulted . . . they are being kicked about like dogs.'

On the train to Welkom, the men's attitudes appear to change completely. They seem both fearful and exultant, becoming coarser and more boisterous, shouting lewd remarks to women walking along the railway line and singing chants of how they have left the land they love to go underground like rats. There is a fatalism about the words:

Lesotho, now I leave you with your mountains, where
I used to run
I am going to the white man's place – the tableland.
Keep our children so that they may grow up at your
sides as we did ourselves.
I am leaving you in Lesotho
I will never see your men with their beautiful
mountains
I am going to the white man's land – with electricity
I am leaving all the dark places here
But I still prefer the mountains of Lesotho.

At the Welkom centre they strip again, shower in cold water and are examined, X-rayed and fingerprinted before being bussed off to their mines. Then comes the induction process where the men are told about pay and conditions, rules and regulations. They understand barely a word because they are spoken to in the lingua franca of the mines – a combination of Zulu, English and Afrikaans called *fanakalo*. Novices are only given lessons after induction. The worst, however, is yet to come. In order to cope with the very high temperatures underground, the black miners (though not the white) go through the 'acclimatisation procedure'. This starts in the changing-room, where the men once again have to strip naked. Moving through to the scale room, they have their temperature taken and weight recorded, and a supply of vitamin C tablets is handed out. It is only then that each man is given a skirt for the climatic chamber, where the temperature rises to 34 degrees Celsius. For four hours a day for five days, the men are made to walk up and down concrete steps, twenty-four steps a minute to the beat of a drum. Every thirty minutes, they drink from a hose pipe. Every hour, their temperature is taken. Sometimes the supervisor insults or manhandles trainees for marching out of step. They are not allowed to go to the toilet during each session and some have to relieve themselves on the chamber floor.

Acclimatisation of some sort was considered necessary, although in recent years its need has diminished on some deep mines with the installation of ventilation cooling systems. But even a mile down, the pressure and the heat cannot be completely ameliorated. At that depth the rock face feels warm to the touch and, when the drilling starts, the noise and the dust blanket out all other sensations. With South Africa's low-grade, labour-intensive ore the work is especially hard. The Chamber of Mines has described the seams thus:

> Imagine a solid mass of rock tilted . . . like a fat, 1,200-page dictionary lying at an angle. The gold-bearing reef would be thinner than a single page, and the amounts of gold contained therein would hardly cover a couple of commas in the entire book. It is the miner's job to bring out that single page – but his job is made harder because the 'page' has been twisted and torn by nature's forces, and pieces of it may have been thrust between other leaves of the book.[25]

Many studies, Anglo's among them, have identified the white miner as being the major source of tension underground. One miner told the authors: 'He just sits there on his box, drinking tea. At the end of the shift, the team leader reports what has been done and the white miner signs it. He gets the bonus out of what you do and the poor Blacks are getting nothing out of their sweat and toil.'[26] Assaults by white miners on black workers were commonplace, although in the past five years the power of the new union has curbed some of the worst excesses. In the hostels, Anglo researchers found that the personnel assistants who controlled promotion were easily bribed. The *indunas*, tribal representatives appointed by management, often practised homosexuality with young recruits and used that relationship to favour their friends and victimise their enemies. Most black miners felt that the black officials failed to pass on their complaints to management, who were seen as either inaccessible or despotic.

These revelations came as a genuine shock to the Anglo

executives at 44 Main Street, who had previously little
conception of black miners' attitudes to the degradations of
the migrant labour system. Above all, the difficulty in
identifying grievances and finding a way to resolve them
forced the question of recognised trade unions up the
agenda. The sticking point had always been the white Mine
Workers' Union (MWU) which fiercely protected its privi-
leges against encroachment by the Blacks. Its principal
weapon was a blunt refusal to allow Blacks to obtain a
'blasting certificate', the key to promotion. Attitudes in the
MWU had not changed since it raised the notorious 1922
slogan, 'Workers of the world unite – and fight for a white
South Africa.' Arrie Paulus, the union's general secretary,
told the *New York Times* in 1979: 'You have to know a
black. He wants someone to be his boss. They can't think
quickly. You can take a baboon and learn him to play a tune
on the piano, but it's impossible for himself to use his own
mind to go on to the next step.' Challenged about the
offensive nature of these remarks on his return to South
Africa, Paulus retorted: 'All the Kaffirs can go and get
stuffed.'

Uncompromising union leaders like Paulus – who was
brought back from retirement by his union in 1985 – did
not prevent some white unions from recognising the need
for an organised, if subservient, black labour force. As the
economy expanded in 1970s, skilled workers were in short
supply and several white manufacturing unions encouraged
the formation of 'parallel' black unions in order to increase
their industrial muscle. At the same time, the industrial
unrest of the early 1970s and the Soweto uprising of 1976
gave an impetus for the creation of unregistered independent black unions. Although black unions had never been
illegal and had a tradition of militancy going back half a
century, their ability to organise had been severely curtailed
by constant police harassment and arrest of officials.

By 1979 the government bowed to economic pressure and
worker militancy by accepting the recommendations on
formal recognition by the Wiehahn Commission of Inquiry
into Labour Legislation. A government White Paper on the

report commented that 'the trend towards uncontrolled and disorderly development [of trade unions] constitutes a threat to labour peace and must make way for the acceptance by all workers' organisations of the responsibilites, duties and limitations imposed by the statutory system'. Or, as the report itself put it, the time had come to impose a system of 'discipline and control'.[27] One of the Wiehahn Commission's members was Christian du Toit, Anglo's industrial relations consultant at head office at the time and an Anglo employee since 1969.

Yet the case of Elandsrand vividly illustrated that Anglo's priorities remained production and profit at the wilful neglect of working conditions. The evidence for that accusation comes from a 'strictly confidential' Chamber of Mines report on the riot at Elandsrand mine in April 1979. Handwritten on the cover is, 'Not for circulation please.' It is a document that Anglo would prefer to forget.[28]

Elandsrand on the Far West Rand was the first gold mine that Anglo had sunk in fifteen years. Its proven ore reserves – always a conservative estimate – were 1,000 million troy ounces. Compared with the other thirty-eight gold mines in the country it had the potential to be above average in terms of working profit. It was designed as a model mine, with dormitories radiating out from the administration block in a clover-leaf pattern. The *Financial Mail* commented approvingly: 'If there is anything that makes for compound confrontation it is densely populated laagers which can easily be seized and closed to the police.' Anglo was in a hurry to bring the mine to production and a grand opening was arranged for 10 April, thirty-one months ahead of schedule. Two days before, about 700 miners rioted and caused 750,000 rand of damage to the hostel rooms, dining-halls, administrative offices, the beer hall, mining stores, a change house and several vehicles, including the complex administrator's car. The following day only 100 black workers went underground and groups of protesting miners sitting on the surrounding hills were driven back to their hostels by a police helicopter and security guards with dogs. In the evening a full shift went down but nearly 1,000 miners who had refused to work the previous day were laid off and sent home. The Anglo management again claimed that they could not establish what the men's grievances were, although they hinted that outside agitators might have been at work – particularly members of the Lesotho opposition party.

In fact, 44 Main Street had had 'vast amounts of data available on the mine which could have been used as indicators of the potential trouble brewing'. Between February 1977 and April 1979, the workforce had been rapidly increased from 300 to 4,500. In May 1978, a large number of workers refused to go underground, protesting that their complaints over bonuses and overtime were not being dealt with. In March 1979, workers who had been transferred from neighbouring Western Deep Levels complained about lower pay and poorer living conditions. More significantly, Anglo head office had been receiving monthly returns which showed an alarming rate of absenteeism and desertion, serious overcrowding and general unrest. The mine personnel manager was so concerned that he asked for a qualified industrial relations officer. His request was turned down. Behind these rumbles was an 'imbalance between production planning and planning for services' that led to 'a break-down of human relations on the mine'.

The catalogue of failure was comprehensive. A new computer system to clock men into work was faulty. It often booked them absent, or failed to register working time if men were transferred from one gang to another. The bonus system, based on new criteria of metres advanced rather than holes drilled and payable to an entire team rather than just to machine operators, was deliberately not explained until the administration was finalised. 'Throughout the management hierarchy of the mine men claimed that they did not know how the bonus was calculated.' Complaints from the men were not dealt with, since no-one was made responsible for handling them. Because of the drive for production, the miners had to work a seven-day week and those who refused were demoted. Because only one shaft was in operation, there were delays at the cages, with men often missing their team at a particular level. Including travelling time, men were at work for up to thirteen hours a day. After the shift, black workers had to wait until their white supervisors were caged up first. Records of assaults by Whites on Blacks were 'extremely high', with fifty such incidents out of a total ninety-four in the nine months before the riot. Miners arriving back at their hostels late often missed their meals because the kitchens had run out of food or the dining-halls were closed. As there was no broadcast system installed to wake them, men would rise earlier than usual to avoid delays at the computerised 'crush' or in the cages, and as a result would miss breakfast. There were no meal breaks underground and one white supervisor reported that his team had not eaten for three days. A black team leader said he had not eaten breakfast for a week. In the dining-halls men complained that the food was cold, inedible, and often contaminated with foreign matter. There was a shortage of mugs and dishes. The twenty-four-hour shift system meant that some workers would arrive for their dinner to find a breakfast meal of porridge. For the entire workforce there were two cooks who worked a twelve-hour shift.

The hostel-building programme was three months behind schedule and men had to share bunks. Overbunking began in May 1978, with 68 men having to share. By February 1979 the figure had risen to 710. Just before the riot it was 436. The Chamber's report commented: 'Overbunking appears to have had a number of undesirable consequences, including theft (resulting from a shortage of lockers), pressure on change houses and dining halls attached to hostel complexes, assaults in rooms, strain on staff and disorganised waking procedures induced by overcrowding.' An informal practice had developed of punishing workers by making them sleep on the floor. There were further frustrations, humiliations and pain. The water temperatures in the change house showers were either too hot or too cold. The beer hall accommodated only 2,500. Men who wanted to visit their friends in Western Deep were not allowed to walk the shortest route through the white mine workers' village without a permit.

A system of sorts was in place to deal with grievances, but

it was so overworked and inefficient that few complaints were settled. A Black Employees' Council, which met every two months, was chaired by the white manager, whose decision on disputes was final. The first meeting concentrated on the machine drillers' bonus payments and cage times. The report commented: 'It was only after the disturbances that adequate attention started to be paid to these matters.' It concluded that 'black workers currently have no power to bring about changes in matters that cause them concern: in the current industrial relations climate in mining they are not given opportunities to negotiate to bring about changes'.

For Anglo Elandsrand proved a great success. During 1984, 343,816 ounces of gold were mined, giving a total profit of 101 million rand. Asked in 1986 about the conditions leading up to the riot, Bobby Godsell told the authors: 'Management got its co-ordination wrong and badly wrong. As opposed to sinking that shaft and bringing the social services on stream at the same time that was not well done. But it's news to me that 700 people had nowhere to sleep. I would be prepared to bet money that nobody sleeps on the floor in our hostels.'[29] Perhaps Godsell, although head of industrial relations, was among those people to whom the Chamber's report was not to be circulated. A garrulous young graduate from the University of Natal, he is vehement about his concern for his workers. 'We would like to pay our workers properly so that they can have decent houses, decent communities and send their kids to decent schools. From a skills point of view it makes sense, from a social control point of view it makes sense.' He is keen on control. The latest Anglo research on inter-group violence on the mines refers repeatedly to the miners' resentment of the *indunas* as corrupt tools of management. 'We don't have an *induna* system. We haven't had one for ten years,' he says. Pressed, he goes on: 'We don't employ anybody called *induna*. Our hostels are run by a system of room prefects and unit supervisors. People who were previously *indunas* have become unit supervisors. In some hostels, unit supervisors have continued to play certain *induna* roles.' Connoisseurs of South African doublespeak will savour the difference.

Working in the gold mines has long been unpopular among Blacks, with the low wages, unpleasant conditions and job insecurity. In the 1970s, 423 were injured in Anglo mines and 68 killed in clashes with police and security officials. Deaths from accidents remain at about 700 a year.

Most official studies of mining safety in South Africa have argued that accidents are the result of individual error or uncontrolled events. The first investigation into black miners' experiences, published by the University of Witwatersrand in 1985, came to a different conclusion.[30] 'Over half our informants injured in reportable accidents (involving more than fourteen days off work) believed these accidents could have been prevented,' the report said. The informants, all experienced miners, came from four mines, two of them owned by Anglo. One miner described what happened just before his accident:

> The hanging fell where there was not support. We had reported this matter to the team leader. The team leader went to the white miner. Then the white miner told the team leader to 'tell those people if they do not want the work, they must take their clothes and go to the surface,' that is to discharge. Because the miner forced us to work there and threatened to discharge us, so we just had to work without putting in packs. There were sticks there, but we told the team leader that they served no purpose because when we started to drill there it started to shake. So we asked the team leader to put in a pack because it was a big place, then the white miner forced the issue. I do not know if the white miner got into trouble because I was away in hospital.[31]

The survey found that most white miners failed to carry out their statutory safety inspections and neglected the regulations for the use of explosives. Most of this work was carried out by the black team leader and his assistant. Production bonus payments on the mine showed a huge gap between black and white workers. They are called 'kom-a-kom', literally 'come, come'. Rates for Blacks were generally about 20 per cent of the basic wage; for Whites 80 per cent. Black machine drillers, for example, earned an average of between 30 and 40 rand a month in bonuses. Some white miners received over 2,000 rand. One striking conclusion about bonus payments is that very few black workers knew how they were calculated. Attempts to find out led to frustration. 'I once queried one time,' said one miner. 'I was told that I don't know where the money is coming from, I must just be thankful. I asked the white miner, the shift boss and the PA [personal assistant].'

An unpublished research paper prepared for the Chamber of Mines in 1982 reached the same conclusion:

The policy of rewarding efforts, generally, was not understood by workers. Responses were similar, whether less complex or more complex schemes were used, whether earnings were dependent on individual efforts or on team leaders.[32]

Such a lack of communication cuts across Anglo's new policy of explaining the bonus system to workers in order to increase production.

Many black miners said the white miners insisted on work going ahead in potentially dangerous conditions so that the Whites could collect their supervisory bonuses:

What happens is that the miner, since there are phones, if you refuse to work he phones the shift boss and tells that a certain COY [company member] must be blocked because he does not want to obey instructions. So when you come to the surface they do not ask if it's dangerous, they ask you why do you refuse to obey instructions. So that's why I feel I have to work.[33]

The intense hostility between black and white miners has not gone unrecognised by the Chamber of Mines; another unpublished report said in 1983:

It would appear that autocratic and arbitrary supervision is likely to give results that are satisfactory in the short term but to be counter-productive in the longer term. Given the need to stabilise the workforce, particularly at gang level, short-term solutions need to be avoided. This suggests that the team leader (and miner) will have to be taught where necessary to avoid arbitrary and punitive behaviour.[34]

When the National Union of Mineworkers began organising in 1983, black miners found a powerful voice to challenge these practices. Within three years it was the recognised negotiating body in thirteen of the country's fifty-one goldmines, with a membership of 110,000 out of a total gold mine workforce of 451,000. Eleven of the organised mines were owned by Anglo. The union has shown itself to be a well-led, tightly disciplined and sophisticated organisation. For the first time, thousands of Blacks were involved democratically in a struggle to improve their wages and conditions. With the start of the present township uprisings in September 1984, the union has also begun to play a more overtly political role, joining in consumer boycotts and striking for the release of union officials detained under the 1986 emergency. Some of the mining houses, such as Gencor and GFSA, have resisted union organisation by driving organisers off the mines. AAC's willingness to recognise the union on many of its gold and coal mines has not been without a struggle. While Anglo understands the need to have effective communication with its workers through regulated channels, it also recognises the need to keep the NUM under pressure so that it will be pliant when it begins to challenge management prerogatives. In the face of concerted union action, the group responded with the predictable arsenal of reprisals – tear gas, bullets and dismissals.

At the beginning of 1985, faction fighting on the Free State goldfields broke out again, the most serious clashes for ten years. Several workers were killed over a dispute involving control of illegal liquor sales at Western Deep.

Further north, at Vaal Reefs, four team leaders were killed. At the same time, Vaal Reef workers had started a boycott of liquor outlets and concession stores in protest over the high prices and low wages. The union, which had organised a majority of the 43,000 workers on what was then the largest gold mine in the world, were also campaigning against the *induna* system, hostel management and lack of overtime pay for Sunday work. In April, as the union was gearing up for its annual pay battle, Anglo American decided to get tough. Faced with five weeks of disruption at Vaal Reefs, the company summarily dismissed 14,400 black miners, one-third of the workforce. It was the biggest sacking in mining history. In the process, at least two miners were killed and many injured by the police and security guards.

The specific catalyst of the dispute was a decision in January 1985 to give a 10 per cent increase to a small group of monthly-paid black and white officials. The NUM wanted it extended to the rest of its members but the company argued that wages were a matter for national negotiation with the Chamber of Mines. The conflict came to a head in the week of 21 April, when 300 men were dismissed for refusing to work on Sunday without extra pay. The next day, machine operators at two of the ten shafts refused to charge up at the rockface, claiming that this was a job reserved for Whites and that they were not being paid the rate. In the next three days, several hundred men were dismissed. Nicholas Mkhwanazi, the 25-year-old No. 8 shaft steward who had played an important role in unionising the mine, described his last attempts at negotiation with the mine manager, Mr Smith.

> Smith was very hostile. He said he was not prepared to re-engage those who were dismissed. Instead they should take their belongings and quit the mine. Those who did not do charging up would be dismissed. Things must go back to normal, he said. He added that this was the last time he was prepared to speak to shaft stewards. I reminded him of our meeting with

the general manager, Mr Williams, where it was agreed shaft stewards could make representations as friends, but he said he was not interested. Production was down 50 per cent and approximately 20 million rand was lost, he complained.[35]

On Saturday, 27 April, the 18,000 workers on the South Division, which comprised shafts 8 and 9, refused to work and helicopters circled overhead dropping leaflets informing the workers that they were dismissed. The hostels were surrounded, road blocks set up and the South African police called in. NUM regional officials and the management failed to reach an agreement and the next day the stick came out. Mkhwanazi recalled:

> At about 10.10 am the mine security arrived and took off the main gate of the hostel and loaded it on a truck. They arrested a shaft steward, on watch, when he wanted an explanation for their action. I was in a meeting with the other shaft stewards. We assembled all the workers in the arena. We could hear big lorries and helicopters arriving and orders being shouted. SAP reinforcements also arrived. From the helicopter it was announced that everyone should go to the Ernest Oppenheimer stadium. I tried to explain to workers what this meant and what was likely to happen. I appealed to them to sit quietly – not to sing or chant. Without warning the security police fired tear gas and bullets and started charging into the crowd. It was then that the two known deaths occurred. There were thousands of workers. The tear gas was overpowering and workers tried to run away. I surrendered myself to die, but some of the workers dragged me away, because I refused to run.[36]

He managed to escape by dressing in a traditional Basotho blanket and hat. Once outside the gate he was put inside the boot of a car and driven to safety. The rest of the workers were bussed back to their bantustans or neighbouring states.

Anglo issued a press release 'regretting' the action.

Bobby Godsell, in fine form, said: 'Our motivation in dismissing this very large number of people was guided by one concern only, and that was to prevent any further deterioration of order on the mines. . . . We involved the police on our mines as a last resort and are conscious that often the involvement of the police means violence.' Godsell must have read at least one of the company's reports into mine disturbances. An investigation into the serious riots on the gold mines in January 1975 against the imposition of deferred wages by the Lesotho government concluded: 'In cases of large-scale disturbances we cannot always look to the South African police for the prevention of loss of life and the protection of mine property.'[37]

In a separate dispute at the same time on a gold mine owned by Anglo-Vaal, in which Anglo has an investment, another 3,000 Blacks were sacked after protesting against the dismissal of four shop stewards. As the men were being sent back to their homelands or surrounding countries for taking part in an illegal strike, the two mining houses felt a more urgent form of black anger. At their headquarters in Johannesburg two limpet mines exploded, shattering hundreds of windows in the area. No-one was injured. Although most of the miners were eventually reinstated, the dispute shocked liberal South African opinion. Even the Oppenheimer-financed Progressive Federal Party said it was extremely disturbed that the two sides could not sort out their differences through normal channels.

Determined to rehabilitate its image and anxious to avoid a damaging official strike, AAC led the way four months later in meeting the NUM's annual wage demands. In raising their offer by 2.8 per cent to 22 per cent, AAC, JCI and one other mining house once again broke away from the recommended Chamber of Mines offer. It was a cunning move, since 80 per cent of the NUM's claimed membership of 150,000 worked on AAC mines. When the union called out its members at the ten mines of GFSA and two other companies which refused to improve their offers, the strike collapsed after two days. A combination of dismissal threats and the use of tear gas and rubber bullets by mine security guards against striking workers persuaded the union to call it off. They insisted on one condition: that the Industrial Court decided whether legally striking miners could be dismissed from their jobs and evicted from the hostels. Two months later, in November, the court ruled in the union's favour. In the circumstances it was a considerable victory for the union and its general secretary, Cyril Ramaphosa, a young lawyer, who had already spent seventeen months in prison for his political activites.

Ramaphosa was thrust into an even more prominent position that November when he delivered the inaugural address of a new united trade union front, the Congress of South Africa Trade Unions (COSATU). At the meeting in Durban COSATU claimed a signed-up membership of 500,000. Its first president, Elijah Barayi, was a former vice-president of the NUM, who demanded the abolition of the pass laws. COSATU signalled a more explicitly political stance from the unions which, since the beginning of unrest in September 1984, had gone through a period of impressive growth, particularly in the industrial sector. This was a significant shift for future labour relations. COSATU's predecessor, the Federation of South African Trade Unions (FOSATU), had taken a very clear position on the position of unions within the liberation struggle. Politically it distanced itself from what it called 'the honeypot of popular activity'. FOSATU argued that the principal role of the unions was to build a democratic, organised working class which would be able to challenge the economic structure of the apartheid regime. The popular struggle, while equally important, had a tendency for decisions to flow from the leadership rather than from the grassroots. But the explosion of unrest in the townships, especially those close to industrial centres in the Eastern Cape and the Transvaal, inevitably rubbed off on trade union perspectives. The extent of co-operation between the unions and the United Democratic Front affiliates in the townships was often subject to different levels of enthusiasm. But with the launch of COSATU many of those differences had been reconciled in the face of the onslaught from the state. Many of the NUM's actions – the guerrilla battles against discrimination, the boycotts and the wage protests – were becoming inextricably linked with the spreading popular uprisings.

In its first policy statement COSATU endorsed disinvestment, nationalisation of the mines, the abolition of discriminatory legislation, the unbanning of political organisations and a unitary state with 'one person, one vote'. It also adopted a commitment to women's rights, both in the workplace and in their daily lives.

In an unprecedented exchange in the summer of 1986, Ramaphosa had an opportunity to tell Harry Oppenheimer to his face what he thought of Anglo's wage policies and the role of the mining houses. The occasion for this, their first meeting, was a genteel affair on the surface – the first anniversary of the radical *Weekly Mail* newspaper, which was held in the relaxed multi-racial atmosphere of the Market Theatre in Johannesburg. The Market has established itelf as an oasis of cultural independence and dissent, although the long arm of Oppenheimer is even there unavoidable. Part of its funding comes from the Ernest Oppenheimer Memorial Trust and AAC. Ever ready to associate himself with symbols of opposition Oppenheimer had put 5,000 rand into the paper. The white wine and the canapés and the presence of Anglo public relations executives, together with a few black professionals and union employees, eased the historic tensions. Despite a tiring day at wage negotiations at the Chamber of Mines, Ramaphosa was in an attacking mood. His prepared speech, hurriedly typed out on the union's word processor the day before by his hard-working press officer, Marcel Golding, was a wide-ranging assault on the small, urbane man who sat next to him. 'The mining industry is left unchallenged by the press,' he said. 'The mining industry is least able to convince people of its support for social change. It is the industry which provided the furnace in which race discrimination was baked and the press knows this. Today it relies absolutely on the exploitative migrant labour system and on police oppression to operate. It pays black workers the lowest wages of any major mining company in the world, with the exception of India. . . . All you hear the mining industry barons say is that they are hamstrung by the law. Big business has been breaking innumerable laws to make big profits, but they have avoided breaking unjust laws that would help destroy the migrant labour system and allow workers to live with their families.'[38]

Oppenheimer was having none of this. 'I differ a little bit from Cyril Ramaphosa,' he began, 'in thinking this ought to be fun. I think it should be rather a cheerful occasion.' His response to Ramaphosa's analytical and passionate speech was so dismissively patronising as to amount to an insult. 'The fact that Mr Cyril Ramaphosa is here to talk as he did talk tonight – a most touching and moving speech, made all the more touching by the neglect of the facts – the fact that we were both here to talk together is something which gives me very great pleasure.' He suggested that Ramaphosa had got it wrong, because 'in some sections anyhow in private enterprise he has powerful potential allies in his battle against racial discrimination'.[39]

The facts of AAC's wage levels on the gold mines, compared to the official indices of poverty in South Africa, were easily arrived at. From July 1985, the take-home pay of underground workers ranged from 214 rand a month to 660. For surface workers it was 180 to 587. There are three minimum poverty lines. The minimum living level (MLL) for a family of four or five is calculated by the Bureau of Market Research at the University of South Africa, paid for by the Chamber of Mines, and the mining houses. For Johannesburg in February 1986 it stood at 391 rand. This was reckoned to be enough just to survive. The supplementary living level for 'a modest, low level standard of living' was 506 rand. A European Economic Community level for firms with South African subsidiaries is the MLL plus 50 per cent, that is 587 rand. On this basis AAC was paying poverty wages for most of its workers. However, there are two more ingredients in the sophisticated business of defining hunger and deprivation. Anglo argues that the free food and accommodation amount to 100 rand a month per worker. The Chamber further argues that single migrant hostel dwellers do not have to support a family so the three official levels are reduced. This brings the MLL down from 391 to 271 rand, although by no means all the migrant workers are single. The company's minimum wages, therefore, skated around the lowest wages that were deemed to be able to support people at the meanest standard of living.

An unpublished survey sponsored jointly by AAC and the NUM in 1986 contained yet another warning of things to come. 'The mines cannot be expected to be separated off from the wider conflicts occurring in South Africa at present, and . . . until real and vigorous moves are seen to be made by the various mining houses to put an end to the discriminatory and exploitative practices currently exercised, the level of conflict on the mines will rise, not fall.'[40] It was a prescient warning. Before the year was out another, more serious, wave of faction fighting broke out primarily on Anglo's gold mines. By February 1987 more than 130 workers had been killed, the majority at Vaal Reefs and President Steyn. In one incident at Vaal Reefs 20 miners were killed and 72 injured when the *indunas* attacked shaft stewards co-ordinating the NUM-sponsored bar boycott. Anglo refused to accept any responsibility. Taking out a newspaper advertisement to distance itself from the violence, the company blamed the state of emergency, general unrest, frustration at the lack of career advancement, reports of repatriation for Mozambique migrant workers and union intimidation. It announced a 'major' housing programme for married workers. The NUM blamed the conflict on the institutionalised oppression of the migrant labour and hostel system, responding in its own advertisement in the *Weekly Mail* (9–15 January 1987):

The NUM and mineworkers are not fooled by the Anglo American Corporation's public advertisement, particularly when the lives of its members are at stake. . . .

Let it be known once and for all that the source of

conflict is rooted in the institutions of oppression and exploitation which exist in the mining industry. The hostel system, migrant labour and induna system were pioneered at the turn of the century by the mine-owners to ensure maximum exploitation and control over all aspects of mineworkers' lives. It is from this brutal and draconian system that AAC has benefited. Over time these structures have been refined but kept intact.

AAC has identified and acknowledged some of the issues which have caused the tensions. But what has it done? AAC wants industrial relations to be sound and orderly yet it is not prepared to remove the archaic structures which are the source of conflict.

In this war of words there were more complex undercurrents. The 60,000 Mozambican migrants, many of them with long service, had been threatened with repatriation following a land-mine explosion near the border which injured six soldiers. After the January coup in Lesotho, the 109,000 Basotho miners who often held the higher-paid jobs were told not to get involved in South African politics. Their caution coincided with vigorous union recruitment among the militant Xhosa, at a time when the union itself was becoming more politicised. Crammed into their bleak and isolated hostels, the gold miners were seething cauldron of resentments, rivalries and fears. As a poignant reminder of the low esteem in which they were held, a list of eight dead men was issued from President Steyn after fighting on Christmas Eve. There were no names, just six-figure work numbers.

The NUM's adoption of a leading role in the liberation struggle became more apparent at its fourth annual conference in February 1987 when it pledged to get rid of the single-sex hostel system. '1987 will be the year that the miners take control,' James Motlatsi, the NUM president, told a gathering of 15,000 members in Soweto's Jubulani Stadium. It was the largest 'political' gathering since the State of Emergency was declared nine months before. A giant (illegal) poster of Nelson Mandela – elected the previous year as honorary life president – was displayed as the conference endorsed the Freedom Charter, a formal, if symbolic, commitment to the nationalisation of the mines. Cyril Ramaphosa, however, gave a measured interpretation to the vote. Much work had to done, he said, before specific plans were drawn up. In line with current ANC thinking – so difficult for white South Africans to read about in the censored media – Ramaphosa appreciated that in any new dispensation the wealth of the country should not be diminished by hasty ideological gestures.

Motlatsi's declaration was followed in March 1987 with the NUM demanding a statement of intent from the Chamber of Mines to dismantle the hostel system. It was a forlorn ultimatum but it set the tone for a series of actions on Anglo's mines which began to challenge the degradation of the system. In April about 250 wives moved into four Anglo coal-mine hostels in defiance of the mine managements, who warned they were trespassing. One manager circulated a statement that the hostel's food and facilities were for employees only. 'You will not be treated like a lady,' he said. In the event, the occupation went off quietly and Anglo pressed ahead with its scheme, announced in January, for the construction of 24,000 houses for married gold-mine workers. But the bulk of the labour force, the foreign migrant workers, were excluded on instructions from the government. Another discriminatory practice was highlighted by industrial action on several of Anglo's larger gold mines. Shaft stewards objected to the use of 'picanins' – black miners whose job was to carry the satchel of the white 'master' with his food, newspapers and comics. The fact that such a system still existed in 1987 showed how entrenched racist structures were on the mines. According to Ramaphosa, some white miners at Vaal Reefs were so dumbfounded when their picanins were withdrawn that they resigned and moved to other mines.

Meanwhile, the 1987 pay negotiations were grinding to a halt. On 1 July the Chamber of Mines unilaterally imposed increases of between 16 per cent and 23 per cent, refusing to

move closer to the union's demand of 30 per cent. Peter
Gush, Anglo's gold division chief, said there would be no
more on offer. The scene was set for what became the
biggest strike in recent South African history and from
which Anglo emerged with its reformist image in shreds.

The mining houses never expected such a show of
strength and organisation. Experience of the previous two
years had shown that the NUM could at best muster a brief
and fragmented display of solidarity. But this time they
were claiming a membership of 262,000, over half of the
country's mine workforce, and 80 per cent on Anglo mines.
The strike began on 9 August. At the end of the first full
day, with widely differing claims of the numbers involved,
a tragic pattern began to emerge. At Anglo Vaal's Loraine
mine the first black miner was shot in the legs by security
police. At the end of the three weeks, nine had died, up to
500 were injured and another 400 arrested.

For most of the dispute, journalists were barred from
mine premises and as the violence raged along the golden
arc between miners and security police and – in a few cases
– between strikers and working miners, the two sides dug
into their respective bunkers. Ironically the new government, returned in the Whites-only election in May 1987,
chose the first week of the strike to abolish the job-
reservation rule that denied blasting certificates to Blacks.

The Labour Monitoring Group of academic researchers
put the best estimate of the numbers on strike at a massive
334,600 men out of a total workforce of 509,800 (the NUM
claimed that 340,000 miners struck, while the Chamber of
Mines insisted it was 240,000). Out of 99 mines, about 40 or
so were affected, with Anglo being the hardest hit. Many
miners pre-empted a threatened call by the NUM to send
all their men home and left the compounds. Only Gold
Fields' mines, where the union had effectively been barred,
remained untouched. Anglo made little effort to restrain its
mine security police: at Vaal Reefs and Western Deep over
80 miners were injured in the first week. The entire strike
committee of 78 men at Klerksdorp were arrested and
charged with conspiracy to murder by the SAP after some

heated speeches. At Ergo, Anglo won an injunction against 400 miners who had occupied part of the site, which led to 23 arrests. In all, 225 men were injured by rubber bullets, tear gas and batons in six days. At the weekend Anglo took stock of the deteriorating situation and Bobby Godsell devised a new approach, half-conciliatory, half-menacing. He invited the NUM leaders to a meeting to seek ways of reducing the violence, and at the same time it was announced that Anglo would have to shut down two gold shafts and Landon coal mine with the loss of 2,000 jobs. They were said to be uneconomical and the men were given a three-day deadline to return to work.

The talks broke down on the second day, with Rama-phosa and his colleagues walking out. They had just heard that the SAP, allegedly without management approval, had opened fire with rubber bullets at the gates of President Steyn. The NUM accused the mining houses of colluding with the state. For the rest of the week the companies began to tighten the screw. Although the miners returned to Landon colliery to try to negotiate a retrenchment deal, Anglo, JCI and Gencor all stepped up their threats to close shafts, discipline strikers or simply dismiss them. Bobby Godsell's assertion that Anglo never sacks legally striking workers was shown to be a shallow public-relations ploy when it was announced that 17,000 Anglo men would be dismissed if they did not return to work by the coming Monday.

In the midst of this mayhem, the Anglo American Corporation held its sedate annual general meeting in Johannesburg. On the basis that a bloody strike was better than workers not being able to strike at all, Gavin Relly serenely told the meeting that the dispute 'was an indication of progress by South African society towards normali-sation'. But he did hold out the chance of more negotiations – not on wages but on holiday-leave bonuses, death benefits and an improved provident fund deal.

There were the usual conflicting claims about black miners' pay. Relly told the meeting that average earnings had increased by 85 per cent in ten years. Elsewhere Johann

Liebenberg, the industrial relations adviser to the Chamber of Mines, was saying that basic pay for unskilled and semi-skilled workers throughout the industry had gone up by 32 per cent over the same period. Bobby Godsell added his calculations to show that average pay for all gold and uranium miners was 12 per cent above minimum rates, with overtime and bonuses included. The majority of Anglo workers were in grade four, he said. All these figures ignored the fact that the 30 per cent demand would in real terms only bring the average wage to just above 1984 levels, according to the Chamber of Mines annual reports. For the increases since the big wage lift-off in 1972 – when the rates were worse in real terms than during the Boer War – peaked in 1983. Grade four did have more workers than any of the other eight, but more than half of the workers were spread between the lowest-paying grades one to three. Only 13 per cent were in the top three grades.

The strike entered its third and final week with speculation about if and how the government might respond, as the millions of rand lost to the mining houses also meant a hefty drop in state tax revenues. Curiously, gold shares only dropped slightly, on the well-founded assumption that the houses had stockpiled both ore on the surface and bullion. President Botha, it was thought, was also privately enjoying the sight of Anglo's liberal reputation being battered.

On the Monday, Anglo and JCI extended their deadlines for dismissals, suggested that miners were drifting back to work, and offered new talks without conditions. In Lesotho it quietly began to recruit new workers. Bobby Godsell put a fine gloss on the state of play. 'This test we're going through is precisely a way where liberal white business is trying to find a sustainable pattern of sharing power with black workers. This is a strike about getting patterns of bargaining – and indeed of striking – that we can live with in the future.'

In four hours of talks at the Chamber of Mines the new fringe benefits suggested by Relly were put on the table: an effective cash increase of 1.3 per cent. Ramaphosa's team reduced their claim to 27 per cent. The NUM said they would have to consult their members, although they left the meeting with no great enthusiasm for the task. Privately they realised that the end was in sight and members were advised that it would be best to accept the new offer. But the membership was in no mood for compromise after the sacrifices of the previous two weeks. On Wednesday, 26 August, mass meetings rejected the new offer and the companies began the sackings: 40,000 on Anglo mines; 20,000 at Gencor; 3,000 at JCI's Randfontein Estates. 'Mine managements,' the Chamber said in a statement, 'will now be pursuing the objective of getting their mines back to normal production.' At Western Deep the union heard that several thousand miners had been ordered at gunpoint to return to work.

For the NUM, and for the wider liberation forces which had been intensely engaged as sideline observers in the development of the strike, it was crunch time. That Wednesday evening COSATU decided that its affiliates could not come out in sympathy action for a dispute that seemed doomed to a damaging failure. The NUM executive had two stark options. Either they could give in and preserve the union for the next battle, or they could watch their members disappear to the homelands and abroad and with them the union's hard-won organisation. The choice was difficult but obvious to the calculating strategists in the Johannesburg headquarters. On Friday, 29 August, the NUM asked to speak to Anglo executives. They had already decided that the best course was an honourable retreat, with priority efforts to secure the re-engagement of dismissed workers. They met in the Carlton Hotel, eventually bringing in Gencor managers and finally the Chamber of Mines. Outside, the sackings went on; the mining houses threatened court action to evict strikers who had taken over hostels; *City Press* reported a confidential document which said that the Reserve Bank was about to cut off the union's foreign funds.

On Sunday, 30 August, the Chamber announced that the strike was over. Bobby Godsell was restrained. 'None of my colleagues are celebrating victory here today,' he said and with good reason. Anglo had been shown to be as ruthless and brutal as the rest of the mining houses. Reduced to its basics, the leading white business critic of apartheid had used starvation, violence and summary dismissal as weapons against its black workers.

The Progressive Federal Party spokesman, Peter Gastrow, opined that labour relations had reached a new sophistication. Manpower minister Pietie du Plessis said the labour legisation had proved its worth so that 'economic forces brought the conclusion of the strike'. For Anglo and the state, that was the crucial consideration: the strike had failed to escalate into an overtly political contest with wider trade union support.

But in effect the union had won a significant political victory in keeping so many strikers out for such a long time. The power of the union and its integrity had been enhanced. Cyril Ramaphosa, who with his executive had remarkably been unscathed by the state's clamp-down on union activists during the state of emergency, called it a dress rehearsal for 1988.

On the next day, Monday, 31 August, the miners went underground. At Gencor's St Helena gold mine in the Orange Free State 57 black miners and five Whites were descending the 1,300-metre shaft when their cage was hit by an explosion. They plunged to their deaths beneath tons of rubble. In the words of the old miners' saying, now the title of the NUM's recently published booklet on safety, it was just one of 'A Thousand Ways to Die' on the gold mines.

Anglo reinstated about three-quarters of the dismissed men and under union pressure agreed to take the other cases to arbitration in the spring of 1988.

Two months after the strike, the real financial impact on Anglo turned out to be rather less dramatic than expected. Production at the difficult Western Deep levels dropped by 34 per cent, but much less at Vaal Reefs and Freegold, the two largest mines in the country. Yet Freegold's profits during the period shot up through working higher-grade ore. Anglo's administered mines still made a profit for the

September quarter of 514 million rand – a drop of only 14 million on the June quarter.

As a postscript to the unbowed might of Pretoria and its gold houses, a magnificent state banquet was held in November to open the new black marble and glass head-quarters of the Reserve Bank. In the vaults were the state's gold reserves, which had more than doubled over the year to 6.2 billion fine ounces. President Botha was guest of honour. Some important critics, such as Chris Ball of the National Bank and Dr Fritz Leutwiler, the former Swiss debt mediator, stayed away. But Harry Oppenheimer was there to give his usual speech about the need for political solutions to South Africa's isolation.

Compared with the miners, Anglo's industrial workers are relatively fortunate. They have found it easier in factories to organise strong trade unions and skilled labour is more in demand. Wages are slightly higher. With the scrapping of industrial job reservation in 1976, Anglo promoted a few black employees to well-paid, skilled jobs in most of its plants. For the rest, wages for Blacks are kept just clear of the various poverty minimum lines and de facto job reservation still exists at plant level. A worker at Anglo's subsidiary, Highveld Steel, explained:

When they employ an artisan [white] they tell him he has to have an artisan helper, to carry the tools for the artisan when he is going to fix something. When they get there they [the artisan] just show him, 'Do this, do this, do this' – the artisan stands watching. That is the general pattern.[41]

Anglo's relations with the industrial unions illustrate just how committed the company is to maintaining its authority. In 1979 the Metal and Allied Workers' Union (MAWU) began organising in Scaw Metals, a wholly owned subsid-iary of Anglo's main industrial investment company. The union was informally recognised in 1980 but the company refused to sign an agreement without a clause tying the question of wages and conditions to negotiations at Indus-trial Council level for the whole steel and engineering industry. Since all fundamental decisions were taken at this level, MAWU's plant negotiators would be left with nothing to discuss except, as one union representative put it, 'the state of the toilets'.

In 1982, the union challenged this system and the 2,000 workers went on strike for a rise in their basic pay to be negotiated locally. After eleven days all the workers were sacked, evicted from their hostels and sent back to the bantustans. Later 1,800 were re-engaged and the union was forced to join the Industrial Council. Bobby Godsell made it clear how far Anglo was prepared to go:

> Scaw was an illegal strike. It was a strike initiated by the workers . . . a strike about where we bargain, at what level. That for management was a very important battle and that's why management stuck fast and actually won the battle. . . . We don't see the purpose of the strike being there to put the business out of business. And so we would say that the employers have the right to retain a kind of absolute last resort, exchanging their labour force or dismissing their labour force in order to protect essential business interests.[42]

Godsell claimed that Anglo had never sacked legally striking workers. Yet many strikers have been fired by companies within the group. Anglo took no responsibility for threatening to sack the 8,500 legally striking workers at four of the giant AECI chemical plants in 1984, though it effectively controls the company with a 39.5 per cent shareholding. The strike was the first legal national stoppage by black workers. Later that year at Highveld Steel, the 3,500 legally striking black workers were told that they could be sacked for breaking their contract. The threat was enough to bring them back to work. About 1,000 of the Highveld Blacks live in the townships; the rest are migrant workers accommodated in hostels. A shop steward told the authors:

> The hostels are cold. There are only two stoves to cook on. With 500 people, it takes about two or three hours to get a pot on the stove. There are only cold showers, and some don't work. It's not clean. There are mice

under the bed. There are no storage facilities, just a small locker. No furniture, no tables, nothing. There are a few windows but some are broken with cardboard in. No ceilings, just an asbestos roof, no heaters. You have to try to get blankets to keep warm. . . . Sometimes, the toilets are dark, the lights don't work. Then the muggers hide in the toilets and when the people come in they take your money. If you haven't got money, he will stab you a little bit with the knife.[43]

For staying in these conditions for the year's contract, each worker in a sixteen-man room has 12 rand deducted from his pay. The price rises to 16 rand for a room for two people, and 21 rand for a single room like 'a small passage with only room for a bed'. Many of Anglo's workers live in these or similar conditions, but the company house magazine, *Optima*, and its annual reports prefer to highlight other sides of the business: pictures of women being taught to type; black apprentices upgrading their jobs; schools built with Anglo's support. The arrival of the union at Highveld persuaded Anglo to renovate the hostel at a cost of 1.3 million rand. 'Workers have been asking for improvements since 1976,' the steward said. 'The company said it couldn't afford it. Then we joined MAWU. After eighteen months we got the money.'

At AAC's head office the women cleaners are paid just above the level set by the Sullivan Principles – the code of practice for American companies operating in South Africa. Their union organiser estimated that about half of the women were single heads of households. The wage level – for a family of six – is calculated by adding estimates of essential expenditure from five categories: food, clothing, heat and cleaning, rent and transport. It allows for a family to consume, for example, a pound of meat a month, 3.5 eggs and 5 lbs of vegetables. Most of the food budget is supposed to go towards mealie meal. There is very little left for education, doctors' bills, books, family emergencies or travel to visit relatives. The women on the night shift leave Soweto at 5 p.m. An organiser told the authors: 'They do a

nine-hour shift starting at 6 p.m. By not taking a meal
break they can finish at 3 a.m. and get two hours sleep on
the floor before catching the bus home – it's too dangerous
before then. Until the union got involved, they didn't
provide any furniture in the cleaner's room – only cardboard boxes – or even tea urns or tea and coffee.' When
they get home the women make breakfast, see the children
off to school and clean the house. Then they sleep until it is
time for the next shift.

At the end of 1986 another organised section of workers
in the Anglo camp experienced the sharp end of management policy. The shopworkers' union called a national
strike at the ubiquitous OK Bazaars general stores. After
long negotiations, the company refused to review its wage
policy in line with increased profits which the union
claimed had been promised. OK adopted a range of tactics,
besides bringing in the inevitable scabs. The company went
to court to prevent strikers going near the stores; on a
number of occasions the police were called to arrest pickets.
On one day alone, 64 workers were arrested and the union
had to stump up bail of 1,000 rand each. General workers at
OK earned 232 rand a month. In Pretoria the police
presence was so strong that organisation became impossible. OK's links to Anglo were not ignored. A shop
steward summed it up: 'Anglo American, through South
African Breweries and Premier Milling, own many shares in
the OK. We are tired of their hypocrisy. They visit the
ANC in Lusaka and then come home to crush legal strikes.'

At the bottom of the heap are the labourers who work on
Anglo's farms. They have no legal wage or employment
protection, and as residents of 'non-prescribed' areas they
are unable to move elsewhere. If a farm-worker loses his job
or retires, he also loses his home and becomes a 'displaced
person'. The only place to go is one of the homelands he
may never have seen. The union have found it difficult to
organise on the farms but the first attempt, by the Orange
Vaal General Workers' Union, began in 1981 at Anglo's
Soetvelde Farms in the Transvaal. The farm's general
manager, A. A. Penberthy, had this to say: 'We have

nothing against them joining a union, provided it goes about things in the right way. But this one seems to be political. They are telling me how to run my business. They send letters making demands about canteens and lunch hours and they question our right to deduct traffic fines from drivers' pay. The individual communication we used to have with our workers is gone since the union arrived.'[44]

This was hardly surprising, according to the union organiser, Philip Masia: 'We never get to see Mr Penberthy. The managers are rude to us and never listen.' Not one demand had been conceded by the management.

A new form of co-option of black workers throughout South African industry was given a high-profile impetus by Ford of Canada when it pulled out in November 1987, leaving Anglo with three-quarters of the holding in Samcor. Just over half of Ford's 42 per cent in the company was placed in a workers-controlled trust with representation on the main board. The deal was agreed after ten months of negotiation with the National Union of Metal Workers (NUMSA, formerly MAWU). Anglo was impressed, since the idea fitted into its philosophy of creating a black sector with personal investment in the capitalist system. Share ownership, as in Britain, gave the appearance of a widening democracy.

However, Anglo decided that its own version of share ownership would bypass any union involvement or participation in decision-making. An Anglo associated company, South African Breweries (SAB), had already shown that the unions could successfully be ignored. Amalgamated Beverage Industries (ABI) is the largest producer of Coca Cola and Fanta in the country. In 1986 the Coca Cola Corporation, which formerly held 82 per cent of the company, disinvested and sold 70 per cent to SAB. A further 19 per cent went to Cadbury Schweppes, and Coke wanted the remaining 11 per cent to be sold to its staff and dealers through interest-free loans. ABI launched a publicity campaign to encourage acceptance of the scheme, but the two food workers' unions and the Soweto Chamber of Commerce rejected it as political tokenism. The Food and Allied

Workers' Union said the 'sale of shares advances and protects the interests of profit-takers, while dividing united action by the workers'.[45] Frustrated by this opposition, ABI appealed direct to the individual staff members and dealers, who vastly oversubscribed the offer. So Anglo knew it was on safe, if controversial, ground when in November 1987 it offered free shares in the Anglo American Corporation.

The initial proposal, partly devised by Bobby Godsell, was to give five shares each to 2,500 staff at AAC's head office who had more than two years of service. Over a five-year period, up to 250,000 workers in AAC and associated companies would then be invited to join the scheme, with the shares held for a minimum of four years in management-controlled trust. If the AAC offer was fully taken up, the 7.5 million shares would represent 3.5 per cent of the equity. Gavin Relly, AAC's chairman, waxed lyrical: 'The future prosperity of the corporation is inextricably linked with the future prosperity of all South Africans in the creation of significant new wealth, in the context of a free and fair economy and society.' The directors of AAC can testify to that; under the long-standing share scheme for them they held 936,100 shares in 1987. The first reaction from the NUM's Cyril Ramaphosa was: 'It stinks.' He went on: 'They refused to grant the pay rises which could have ended the strike and now they are coming in through the back door and offering shares. What matters to the workers is not wealth in the future but wages now.'[46]

But it was not only the unions and black organisations that questioned the Anglo approach. *Finance Week*, in one of its more outspoken editorials, said the scheme smacked of paternalism: 'The established media, much of it controlled by Anglo, can sing the praises of Anglo to the heavens. Newspapers in the black community have not shared the enthusiasm of their white counterparts. . . . So long as black workers perceive the scheme to be more in the interests of their employer than themselves, to be less an attempt to promote a pragmatic synthesis between capitalist and socialist ideologies than an attempt to undermine unionism, it carries risks which threaten the exercise.'[47]

The exercise, in fact, was flawed from the start. Ford and Coca Cola were able to export the ideas of wider sharehold-ding from the monetarist shores of Reagan's America and Thatcher's Britain. But in the South African context, where the economic issues are still inextricably bound up with power and privilege, the matter takes on a much more fundamental hue. Ford, under North American and Euro-pean anti-apartheid pressures, was able to meet some of the collective black demands for a say in corporate decisions. Anglo executives fought shy of what is to them an unaccept-able radically move. The empire was only being true to itself.

10

Playing the Black Markets

When South Africa left the Commonwealth in 1960, it was surrounded by the politically quiescent colonies of European powers. Portugal kept Angola and Mozambique on a tight rein. Swaziland, Basutoland (Lesotho), Bechuanaland (Botswana), the two Rhodesias (Zambia and Zimbabwe) and Nyasaland (Malawi) were all ruled from London. South West Africa (Namibia) was part of South Africa's fiefdom. Ten years later Pretoria's hopes of incorporating the small states into a greater South Africa had come to nothing. Lesotho, Swaziland, Botswana and Zambia had become independent. Rhodesia was controlled by a fractious settler government in open revolt against Britain. The black populations of Rhodesia, Mozambique, Angola, Namibia and South Africa itself had launched liberation struggles. By 1980, the Portuguese colonies had won their independence, the settler regime had been ousted in Zimbabwe and the wars in Namibia and South Africa had escalated. From being surrounded by sympathetic administrations, South Africa found itself at odds with the often hostile governments of the 'frontline' states, many of which were prepared to give active political and material support to liberation movements that were fighting the South African state.

These changes created real problems for South African capitalists like Harry Oppenheimer. Southern Africa had for years regarded them as a limitless supplier of cheap labour, a vast and largely untapped source of primary materials and a ready market for South African goods, so it came as something of a shock to them to find doors slammed in their faces wherever they went. The fact that many back doors remained open meant that business continued, but on far less comfortable terms. In particular, South African companies like Anglo were deprived of the close associations they had enjoyed with the Portuguese, most of whom had fled taking every last stick of furniture with them. The Portuguese connection, however, was to be maintained on two fronts. In the first place, Portuguese business continued to assist in the destabilisation of the former colonies; and many Portuguese transferred their assets not to Lisbon but to Brazil, which had remarkably similar advantages to South Africa in terms of cheap labour, rich mineral resources and authoritarian regimes. Anglo's entrée into Rio was through these very channels, and the head of their Brazilian operations, Dr Mario Ferreira, once in charge of Anglo's interests in colonial Mozambique, now sits on the main AAC board.

The danger presented by the disintegration of the colonial *cordon sanitaire* led many South African businessmen to take clear political stances. Oppenheimer spoke for most of them in October 1984 when he explained his views about independent black states and the lessons for South Africa to the Foreign Policy Association in New York:

The idea that a just political settlement in South Africa should necessarily take the same form as in other southern African states is quite unrealistic and, indeed, preposterous. Although I have spent a lifetime fighting against policies of racial discrimination in South Africa, I certainly would not willingly accept a political settlement which involved any serious risk of South Africa's developing into a Marxist-orientated, one-party state. And who can say that in

African conditions the establishment of a Westminster-type constitution based on one-man-one-vote would not involve such a risk?[1]

South African companies know that they can work on one level with independent governments of Africa. Even before Mozambique had become formally independent, Anglo's Gordon Waddell flew to Maputo to discuss with the provisional government 'matters of mutual interest'. Throughout the Angolan civil war, one of the few foreign companies to continue paying taxes to the MPLA liberation movement was De Beers, through its diamond interests there. AAC and De Beers have operated continuously in Tanzania, Zambia and Botswana. At the same time, economically independent countries have, albeit reluctantly, supported South Africa's attempts to tame its more radical neighbours and have been obliged to withdraw their support for the African National Congress (ANC) and the South West Africa People's Organisations (SWAPO) in Namibia.

South Africa's attempts to reverse the defeats of the 1960s and 1970s have led to the destabilisation and impoverishment of the whole southern African region, something not at first sight in the interests of the South African companies operating there. Evidently, though, they have seen the situation as a choice between some disruption to their business outside South Africa, and the potential total disruption of their operations inside the country. Without exception, the business community shares the government's perception of events in independent Africa as being threatening to their interests. In his 1980 chairman's report, Premier's Tony Bloom, a rising Anglo star, applauded agreements which had been extracted by a mixture of force and economic sanctions: 'Political developments during the year have been most encouraging. The recent agreements signed by Mozambique and Swaziland represent a major foreign-policy achievement for South Africa and will hopefully form the basis for the broader regional co-operation in the whole of the southern Africa region.'

In 1975, the South African army invaded Angola in an attempt to secure victory in the civil war for groups sympathetic to its interests. It was forced to withdraw, and a reassessment of tactics led to the adoption of a strategy of gradual attrition against states regarded as hostile.

In Angola the South Africans rearmed and retrained the defeated forces of Jonas Savimbi's Union for the Total Independence of Angola (UNITA), which then began systematically to sabotage the infrastructure of the country, to attack rural mines and settlements and to abduct or kill Angolans and foreigners living in remote areas. From time to time the South African army made further incursions into the country to establish UNITA in new areas, to attack Namibian refugee villages and SWAPO bases and to destroy Angolan defences. Through the 1980s, South African forces maintained a presence on Angolan territory in the south of the country. By 1984, 70 per cent of Angola's revenues were being spent on the war. Although Angola is potentially one of the richest countries in Africa, with deposits of oil, diamonds, iron, copper, uranium and other minerals, as well as plentiful supplies of fertile land, Angolans are forced to queue for food at street kitchens.

A similar strategy was pursued in Mozambique. Lacking an existing organisation to arm and provision, South Africa created its own 'rebel' force, the Mozambique National Resistance (MNR), out of the ex-Portuguese colonial force and secret police and ex-soldiers and malcontents of the Rhodesian regime. Operating initially from bases within South Africa, and later supplied by South Africa, the MNR effectively disrupted attempts to rebuild the shattered and plundered Mozambique economy. At one time Maputo harbour was mined. In January 1981, South African special forces raided an ANC house, killing a dozen people. Two years later South African jets bombed houses and a factory in Maputo; only one of the six people killed had any ANC connections. One of the most notorious cases where South African involvement was alleged but never proved was the letter-bomb assassination in Maputo, on 17 August 1982, of Ruth First, the anti-apartheid campaigner and wife of the

ANC military strategist Joe Slovo. On the propaganda front, the Portuguese businessman, Jorge Jardim, a former associate of Anglo's Ferreira, helped to finance the MNR's radio station.[2]

The military and covert operations were accompanied by economic pressure. This was made possible by the dependence of these countries on trade with South Africa and its transport system and on labour exports, and by the domination of their economies by South African-based interests, many of them run by Anglo companies.

In 1985, the republic sold 2 billion rand of goods to the rest of Africa, about four times the value of imports. The imbalance has consistently grown since the mid-1970s. According to the International Monetary Fund, Zimbabwe is South Africa's biggest trading partner, taking $337.7 million of South African exports, compared with providing imports of $190 million. When Zimbabwe became independent, South Africa unilaterally cancelled a preferential trade agreement dating back to 1964. In 1982, Malawi had a $95 million deficit with South Africa, and Zambia's exports to South Africa represented only 6.5 per cent of a two-way trade of almost $87 million. Of Mozambique's imports, excluding fuel, 19 per cent came from South Africa, and in 1984, the last year for which full statistics are available, almost 50 per cent of the imports of the vulnerable six land-locked SADCC countries came from their apartheid neighbour. For all SADCC countries total South African exports came to $1.7 billion, ten per cent of all South Africa's export sales.

This dependence was exacerbated by the effect of the drought in the early 1980s. Of South Africa's total maize imports in 1984 of 5.5 million tonnes, 29 per cent was for transhipment to Zimbabwe, Zambia, Lesotho, Botswana and Swaziland. Much of this trade is covert, with false certificates of origin and double invoices to conceal their place of manufacture. The result is that the goods of Anglo's industrial companies end up on the shelves of retailers throughout Africa.

Anglo's companies are in the forefront of developing this

trade. One of them, Premier International, 'undertakes invaluable work in spearheading South Africa's attempts to develop trading relationships throughout Africa', according to its chairman, Tony Bloom. By the end of 1983, Premier's exports represented 10 per cent of total South African exports to other African countries and were worth about 100 million rand. The group claimed to have overcome political animosity, poorly developed financial infrastructures, chronic shortages of foreign exchange and unreliable transport services to achieve its export success.

Another Anglo firm, Freight Services (now called Rennies Freight Services), was able to offer just the connections that Premier needed. A major freight-forwarding and shipping group, Freight Services (FS) had subsidiaries all over southern Africa. It became expert at overcoming obstacles to trade, and for fifteen years it played a central role in supplying the rebel Rhodesian regime of Ian Smith with oil, which was transported from the Shell terminal in Laurenço Marques (now Maputo), Mozambique. In 1974, after the revolution in Portugal, it was obvious that it was only a matter of time before the Mozambique Liberation Front (FRELIMO) government took over in Mozambique. Representatives of the oil companies that had been supplying the oil to FS met with South African ministers to discuss the possibility of routing oil through South Africa and Botswana in the event of FRELIMO terminating the trade. A complex swap agreement was arranged with the South African Coal, Oil and Gas Corporation (SASOL), the parastatal oil-from-coal producer. The companies would supply a greater proportion of South Africa's needs, thereby freeing SASOL oil for Rhodesia.

Hand in hand with this, Anglo agreed to merge FS with Aero Marine Investments and Manica Holdings, both subsidiaries of another parastatal, the South African Marine Corporation (Safmarine). Anglo's 77 per cent, through its industrial arm, Anglo American Industrial Corporation (AMIC), was reduced to 40.3 per cent in the new company, Aero Marine Freight Services Holdings. But Anglo insisted on retaining joint control. AMIC and Safmarine split the ownership of a holding company, Redbury Holdings, between them, and Redbury in turn took a controlling interest of 50.8 per cent. In effect, at a time when the South African government was forced to become directly involved in the supply of oil to its ally, Anglo entered into an equal partnership with the state.

Freight Services' central role for over ten years was finally revealed in the British government's investigations into the trade, published in 1978 as the Bingham Report.[3] By then, however, FS had expanded into other clandestine fields. It had begun to set up an international freight and procurement network of sixty companies against the day when they might become necessary to evade sanctions against South Africa itself. The most important step was the acquisition of an established and respectable British freight-forwarding company, Davidson, Park and Speed of Glasgow. Through a series of carefully planned manoeuvres, FS took over the company without revealing to its staff or directors that a South African company was involved. It was not until a major exposé was published in the London *Guardian* newspaper in March 1984 that they discovered the truth. Through the Glasgow firm, FS acquired freight companies in virtually every African country, allowing the export of South African goods without revealing their origins. An explanation of FS's activities was given by the managing director of Davidson:

> There was commercial concern that an active South African involvement in freight companies here might prejudice business to areas that did not get on with South Africa. Initial secrecy, if there was any secrecy, was purely commercial, not for any devious reasons.[4]

The most recent chapter in the Freight Services story has placed it in an even stronger position. In September 1984 Safmarine merged with a major South African hotel, casino and shipping company, Rennies, to form Safren. Anglo, in turn, agreed to a merger of FS with Rennies but only so long as FS did not become a Safren subsidiary. It was arranged, therefore, that Redbury Holdings would keep a

controlling interest with AMIC, sharing ownership of Redbury with Safren. The result of this complicated deal was
that FS became buried in a major conglomerate with assets
of 1.2 billion rand. The extent to which Anglo stuck in its
heels over the merger was a measure of the importance it
attached to this relatively small, but strategic, part of the
empire. South Africa's domination of the whole region's
transport network explains just how important.

A web of rail and road links connects the country's
industrial heartland to Zaïre, Zambia, Zimbabwe, Malawi,
Mozambique, Namibia, Botswana, Lesotho and Swaziland.
The internal arteries end at the ports of Saldanha Bay, Cape
Town, Port Elizabeth, East London, Durban and Richards
Bay, which handle the bulk of South Africa's trade with the
outside world. Most of the alternative routes are also either
controlled or blocked by South Africa. Lobito in Angola
has been cut off from the rest of Africa for long periods,
owing to continuous sabotage of the Benguela railway line
by South Africa's protégé, UNITA. Walvis Bay in Namibia
is under direct South African rule. Maputo in Mozambique
remains the main railway port for the eastern Transvaal,
while the Mozambique National Resistance Movement
(MNR) ensures that traffic between Beira, the country's
other port, and Zimbabwe is constantly vulnerable. The
only alternative port, Dar es Salaam in Tanzania, is connected to Zambia by the Tazara railway line, an extremely
long, over-burdened single-track line subject to chronic
disruption and delay.

South Africa has frequently wielded its control of transport routes to coerce countries into compliance with its
wishes. Mozambique is financially dependent on the revenue provided by the movement of South African freight
through Maputo, South Africa's third largest shipping
outlet, and Pretoria was able to use this as one of the levers
to force Mozambique to sign the Nkomati Accord of 1984.
The volume of traffic through Maputo was drastically
reduced from 6.8 million tonnes in 1973 to 1.1 million ten
years later. In addition, South Africa diverted a higher
proportion of low-tariff minerals such as coal through

Maputo, while routing the high-tariff chrome, copper and nickel through its own ports. Movement of steel through Maputo was totally ceased by 1982. Following the signing of the Nkomati Accord, tonnage was expected to double. The Mozambique National Planning Commission estimated that between 1975 and 1984 the joint effects of the Zimbabwean war of independence, the activities of the MNR and South African sanctions had altogether cost the country, one of the world's poorest, 7 billion rand. Anglo companies concurred with the strategy. Highveld Steel, a major exporter, is in the eastern Transvaal, and Maputo is the obvious port for exports to South-East Asia. Despite this, no steel or related products have been sent through Maputo in recent years. Such boycotting was maintained despite a potential saving of at least $10 per ton, compared with other routes.

On one occasion some Anglo employees assisted with a direct South African attack on Beira in 1982. On 9 December, a boatload of South African-trained commandos landed at Beira and attached limpet mines to the oil tanks, causing US$20 millions' worth of damage. The week before the raid, the staff of Manica Freight Services – 40 per cent owned by Anglo, the rest by Safmarine – were told to fill their cars because of a likely shortage of petrol. The Mozambique authorities discovered that Manica's director, Dion Hamilton, a Briton, had provided information for the raid while his deputy, a Portuguese called Benjamin Fox, had supplied arms to the MNR. Their office was, in effect, an MNR intelligence post. They were sentenced respectively to twenty years' and eight years' imprisonment for knowing about the raid in advance. Hamilton, who had worked in Beira since the beginning of sanctions, was also found guilty of 'acts amounting to terrorism' and of possession of guns.[5]

The 1985 coup in Lesotho is a good example of South Africa's economic power. Chief Leabua Jonathan, the ruler of this small, mountainous enclave, had come to power in the 1965 elections with South African financial support. He was even permitted to enter the gold-mining areas to campaign among the Basotho migrant workers, who make up about a third of Lesotho's adult male labour force and contribute up to 40 per cent to the country's gross national product. He later visited Verwoerd, who received him as an independent head of state.

Relations began to deteriorate after the 1970 elections, when Chief Jonathan, a shrewd and ruthless politician, realised that he was losing. He suspended the constitution and locked up the opposition. Aware that his pro-South African stance had lost him support, Chief Jonathan increasingly took a hostile attitude to apartheid, refusing to recognise the 'independent' homeland of the Transkei. He incurred particular South African displeasure by claiming large tracts of land in the Orange Free State. The mountains of Lesotho had long been a refuge for ANC exiles, and their numbers swelled after the Soweto uprising.

Pretoria's destabilisation began first of all with covert support for the Lesotho Liberation Army, the military wing of the opposition Basutoland Congress Party (BCP), which has launched numerous attacks from across the South African border. We have seen in Chapter 9 how the intelligence service BOSS recruited agents to organise the BCP on the Free State gold mines. In 1982, commandos flew into the capital of Maseru by helicopter and killed forty-two people, twenty-seven of them ANC refugees. Chief Jonathan responded by turning for assistance to the east, inviting Russia, China and North Korea to set up diplomatic missions. The North Koreans trained Jonathan's new Youth League, which began to take on the characteristics of a revolutionary guard.

By 1984, however, South Africa was becoming more impatient with the erratic mountain kingdom, especially as it was resisting the sort of security pact that had been signed with Mozambique. One point of pressure was an attempt to renegotiate the South African Customs Union, a long-established form of compensation for the economic dependence of Lesotho, Botswana and Swaziland, which provided up to 70 per cent of Lesotho's revenues. Another economic lever was South Africa's successful opposition to the setting up of a Honda car-assembly plant that would rival South African production. As the unrest grew in the South African townships, more young Blacks took to the Lesotho hills, en route to the ANC-run Solomon Mahlangu training college in Tanzania.

In December 1985, another white commando raid, widely believed to have been carried out by the South African Defence Force, entered Maseru and killed six people at a Christmas party. Two weeks later, South Africa imposed a virtual economic blockade, with deliberately lengthy and rigorous border checks on all traffic. It amounted to a stranglehold. Lesotho gets 90 per cent of its imports from South Africa, including half its food and all of its fuel. Jonathan dispatched his armed forces chief, Major General Justin Lekhanya, to Pretoria to negotiate, while at the same time announcing that he was thinking of turning to the Eastern bloc for weapons. Pretoria's conditions were the expulsion of the North Korean military trainers and the handing over of named ANC activists. Precise details of the talks have not emerged, but on his return General Lekhanya seized power and, in an apparent compromise, began to deport the ANC refugees to countries of their choice. Lekhanya may well have shared Pretoria's fears about the increasing role played by communist countries, but he was also aware that the Youth League had called for his retirement. In any event, South Africa had got its way.

The presence of a large number of foreign migrant workers on the gold mines was another important factor in South Africa's relations with its neighbours. Both the mining houses and the government were anxious about the vulnerability of supplies as more countries became independent. Zambia and Tanzania banned recruitment and the percentage of foreign workers declined from 79 per cent in 1973 to 43 per cent in 1983. Through the Chamber of Mines, Anglo led the trend, primarily because it could afford to pay higher wages to South African Blacks from its richer Orange Free State mines and because it wanted to break the power of the white mineworkers' union by encouraging more locally skilled men.

While the South African government disapproved of the impact this had on its influx policies, drawing more Blacks from the land and the homelands, it helped the process for wider political considerations. It has used threats to end labour recruitment to pressurise Lesotho and Swaziland to expel ANC members from their countries. The financial effects of this can be judged by the value of deferred pay and remittances to the homes of miners: the five major countries, which supplied 186,000 miners in 1983, remitted 211 million rand. By arrangement with South Africa, a significant proportion of these payments had been transferred in gold during the colonial period, providing much-needed hard currency. Once the countries became independent, the agreement was unilaterally terminated, thereby further weakening their economies.

Having battered its neighbours into acquiescence, South Africa has begun to plan for a future of expanded trade in Africa with greater confidence. The South African Association of Chambers of Commerce (Assocom) announced in April 1984, after Nkomati, that a number of 'business safaris' were being organised to explore new trade routes. The intention, propounded by P. W. Botha in 1979, was to recreate the 'constellation of southern states' – a South African production area with a captive market. While this was initially attractive to trading companies looking for new markets, the big South African mining and investment companies stood back. As one Anglo director said in 1983: 'It would take very special circumstances to get us to invest substantial funds in a black African country.'

Anglo's existing operations in Africa fall into three main categories. First, it is the dominant corporate presence in those countries whose economies are largely integrated with that of South Africa. The main countries in this group are Botswana, Lesotho, Namibia and Swaziland. Anglo has significant holdings in a second category for mainly historical reasons and has been open to the sale of an increasing share of its activities to host governments. This group includes Zambia and Zimbabwe. The third category comprises those countries with which Anglo has a marketing relationship, through its manufacturing subsidiaries or through the De Beers' Central Selling Organisation (CSO). Other interests have been acquired inadvertently through international take-overs, rather than a conscious decision to get involved. Most important are Angola, Ghana, Sierra Leone, Kenya, the Ivory Coast, Malawi, Mauritius, Nigeria, Tanzania and Zaïre.

In the first group of countries Anglo's dominance is almost as complete as within South Africa itself. The Botswana economy is virtually an Anglo fiefdom. Mining is the most important industry and the group manages the three main products – diamonds copper/nickel and coal. Nearly two-thirds of its foreign exchange and 40 per cent of government revenues come from three diamond mines. One of them, Jwaneng, is among the biggest in the world and, by value, the country produces about as much as South Africa. In the De Beers cartel, Botswana is therefore of paramount importance. As the company's annual report remarked in 1979: 'It is not too much to say that the interest of the Government of Botswana in the stability and prosperity of the diamond industry is virtually as great as that of the De Beers Company itself and I am glad to report that the relationship between the Government and Company is smooth and co-operative.'[6]

In exercising its only real lever of power over its giant neighbour, Botswana was able to negotiate a comparatively advantageous deal with high production levels to maximise revenue. The mines are run by the De Beers Botswana Mining Company, 50 per cent owned by the government, which takes 70 per cent of the revenue. De Beers buys up the entire production and sells it, mixed with stones from other countries, in London. While the arrangement has given Botswana one of the fastest growth rates in Africa, De Beers still controls all the shots. In times of a diamond slump, as in the early 1970s, the country was obliged to stockpile 10–15 per cent of the 12 million-carat production. The diamond-cutting industry, run by Belgium with Tanzanian instructors, is required to buy its rough stones from De Beers with a minimum value of $1 million a month.

The relationship became even closer in July 1987 when De Beers bought the entire stockpile, then estimated at between $300 and $500 million, in exchange for cash and a 5.3 stake in De Beers. Botswana's production then stood at 13.1 million carats, over 50 per cent of the De Beers' overall production. The new minority shareholder was also given the right to nominate two directors – the first Blacks to sit on the board since the company was founded by Cecil Rhodes 100 years ago.

Anglo's 93 per cent owned coal mine at Morupule supplies Botswana's power station, and its copper/nickel mine at Selebi-Phikwe is the largest private employer in the country, with a payroll of 4,500. Apart from beef, the traditional export, these are the commanding heights of the economy. Mining, however, creates relatively few jobs. The total of 8,900 workers represented 8 per cent of the labour force in the formal sector in the 1981 census. And the formal sector, which included 18,000 migrants in the South African mines, was only 20 per cent of the total labour force.

With such a narrow economic base, almost wholly tied to South African interests, Botswana is as valuable as Lesotho. The chances of any sustained industrial growth are similarly curtailed. The history of Selebi-Phikwe is a useful illustration.

In an extraordinarily complex deal Anglo put together a financial package in the late 1960s to develop the copper and nickel deposits. One of its partners was the US mining company American Metal Climax (AMAX), an old Anglo friend. AMAX insisted that the smelted ore should be sent to its new refining plant in Louisiana to bring it to full capacity. The mining companies refused a government request to build a refinery in Botswana. At the request of Anglo's managing company, the rate of corporation tax on the mine was increased from 30 per cent to 40 per cent, thereby allowing the company to benefit from the double-taxation agreement between Botswana, Britain and the United States. No taxes were to be paid, however, until all the capital expenditure had been paid back. The mine has been a technical headache and a financial disaster, showing a substantial loss in most years since it came on-stream in 1973. The collapse of metal prices made the situation worse. In 1981, Anglo announced that it was suspending payment of royalties to the government. However, the group has put in substantial amounts of emergency funds to keep the plant operating, which some observers believe is a way of maintaining access to the all-important diamonds. No one was surprised when, at the burial of Botswana's first President, Seretse Khama, at the Serowe royal cemetery in July 1979, Harry Oppenheimer followed the heads of state with his wreath of appreciation.

Oppenheimer interests in the country are for all to see. The brewery is controlled by South African Breweries. Goods are transported by Renfreight. High-street shops include OK Bazaars and Edgars. First National is ubiquitous.

For all its dependence, Botswana has tried to maintain a distance from Pretoria, aligning itself with the frontline states, criticising apartheid policies, refusing to recognise the South African bantustans and allowing in South African refugees. It has consistently refused to a sign a Nkomati-type pact.

During the 1980s, Pretoria has responded with its usual combination of threats and punitive actions. Border traffic, the country's lifeline, has been disrupted; in next door Bophuthatswana, dams were built that reduced precious water supplies; in June 1985, South African commandos raided ten houses in Botswana's capital Gaborone, allegedly on a mission against the ANC. The South African Defence Force claimed they had attacked an ANC base. Among the dead were a 6-year-old child, a 71-year-old man, two young Botswana girls, a Somali refugee and a woman social worker and her businessman husband. Of the twelve people killed, five had links with the ANC but both the government and the ANC denied they were freedom fighters.

In Zimbabwe – as Southern Rhodesian under the Smith regime – British and South African companies controlled more than one-third of all businesss. Anglo's substantial interests, in the second largest industrial economy in southern Africa, were exceeded only by the state, and they have expanded since independence in 1980. In that year AAC had directors on the boards of 82 companies and exerted control over nearly half of them. In the interests of business, Harry Oppenheimer was prepared to treat with one of his devils incarnate, a black Marxist leader.

Faced with the pressing internal problems of integrating three armies and maintaining a conciliatory attitude to those Whites who chose to remain in Zimbabwe rather than emigrate to South Africa, Prime Minister Robert Mugabe showed an unpredicted tolerance towards foreign capital. It was a decision informed as much by pragmatism as by the urgent tasks of consolidating a new state. Nevertheless, Zimbabwe signalled its wider intentions even before the declaration of formal independence on 1 April. Two weeks earlier, it joined with the five other frontline states plus Lesotho, Malawi and Swaziland in the Southern African Development Co-ordination Conference (SADCC), to 'liberate our economies from their dependence on the Republic of South Africa, to overcome the imposed economic fragmentation, and to co-ordinate our efforts toward regional and national economic development.'[7] In the first six years of its existence, SADCC received more than US$1,100 million in foreign aid, but it had a long way to go.

Three of the largest firms quoted on the Zimbabwe Stock Exchange – Bindura Nickel, Hippo Valley and Zimbabwe Alloys – are in the Anglo camp, and are administered by the Anglo American Corporation Zimbabwe Ltd (Amzim). Bindura and Zimbabwe Alloys are crucial companies in the mining industry, which provides nearly 40 per cent of foreign exchange. Bindura owns the country's four nickel mines and a smelter and refinery; Zimbabwe Alloys, with five mines and a refinery, is the second largest producer of chrome after Union Carbide. The two metals rank fourth and first respectively in terms of the value of mining exports and together they represent 16 per cent of the value of all exports. Anglo also manages and has a substantial stake in the only Zimbabwean coal mine, Hwange (Wankie) colliery,

which it co-owns with the government; it dominates ferrochrome production through Zimbabwe Alloys. It has
significant operations through dozens of subsidiaries in
property, farming, timber, food-processing and financial
operations in the country. It owns RAL Holdings Ltd and
through AECI in South Africa it controls the production
and distribution of fertilisers. Anglo has a 24 per cent stake
in the country's largest miller, National Food, and the
group's sugar mill produces the 15 per cent ethanol which is
added to Zimbabwe petrol.

As with many of its operations in black Africa and
elsewhere, Anglo's Zimbabwean business has a deliberately
low profile. Amzim has not been quoted on the stock
exchange and details of the Zimbabwe operations were
entirely removed from the 1985 AAC annual report,
whereas three years earlier they were classed as a principal
investment. This trend towards concealment underpins
Anglo's ambiguous relationship with black Africa and
particularly with Zimbabwe, the strongest frontline state,
where the Oppenheimers still maintain their holiday ranch.

Equally important, however, is the peculiar position of
Zimbabwe in the rather sleazy world of international mineral and metal marketing. For fifteen years under the Smith
regime Rhodesia's mine production and exports were a
closely guarded secret. The principal mining companies –
RTZ, Union Carbide, Anglo and Lonhro – collaborated
with the regime in a sophisticated sanctions-busting exercise, as well as co-operating with a crash programme of
import substitution. The nickel refineries, for example,
meant that value-added pure metal of less bulk than raw ore
could more easily be shipped to Europe, the USA and
Japan. All the multinationals sold their products through
agencies in Europe, principally Switzerland. To a casual
observer, the agencies were owned by Swiss nationals, but
insiders in the metal business knew that some of them were
really owned by the mining companies. Anglo's agency in
Switzerland was called Salg.

After independence, Zimbabwe set up the Minerals
Marketing Corporation, which at first was described as only

an information-gathering agency. Prime Minister Mugabe and his Minister of Mines, Maurice Nyagumbo (who had spent eighteen of the previous twenty years in prison), were both anxious to assure the companies that the government had no intention of nationalising the mines. At the most, they looked forward to some form of minority government participation, but only after essential development priorities were met and funds became available. At the Zimbabwe Economic Resources Conference in 1980, Nyagumbo suggested that a 35 per cent participation might be a reasonable objective. Recruitment to the Corporation's management inevitably involved some patronage for friends and relatives of Mugabe's victorious ZANU party; but the surprising appointment was that of Mark Rule, a veteran white Rhodesian sanctions buster, as general manager. The old system of selling to the same European agencies was maintained and the corporation acted as a rubber stamp for the mining companies' unimpeded and greatly expanded business, after the lifting of sanctions. Neither the price of the metals nor the name of the customer was given to the corporation; one highly placed inside source estimates that Zimbabwe has been losing up to 20 per cent of its mineral wealth, from a trade that amounts to about US$500,000 a year.

The name of the game is transfer pricing, a routine device used by mining companies in developing countries to export money. The most common method is for the metal to be sold to a company in a foreign country at lower than the market price, with the difference being deposited in one of the producer's foreign bank accounts. The setting up of the Minerals Marketing Corporation was designed to prevent this. But there is more than one way of shifting metals around the world. In 1985 Anglo and RTZ entered into what are called toll-refining contracts with two separate companies in Switzerland to refine nickel and copper matte in Zimbabwe from the Selebi-Phikwe mine in Botswana, jointly owned by the American AMAX company and Anglo. The mine had made large losses in the previous three years. A puzzling aspect of the contracts was the generosity on the part of the mining companies to what are relatively small and unknown metal agencies in Switzerland. The background to the deals was principally the dramatic fall in the real value of the two metals: copper fell by 54 per cent and nickel by 64 per cent from 1970 to 1983. AMAX pulled out of Port Nickel, the refinery in Lousiana which it had foisted on the Botswana government; and RTZ closed its loss-making Empress nickel mine in Zimbabwe in 1982, leaving its refinery at Eiffel Flats redundant. Anglo's Zimbabwe refinery at Bindura also had excess capacity.

The contracts were between Anglo's Bindura Nickel Corporation and a company called Incontra AG in Zurich and RTZ's Empress Nickel Mining Corporation and a company called Centametall AG in the Swiss canton of Zug, a favourite base for brass-plate commodity traders who can hide behind the impenetrable company secrecy laws. Both fall outside the Zimbabwean laws to control transfer pricing, since the metal was bought direct from Botswana by the Swiss agencies. Bindura agreed to refine 14,800 tons of matte over five years and Empress promised the delivery of 105,000 tons over ten years. Taken together, the amount of matte represented about half of the two companies' refining capacity yet the price each company charged for the refining was ridiculously cheap. Empress's tolling fee was half what would normally have been charged by other big refiners such as Falconbridge or Inco, and Bindura's was less than two-thirds that of Empress. Bindura also agreed to ship the metal to Rotterdam at its own expense and the delivery dates of the contracts meant that the Swiss companies were given at least thirty days' credit. More extraordinarily still, if Empress failed to fulfil the contract, the company agreed to place US$7.2 million at the disposal of Centametall in New York. The effect of these agreements is that the Swiss companies are getting their metal at extremely favourable rates, well below the world market price, and therefore stand to make handsome profits. In addition, the low prices mean that both Botswana and Zimbabwe will find it difficult to compete with their own metals, especially as the refining capacity in Zimbabwe is being taken up with these toll contracts. And finally, both contracts are outside the control of the Minerals Marketing Corporation. According to informed metal traders, the explanation is simple. Incontra and Centrametall are ultimately controlled by Anglo and RTZ.

Such activities in Zimbabwe can only assist Pretoria's general strategy of regional destabilisation, and the creation of ever more areas of dependency. On other occasions, however, the group has shown confidence in some sectors of the economy by expanding investment and co-operating with national goals of increasing local control.

On the first count, few things were more damaging than the commando raid on the Beira oil terminal in 1982, in which Freight Services personnel played a sinister role. The effect was an acute shortage of fuel in Zimbabwe, forcing the government to make a three-year fuel import deal with South Africa. Freight Services in Harare acted as the Zimbabwean agent for the South African state-owned Safmarine and purposely chose or advised clients to use South African ports in preference to the cheaper route via Beira. The trade was significant; South Africa provided 19 per cent of non-oil imports in 1984 and took 15 per cent of exports. Exporters were encouraged to containerise, pushing more trade towards the new Durban container port. Freight Services, which managed the container pool, was reluctant to release containers for exports through Mozambique or to provide insurance. The company's gloomy reports about the lack of safety on the Beira line because of South Africa-backed MNR attacks were matched by dismal forecasts for investors from Anglo's RAL bank.

There were other actions which amounted to economic sabotage, although they were probably made simply for commercial reasons. For several years, Anglo's South African steel rod and wire company, Haggie Rand, conducted a campaign against competition from Zimbabwe's rival producer, Lancashire Steel. Yet SAB, under its new Anglo direction, has declared its determination to stay and expand, rather than pulling out in fright as it did under its previous conservative management in Angola and Mozambique.

There is a rationale behind these complexities. On a basic level, Anglo remains in Zimbabwe because its valuable investments either make or have the potential to make lucrative profits. At the same time, it is a crucial base in South Africa's most economically important neighbour. For Anglo, it provides an excellent channel for credible communication with the rest of black Africa. What is more, Anglo's activities simply sustain dependency on South Africa. Pretoria could hardly wish for a better partner.

Similarly in Zambia, where Anglo enjoys a close relationship with the state-owned Zambia Consolidated Copper Mines, the company is not averse to apply the economic armlock when its interests are threatened. At the height of the sanctions debate in 1986 President Kaunda announced that ZCCM would stop buying its spare parts and mining equipment from Johannesburg. One of the first moves was to switch to England as a source of detonators. Since 80 per cent of copper exports were already being carried along the Tazara railway to Dar es Salaam instead of South African ports, both Pretoria and Anglo had good cause for concern. One of Anglo's dozen or so companies in Zambia is a subsidiary of Scaw Metals which sold parts to ZCCM. Suddenly Scaw said they would have difficulties in maintaining their supplies. ZCCM looked elsewhere. They turned to another Scaw company in Zimbabwe which also said they could not oblige. Furious ZCCM officials, many of them white expatriates from Britain, decided that they would make the parts themselves. Scaw in Zambia promptly had a change of heart and the supplies became available. In the northern copperbelt towns, with their miserable workers' townships clustered around the huge mine workings, the old lifestyle of Anglo executives is still very much apparent. The graceful white lodge in Kitwe, built in the 1930s, is the finest building in town. ZCCM executives, black and white, repair to its elegant rooms for lunch; the company, a virtual state within a state, knows nothing of shortages in a country on its economic knees. This is where Sir Ernest would stay on his journeys north. The privacy, service and comfort of the lodges are used today by Kaunda on his perigrinations through the copperbelt.

Further north, De Beers' diamond operations market the output from Angola, Ghana, the Ivory Coast, Sierra Leone, Tanzania and Zaïre. Freight Services is everywhere, and there are direct but smaller Anglo operations in Nigeria, Kenya, Mauritius and Malawi.

Despite its frequently expressed and downright hostile reservations about black states, Anglo is often seen as the acceptable face of capitalism by many African governments, although those with diamonds have little choice. Harry Oppenheimer himself enjoys a warm personal relationship with Zambia's President Dr Kaunda, and is reputed to get on well with Zimbabwean Prime Minister Mugabe, despite South African funding of his rival, Bishop Abel Muzorewa, in the independence elections. In October 1983, when President Samora Machel of Mozambique was on a European tour Oppenheimer had a three-hour meeting with him. Anglo's political proxies within the Progressive Federal Party also frequently visit African countries and are regularly received by their heads of state.

In the scale of the empire, treating with the rest of Africa may be small beer. But it is on the increase – from 2 per cent of investment earnings in 1982 to 7 per cent in 1986. When majority rule does come, that will no doubt be another mild insurance for Anglo's survival.

In the meantime, there is also the El Dorado across the Atlantic.

*   *   *   *   *

When Harry Oppenheimer goes shopping for business abroad, he is regularly received by the highest in the land. So it was in 1975 when he met President Geisel of Brazil. Oppenheimer's visit was nicely timed. A month later, a parliamentary commission of inquiry was due to convene to examine the role of foreign capital in the country. The Chamber of Deputies had also set up a second inquiry into Brazil's mining policy. Both of them were planning to investigate Anglo's purchase of a 49 per cent share in the country's biggest gold mine, Morro Velho.

While some deputies were apprehensive about the South African connection, the Minister of Finance, Mario Simonsen, a banker and industrialist in his own right, was optimistic. Government policy at the time was to denationalise certain industries. In evidence to the Commission on Multinationals, the Brazilian Minister of Mines and Energy explained the technical reasons for acceptance:

> It's really only Anglo American which has the best knowhow for exploiting the gold at this depth. . . . We hope that with this association gold production will increase. The deal was signed a year ago. I believe the national group made the deal on excellent terms because gold has since dropped in price from 200 to 130 dollars.[8]

His evidence was incorporated into the report of the commission as part of the chairman's overall summary of the situation. Called before the Commission into Mining was Walter Moreira Salles, one of the three Brazilian owners and a former ambassador and cabinet minister. For reasons that have never been explained, the part of his deposition that specifically dealt with the deal was excised from the final report. In the event, Anglo escaped all criticism and the gold mine provided the springboard for further acquisitions, in which Simonsen, having left the government, had a hand. It now has a continent-wide conglomerate involved in mining for copper, nickel and gold, petrochemicals, fertilisers, heavy industry, banking, steel and agriculture.

Anglo's choice of Brazil for overseas expansion and direct investment was interesting for a number of reasons. It had already participated in a joint prospecting venture with Brazil's leading private mining financier, Agosto Azevedo Antunes, who had made his fortune in manganese with the US giant, Bethlehem Steel. The group started its first company in 1973, when Anglo had widely diversified into the South African economy and still had gold revenues to spend. It had an insatiable appetite for exploration around the world, not least because many of these projects have been abortive.

The bloody dispute at Anglo's Carletonville mine and the massive series of strikes by black workers living below the poverty line also took place in 1973. Politically, Vorster's policy of détente towards black Africa had virtually collapsed as the contradictions of apartheid led to increasingly trenchant black demands. The South African government, diplomatically isolated and with few overseas markets, began to establish closer ties with other unpopular countries sympathetic to its embattled position. These countries included Israel, Taiwan, the Shah's Iran, South Korea and a number of Latin American dictatorships. One of its major preoccupations in doing so was to secure sources of supply for its growing armaments needs and manufacturing capability. The young nuclear industries of Israel, Argentina and Brazil were seen as potentially collaborative, especially in view of South Africa's vast access to uranium. Pretoria invested most of its efforts in Brazil.

Despite rhetoric against apartheid, Brazil's generals were keen to sell their goods and to buy oil in Africa. South African Airways inaugurated its first weekly flight from Johannesburg to Rio in 1969 and the Brazilian airline Varig reciprocated a year later. South Africa's rather unadventurous exporters were encouraged to take an interest, with government lines of credit established in several Latin American states. A submarine telephone cable between Brazil and the Canary Islands was laid in 1973 to link up with the London–Cape Town cable. At first the trade was very much one-way out of Brazil, until Anglo moved in.

The purchase of Morro Velho in the state of Minas Gerais was an important acquisition. Brazil was the world's largest gold producer in the eighteenth century and the mine was sunk over 150 years ago. It was Brazil's primary source of underground gold. When Anglo bought the mine, it was run down, with outdated equipment, a large labour force and serious technical problems resulting from its great depth. The lower levels, down to 2,450 metres, had become

overheated, and drilling was impossible. The expertise of
Anglo, personally represented by Harry Oppenheimer, was
enough to attract powerful and discreet support.

By 1985, the mine produced 5.6 tons of gold, 10 per cent
of the country's production, and Anglo had spent US$160
million dollars on its modernisation. A further $60 million
was spent on opening a new gold mine at Jacobina in Bahia,
1,000 kilometres to the north. In 1986, Anglo American of
South America (AMSA) and its gold mining subsidiary,
Mineraçao Morro Velho SA, acquired an interest in and
management of the Crixas gold project in the state of Goias.
This new mine, plus the expansion of Jacobina, is expected
to increase AMSA's gold production to over fourteen tons
in 1992. Crippled by international debt, the Brazilian
government is very amenable to the idea that a gold
bonanza could save the economy. Its Mineral Resources
Research company optimistically predicted in 1980 that
production could rise to 200 tons within five years. An
Anglo official was sceptical: 'You need a big capital programme. It's not just a question of digging holes.'

But in fact most of Brazil's gold is mined in exactly this
way by *garimpeiros*, gold diggers working local claims. If the
government and the corporations have their way, the
garimpeiros will be persuaded off their claims, in the same
way that the small-time South African prospectors were
removed in the last century. Anglo's house magazine,
Optima had this to say in December 1984:

> Meanwhile, the activities of the unemployed-turned-
> goldminers is seriously hindering the development of
> some capital-intensive mining methods. The nature of
> Brazil's known gold deposits is such that mining might
> be carried out in some areas using open-cast pit
> methods, while in other areas only underground meth-
> ods are feasible. Either approach requires that the area
> be clear of small-time miners.[9]

Anglo was able to extend its control over Morro Velho
with the help of the former minister Mario Simonsen, to
whom a fulsome tribute was written in *Optima*.[10] After

another visit to Brazil by Oppenheimer in October 1979, the holding company Anglo American Corporation do Brasil Limitada (Ambras) acquired a 49 per cent stake in a steel-manufacturing firm, Siderugiga Hime, part of the Bozano Simonsen group, ostensibly in order to have a research base for prospecting non-ferrous metals. However, Hime also had 1 per cent of Morro Velho, which shareholding was increased to 51 per cent, giving Ambras effective control.

Such a high profile for a South African company proved to be too much for Brazilian financiers. Thus, in 1982, an application for government funds was rejected on the grounds that the mine was controlled by a foreign company, despite the 51 per cent Brazilian ownership. Within one year, Ambras had apparently reduced its share, giving the appearance of national control. However, it still retained 45 per cent through cross-holdings, and at the same time Ambras continued to build up its interest in Simonsen's bank and industrial group.

Paralleling its activities in South Africa, Anglo also obtained significant holdings in Brazil's explosives industry. Its methods here were even more complex and controversial. Private Brazilian firms had been suffering from the effects of old technology, difficulties in getting finance and price competition from Du Pont and from military enterprises. This led to the sale of several locally owned explosives companies, three of them to EMPAR, the subsidiary of a Portuguese firm, Sociedade Financeira Portuguesa (SOFIN), which was owned by a former Portuguese finance minister, Professor Texeira Pinto.

This was a stroke of luck for Anglo, since the group had co-operated with SOFIN earlier on the construction of the Cabora Bassa dam in Mozambique. The vehicle for their new association was another private explosives company, Industria Quimica Matiqueira (IQM). In 1973 it offered a joint venture to ICI America, the US subsidiary of the British chemical giant, which for years had worked in South Africa with De Beers' explosives company. Harry Oppenheimer learned of the prospective deal and persuaded ICI

(UK) to replace ICI America with AECI. The result was the formation of a joint company between AECI and EMPAR, Ibex Participacoes, which bought IQM in March 1974.

Events in Portugal, however, threatened to disrupt Anglo's plans. After the 25 April 1975 revolution, Texeira Pinto relocated his SOFIN operations in Luxemburg and Switzerland, before the government could nationalise them. EMPAR appeared to pass into the hands of its Brazilian directors: Pinto's lawyer Gustavo Capanema, who was the son of a former Brazilian education minister, and Franco Vorresy, an Italian-American who had worked with an Oppenheimer cellulose company based in Angola. The Portuguese government subsequently sued Pinto for selling his interest in EMPAR at far below market value. It believed that EMPAR was still backed by Pinto – a view endorsed by Brazil when it refused to sell an insurance company to Capanema because he was compromised by foreign interests.

Curiously, Anglo and AECI shareholders have not been told about their association with EMPAR in the annual reports. This may be because the joint company, Ibex Participacoes, also owns 100 per cent of one of Brazil's most important armament companies, Companhia de Explosivos Valparaiba, formerly part of IQM. This is a major supplier to the Brazilian military and a major exporter of grenades, heavy ammunition fuses, bazooka and aircraft rockets and submachineguns.[11] There is no evidence that any of these reached South Africa, although Brazil does export hunting carbines and pistol parts for South African farmers, who are now a crucial component in border security commandos.

The Oppenheimer mini-empire in Latin America took a great leap forward in 1981 when the corporation announced that it was buying, for $115 million, a 40 per cent stake in Empresas Sudamericanas Consolidadas, the holding company for the interests of the Panama-based Hochschild group. This included Chile's largest privately owned copper mine, Mantos Blancos, Peru's Arcata silver mine and the Petrosur fertiliser company in Argentina. In Brazil there was the Codemin nickel mine and a producer of fertilisers, carbon black, industrial phosphate and gypsum. The announcement was low-key, considering that the move doubled Anglo's investments on the South American continent. Set against the group's cash reserves of 1,730 million rand, it was relatively modest, but nevertheless significant. In November 1984, Anglo bought the remaining 60 per cent of Empresas and reorganised its whole Latin American structure. Two years later, despite Brazil's 1985 banning of military sales and sporting, cultural and scientific ties to South Africa, Anglo made its involvement far more explicit, renaming Empresas the Anglo American Corporation of South America (AMSA). Through a holding company jointly owned by AAC, De Beers and Minorco, AMSA controls operations throughout South America, with Ambras handling the Brazilian assets.

Within the space of twelve years, Anglo had created a unified, fully owned operation which had a permanent and strategic role in the Brazilian economy, and important footholds elsewhere on the Latin American continent. In this, the Oppenheimer family's old links with the former Portuguese colonies were of vital assistance. Its commitment is further demonstrated by its continuing exploration for gold and silver in Brazil, Chile and Argentina. In 1985 Gavin Relly continued Harry Oppenheimer's personal interest, with an extensive tour of the business. Like Hong Kong and Taiwan, Chile has become a target for South African development in order to evade the effect of sanctions. The state copper company, which earns 10 per cent of government revenues, is one of the principal direct sources of funds for General Pinochet's military apparatus. Foreign investors such as Anglo are subject to a 49 per cent tax on earnings but with no limit on profit remittances. In 1987 trade between the two countries rose by 60 per cent. In October 1987 the South African finance minister, Barend du Plessis, paid an unofficial visit to Santiago and offered the regime this admiring compliment: 'Despite the fact that South Africa is not a capital exporting country, we do permit our businesses to invest in other countries under the same conditions as ours, and from this point of view Chile has great potential.' Anglo's Mantos Blancos mine, which saw a 19 per cent increase in production in 1986, is currently being converted from an open pit to an underground mine. In the same month, as a symbolic gesture of friendship between two international outcasts, the departing South African ambassador was awarded the Bernardo O'Higgins Order of Merit, named after the country's independence hero. Latin America, of course, is on a much smaller scale than South Africa. AMSA had net profits in 1986 of $29.4 million and $14.3 million in dividends.

When majority rule does come to South Africa, in whatever form, many in the inevitable white exodus will probably look to Latin America and particularly Brazil. As a country with a similar level of development to South Africa, a good climate and an entrenched racism against those of African descent (the larger part of the population), it could well be home from home. Moreover, Anglo would be there to service them. This is not as fanciful as it may at first seem. In 1978 a group from the far right Herstigte National Party toured Brazil and Bolivia, investigating the availability of farming land. One remarked, on his return to South Africa:

> Obviously we are not altogether happy with the racial situation there. I do not foresee any real problems, however, because, like us, they practise discrimination. The whole economy is ruled by a small minority of white immigrants from Europe who keep the local Indians well and truly in their place. The only real difference is that they do it quietly without advertising it to the outside world. From this point of view, white South Africans will feel very much at home there.[12]

11

The Lair of the Lion

Wearing a floppy white hat and an open-necked checked shirt, Gavin Relly went to President Kaunda's lodge in the Luangwa National Park on 13 September 1985 and talked to Oliver Tambo, the head of the African National Congress (ANC) and former lawyer colleague of Nelson Mandela. 'It was difficult to tell who were the capitalists and who were the revolutionaries,' one of the businessmen who accompanied Relly joked later, using a little colour-blind licence. 'They were all in suits and we went in our bush jackets.'[1] Two years earlier, the idea of such a meeting would have been unthinkable. The fact that it did happen showed that events in southern Africa had undergone a sea-change. For once, the apartheid government and its paymasters were running scared and in different directions.

Only eighteen months before, the government and business had celebrated the high point of the uneasy accord which had been made at the Carlton Centre conference in 1979. South Africa's increasingly belligerent relations with its black neighbours, including a partial invasion of Angola in 1983, were swept away with a series of negotiated accords that left Pretoria able to claim itself a peace-keeping regional power. In February 1984, in Lusaka, South Africa agreed to withdraw its troops from southern Angola. The next month saw the Nkomati Accord, in which Mozambique promised to deny bases to the ANC, and South Africa promised to stop supporting the Mozambique National Resistance (MNR) rebels. There were talks in May between South African officials and the South West Africa People's Organisation (SWAPO), and on 29 May President Botha left for the first visit of a South African head of state to Europe for twenty-three years. Mrs Thatcher invited him to London for an intimate tête-à-tête at Chequers, her weekend retreat.

Nkomati was especially important to Botha because, as well as being about security, economic co-operation was also on the agenda. It had the multiple effect of persuading the Reagan administration (in an election year) and the rest of the West that South Africa was seeking a peaceful accommodation with its neighbours; of cutting the ANC route through Swaziland; and of assuring businessmen that their regional markets were being secured. The leaders of South African businessmen, including Harry Oppenheimer, attended the signing and Botha resuscitated his old idea of a constellation of southern African states, tied to the South African economy, if not to the rand. Botha, quoted in a biography, says: 'The Nkomati Accord was the result of a process which began years ago with our philosophy of total strategy.'[2]

Although Oppenheimer was lukewarm about the prospect of investing in Mozambique, the chief executive of the Association of Chambers of Commerce (Assocom) was, like most white South Africans, delighted. 'We stand closer to the Prime Minister's constellation of states goal than ever before,'[3] he said. Relly described the accord as 'a considerable economic success', although he warned that its durability depended on internal reform as well as a resolution to the Namibian problem.

Within a few brief months the euphoria and Botha's grand design collapsed in tatters. In the region it became clear that South Africa had reneged on its agreements with Mozambique and Angola: clandestine support for the MNR continued and South African troops continued to occupy a strip in southern Angola and stepped up their support for the UNITA rebels. Internally, the boycotting of the August elections for Botha's Indian and coloured parliaments was followed by renewed uprisings in the black townships starting ominously with Sharpeville, and leading for the first time to the deployment of the army on the streets. ANC activity was not curbed by the expulsion of militants from Mozambique, and in November black civic groups under the anti-government umbrella organisation, the United Democratic Front (UDF), joined with trade unions around Johannesburg to organise a two-day general strike or 'stayaway'. On gold mines in the Klerksdorp area thousands of miners, dissatisfied with their wages, started boycotting taxis, company shops and liquor stores. The arrest of twelve trade-union leaders and 2,000 others on the eve of negotiations finally prompted a public rebuke from the business community that included the pro-government Afrikaner Handelsinstitut (AHI) as well as the liberal Assocom and the Federated Chambers of Industry (FCI).

It was an unprecedented move from organised business which enraged the government. Louis le Grange, the law and order minister, summoned the heads of the three groups to his office for several hours of heated exchanges that ended in disagreement. This was followed in January 1985 with a memorandum on reform signed by organisations representing 80 per cent of the national workforce. Besides the FCI, Assocom and AHI, the signatories included the Chamber of Mines, the black National African Federated Chamber of Commerce (Nafcoc) and the Steel and Engineering Industries. It was finally endorsed by the South African Foundation (SAF). The memorandum called for political participation for Blacks, common citizenship, an end to forced removals from 'illegal' squatters' camps and the scrapping of the Pass Laws. It went on to state their opposition to boycotts and disinvestment and, in a pointed gesture, the document was presented to Senator Edward Kennedy to demonstrate their commitment to reform.

This rift was not so straightforward. The problem for South African business, and for Anglo in particular, was that Botha's initial preparedness to reform the apartheid system, together with increasing black political demands,

266   *SOUTH AFRICA INC.*

had left them unsure of what to call for and how much
pressure to put on the government. Relly's inability to call
for 'one person, one vote' revealed how much this remained
a problem within Anglo. Since Harry Oppenheimer's
retirement, the group drifted politically, seemingly partici-
pating in a gentle two-step with Botha across the tangled
morass of South African national politics.

Things were quite different under Harry Oppenheimer.
As one of the world's richest men, with a classical English
education, he was able from the start to see South Africa
with all its warts. The family wealth and international
connections enabled him to adopt relatively liberal politics
within the South African context. When the Nationalists
and their apartheid policies were confirmed in power in the
late 1940s, he could speak out from the protection provided
by the millions that his father was then drawing into the
country for investment in the Orange Free State. With the
collapse of opposition to the Nationalists in the 1950s, the
danger for business in following an untrammelled apartheid
route became daily more apparent. Strong and effective
opposition was vital, and Harry Oppenheimer was able to
finance it through the Progressives. This was the product
not of inspired political analysis but of the patent need for
an effective opposition to any system that throttled economic growth.

Harry Oppenheimer was very much his own boss. He
could decide what line to follow both economically and
politically, and be the sole judge of the consequences. Gavin
Relly is in no such position. Unlike Oppenheimer, Relly's
sole claim to fame is his job: without it he would be,
relatively speaking, nothing. For his words to carry weight,
he has to speak with the authority of the chairman of AAC.
That means gaining the approval of at least his inner cabinet
and more likely the executive committee. Relly's political
position will automatically be pushed towards the highest
common factor in this situation. At the very least, his
decisions must be agreed by Slack, Ogilvie Thompson and,
last but certainly not least, Nicky Oppenheimer. Politically
he has to carry Zach de Beer, the group's diplomatist who

has taken over some of the more delicate political tasks at which Harry Oppenheimer was so adept. Only on the most fundamental group commercial decisions is Oppenheimer consulted. In this situation the short-term economic perspective tends to dominate. This is hardly surprising, since profits and losses can be measured whereas there is no such measure in the political balance sheet. This in turn means that, without abandoning the liberal Anglo tradition, the emphasis has to be to a far greater extent on maintaining output in the mines and factories in order to protect profits now, rather than fighting for change that will protect the group's huge capital base in the longer term.

As one of the most sophisticated of the world's international business élite, Harry Oppenheimer may just be able to see that a commitment to 'one person, one vote' within the next five years is the only promise that could now assuage black demands for more radical change and protect his investment. He cannot, however, now tell Anglo's current management that they have to back such a call, and without their backing it would be meaningless. Harry set up the management by committee because he recognised that it was too dangerous to leave all the family's wealth and power in his son Nicky's hands. This was partly because the organisation had grown too large to be one person's fiefdom any longer, and also because Nicky was not seen as strong enough to control it alone. Under a new leader, the family could easily become susceptible to a coup against the Oppenheimers in which senior management moved their allegiance to the second largest shareholder, Old Mutual – an organisation that is richer than the Oppenheimers would be without their control of Anglo. In setting up that committee structure, though, Harry has also had to give them the Freedom of the Bailiwick: tactfully, he can give them his advice but has to let them make their own decisions, so that by the time he really is too old the transition will have been completed and the bulk of the family's influence and power will be intact.

★   ★   ★   ★   ★

This change in Anglo's political approach, and in particular the ascendancy of financial criteria over political considerations, led to the Botha government being given a present it had long coveted. That was the death of the *Rand Daily Mail* at the hands of Gordon Waddell and Gavin Relly. Oppenheimer, once the *Mail's* saviour, acquiesced. The closure on 30 April 1985 of the leading liberal English-language newspaper, with a reputation for investigative journalism, is a story of commercial and political cynicism at the very heart of the Anglo group. It has not yet been fully told in South Africa and it deserves a diversion into the world of the South African media, which will put the trip to Luangwa in to better perspective.

The South African English-language press has always been sympathetic to the mining houses which owned the two main groups. The Argus Group, with the Johannesburg *Star* as its leading daily, was originally controlled by a syndicate of mining capitalists, including Cecil Rhodes. The main shareholders were the Corner House company (now part of Barlow Rand) and Johannesburg Consolidated Investment (JCI). South African Associated Newspapers (SAAN) was formed in 1955 through the merger of the *Sunday Times* syndicate and the *Rand Daily Mail*, established by the mining magnate Sir Abe Bailey. Anglo's interest began with the take-over of JCI in 1960, the year in which the liberal editor of the *Mail*, Laurence Gandar, declared the *Mail's* support for the newly formed Progressive Party.

For decades, the mining houses had been sensitive to accusations of their influence over the newspapers. In the 1930s, the papers were criticised as being mouthpieces of foreign capital, and in the Argus Group a voting trust was set up to distance the owners from the editors. Nevertheless, a Press Commission report in 1962 noted that 'the persons who control the [mining] companies and company groups owning the major urban newspapers are in fact the persons who ultimately determine the policies of the major urban newspapers in the Union'.[4] At the *Mail*, Gandar soon collided with the Nationalists. In 1965 he ran a series of exposés about prison conditions, and the government brought a costly prosecution. The SAAN management took fright and warned their other editors to be more cautious in future. Gandar was gently eased out of his job. By the early 1970s, however, when support for the Progressives was widespread among industrialists, the majority of the English press supported the party. They attacked the bureaucratic restrictions on labour mobility and the refusal to allow official black trade unions as brakes on economic progress. They took a moral position against apartheid. Argus incurred the wrath of Prime Minister Vorster, who threatened to block the group's gradual build-up of shares in SAAN.

The Oppenheimers were the darlings of the *Rand Daily Mail*. After Mary's second marriage to Bill Johnson, her riding instructor, she started the Mary Johnson Column, a weekly canter through South African and London high society. In 1972, when the Progressives tried to persuade Oppenheimer to stand again for parliament, the *Mail* ran a leader under the headline: 'Calling Mr Oppenheimer.' After praising his time as an 'outstanding MP' and recalling his 'brilliant talents' as a businessman, it went on:

He is now a man of 64, and having brought his business empire to this glittering point, will surely have made sufficient provision for others to maintain it. It should, therefore, be perfectly possible for him to retire from daily involvement and instead give himself to the wider interests of the country. Not only is Parliament in need of men of his nature but his entry into Progressive politics would have dynamic effects. It would serve to persuade many who still view the UP as the main vehicle of change that they too should follow their natural bent and give total support to the Progressives. And without doubt, other outstanding individuals would follow his direct political commitment – to the gain of the country.[5]

Oppenheimer declined the offer, but when in 1975 the government tried to take over SAAN and the *Mail* he was having none of it. To head off the government bid, fronted by the National Party industrialist Louis Luyt, Anglo set up the Advowsen Trust, which gave it outright control of the group. In the next year Luyt returned to the attack, with 32 million rand of secret government funds to set up a rival Johannesburg newspaper, *The Citizen*, later exposed as a front in the Muldergate information scandal.

The *Mail*, with the second largest circulation after the *Star*, largely due to the energy of its editor, Raymond Louw, began to feel the squeeze. In 1975 it made a modest loss of 125,000 rand. The advent of television ate into national advertising. But the beginning of the end, according to two former editors, was the appointment of a new managing director, Clive Kinsley. Ignoring the threat from television and abandoning the *Mail*'s regional sales drive by its separate staff, Kinsley centralised both management and marketing for the whole group, ignoring the advice of consultants who urged a concentration on volume retail advertisements. There was another important shift, as the new editor, Allister Sparks, pointed out later in an inquest into the *Mail*'s demise:

> Both Kinsley and his chief of advertising, Nigel Twidale, showed an antipathy to the *Mail*'s black readership. They believed it gave the paper a 'split image'. They held back circulation in the townships and pressed the editors to go for more white women readers. . . . With its many black readers, it did not mesh comfortably with the other group papers. Being the odd one, the ad staff began resenting it because it made their job more difficult.[6]

The property ads for the *Sunday Express* and the personnel ads for the *Sunday Times* were much easier and more lucrative targets.

The *Mail* was reprieved for a while, with the introduction of new technology. Electronic editing and high-speed Goss Metro full-colour presses cut costs and attracted high-value advertising. Record group profits of 9.5 million rand were made in 1981 yet within three years that had been reversed to a 6.3 million rand loss. In its final year of trading the

Mail made a staggering 15 million rand loss. The downturn was accelerated by a fierce circulation battle between the Argus and SAAN groups. Argus launched its early *Sunrise Star* on Saturdays and a *Sunday Star* which kept its cover price and display advertising rates down and began to whittle away the *Sunday Express*'s monopoly of the property market. Kinsley countered with a 10c reduction in the cover price of the *Saturday Mail*, adding 1 million rand to its losses, which were aggravated by SAAN pulling out of the Allied Publishers distribution network and going it alone. Sparks was removed from the editor's chair for his policy of encouraging investigative articles when the directors wanted higher circulation through more 'popular' stories on entertainment and crime.

In 1983 SAAN commissioned a study from the London *Financial Times* on the options available to make the *Mail* profitable, including the launch of a financial daily. When news of the study was leaked to journalists, the chief executive was obliged to make a statement that the closure of the *Mail* was under consideration. In fact that was what the *FT* recommended, cautioning at the same time that there might be opposition from two sources: 'First the representatives of Oppenheimer and other progressive interests could block the move. Secondly journalists sympathetic to the *RDM* could cause a large amount of international criticism.'[7] The *FT* researchers had not done their homework. Although Anglo maintained only one director on the SAAN board – a lawyer with no publishing experience, representing Oppenheimer's Advowsen Trust – the most directly involved executive, Gordon Waddell, had no interest in keeping a loss-maker going. Yet at the same time, as the major shareholder, he refused to intervene between the warring groups. The *Mail*'s ombudsman, James McClurg, argued that the competition had reached levels that were counter-productive to Anglo's interests: 'If the relationship between Anglo and Argus is at arms' length, that between Argus and SAAN could now best be described as at swords' length. Competition, always vigorous, had now developed into open warfare, with Argus

threatening several SAAN newspapers. It is hard to believe
that Anglo could have tolerated this situation indefinitely.
From a business point of view it made a great deal less than
sense.'[8]

Privately, however, Waddell had been approached as
early as 1983 to step in and stop the bloodletting. Three
editors of the *Mail*, Gandar, Louw and Sparks, appealed to
him to save the *Mail* from going under. At different times
over the next two years they made similar appeals. Waddell
was not interested. The idea of a new financial paper was
already on the cards. According to Raymond Louw, Kinsley was convinced of its potential as early as 1982. In
September 1984, Waddell's JCI bought the old Bailey Trust
shares in SAAN, increasing Anglo's holding to 70 per cent.
SAAN informed its staff that the shares were in 'friendly
hands'. But in an interview with one of the journalist
leaders, published as a hindsight after the *Mail* closed,
Waddell was reported to have said: 'Van Zyl [the Progressives' leader] and his friends in Cape Town are more
concerned about the politics. In this office, Ma'am, we're
concerned about the bottom line.' He emphasised that an
opposition press had to be prosperous if it was to remain
viable and that the circulation war had to be stopped with
the position of Argus fully protected.

While he was assuring Van Zyl that the *Mail* would
continue to support the Progressives, Waddell was planning
its funeral. He sought the approval of Relly and on 15
March 1985 the editor Rex Gibson summoned the staff for a
formal announcement. 'When one had bad news to tell, it is
best to tell it quickly,' he said. 'The *Rand Daily Mail* will
close on 30 April.'[9] It would be replaced by a specialist daily
newspaper aimed at an 'up-market readership', which was
to be called *Business Day* and would be modelled on the
Financial Times. There was, inevitably, a deal involved.
Besides the launching of *Business Day*, SAAN took a 50 per
cent stake in Argus's new *Sunday Star* and closed down its
own recently revamped *Sunday Express*. This left *The
Citizen* with one less competitor on the morning market. 'I
would not like to comment on the business part of this

matter. This is a matter for the business people,' said Prime Minister Botha, who might have been expected to rail against yet another Anglo monopoly. He could not, however, disguise his pleasure. 'I would say a new South Africanism is taking control over South Africa and the media will have to take notice of this. A new spirit of national unity is gradually taking control of our country and this will supersede party political differences.[10]

It certainly seemed that the reforming zeal of the *Mail* had become inappropriate to Anglo's purposes in the new climate of black unrest and Relly's closer endorsement of Botha's policies. The effect was that there was less critical edge to the South African press, and the Blacks had lost a sympathetic voice. The South African Society of Journalists did not hesitate to place the blame at Anglo's door:

> In making this decision the SAAN board of directors – and its shareholders – have betrayed the press and the public. We are also dismayed at the role played in this by Anglo American. Anglo is a company which claims a record as having a social conscience and which, in an effort to stem the tide of disinvestment moves, is telling the world it is in the forefront of reform. As the effective major shareholder of SAAN and Argus, Anglo has exercised its power as a monopoly with devastating destructiveness.[11]

The Black Media Workers' Association called it 'a stunning victory for the Nationalist Government which schemed and plotted for a quarter of a century to silence or at least muffle the voice of the *Mail*.'[12]

There was no immediate response from Anglo and the behind-the-scenes manoeuvrings were not public knowledge. In June 1985, Gavin Relly finally broke his silence. At a conference organised by *Business Day*, he accepted that Anglo bore some responsibility for the closure. He said that Anglo was prepared to prevent SAAN from being taken over by hostile forces acting for the government but that it was never the intention of the group to subsidise commercial losses. 'It bears repeating that the corporation is in business to make profits for its shareholders in a socially responsible manner . . . we have to go along with the judgement of the market in its broadest sense. The demise of the *Mail* was a market judgement, however regrettable.'[13]

Many of the *Mail*'s best journalists left or were pushed out. They started the *Weekly Mail*, now the most informative newspaper on what is really happening in South Africa behind the barbed wire and the barricades. Harry Oppenheimer chipped in 5,000 rand.

*   *   *   *   *

With one voice of opposition conveniently silenced, Botha continued his ill-tempered and clumsy attempts to resist black demands and increasingly concerned international pressure. He prevaricated over the release of Nelson Mandela and even his erstwhile ally, Chief Buthelezi, rejected his idea for a 'black forum'. The leaders of the UDF were detained and charged with treason. Then on 15 August 1985 he made his 'Rubicon speech' in Durban. Billed as a major statement on further reform, it ineptly linked Mandela's continued imprisonment with that of Soviet dissidents, and Botha, wagging his finger at the world, declared: 'Don't push us too far.' The speech was a disaster and on 6 September the influential *Financial Mail* delivered its blunt verdict demanding immediate and far-reaching reforms. In an editorial under the heading 'LEAVE NOW', it said: 'All we have to say is do it, and go. And if you can't bring yourself to do it, go anyway.' The *Mail* had also hired a clinical psychiatrist to analyse Botha's body language during his Durban speech. The psychiatrist heaped ridicule on rejection:

> We are constantly aware of truculent, defiant, child-like behaviour in all his gestures. We are aware of anxiety behind the masklike posture. His words have one message. His body language says another . . . it reveals an angry child.[14]

Within a week, Relly was on the Anglo jet to Zambia.

Plans for the meeting with the ANC had been going on for nearly a year. Informal talks in London with ANC representatives took place at the end of 1984 and in January 1985. A key role was played by David Willers, the London director of the South African Foundation, and Hugh Murray, publisher of the glossy *Leadership SA*, who had good contacts in Zambia where the ANC head office was based. In July 1985 Relly visited President Kaunda to discuss the final arrangements, and in August he was meeting Willers in London to discuss tactics. A week before the meeting took place, Willers went on British television with the ANC's London representative, Solly Smith, to argue that there were areas of common interest to talk about.

When news of the impending meeting leaked out, Botha was publicly furious. He denounced the businessmen as 'disloyal'. It was enough to frighten off Anton Rupert of Rembrandt and SAF president Fred du Plessis, and in the end the delegation was something of an Anglo affair.[15] With Relly went Tony Bloom of the Premier group, Zach de Beer, the Anglo executive director, and the SAF director-general Peter de Sorour. There were two newspaper editors, Tertius Myburgh of the *Sunday Times* and Harold Pakendorft of *Die Vaderland*.

The six-hour meeting at President Kaunda's game lodge was with some of the ANC's top political figures, led by its president Oliver Tambo. There was Thabo Mbeki, the 43-year-old director of information and son of Govan Mbeki, a South African Communist Party activist serving a life sentence on Robben Island; Dr Pallo Jordan, the Western-educated head of research, also aged 43; Chris Hani, the political commissar of Umkhonto We Sizwe; and Mac Maharaj, aged 50, the senior Indian on the executive committee.

By all accounts, the atmosphere at the meeting was unusually friendly. Kaunda, who had a long-standing personal relationship with the three businessmen, met the South Africans with warm words: 'I can't tell you how appreciative we are that you have come here today.' When the group settled under the shade of trees, with elephants drinking in the river a few yards away, Kaunda set the conciliatory tone. 'Things that bring men together come from God; the things that divide us are man-made,' He made to leave but everyone insisted he remain as chairman.[16]

The two sides put their respective positions. The businessmen were told that some of South Africa's major corporations would be nationalised by a black majority government, as they represented tremendous wealth in the midst of unspeakable poverty. It was no more than a reiteration of the ANC's 1955 Freedom Charter.

For the businessmen, Gavin Relly said he wanted to see the unconditional release of Nelson Mandela, more reforms of the apartheid system, including integrated education, and negotiations with black leaders. Tony Bloom commented afterwards: 'The point we made was that whatever the political situation in the future it was important to have an economy which was viable and strong and that business therefore had a vital interest in the future.' He was far from pessimistic: 'I got the impression that they were interested in the state owning part of the more important industries rather than in total nationalisation. They have a concern about the concentration of wealth in the hands of the very few. They want to flatten the pyramid a little.'[17] Bloom detected an overwhelming nostalgia among the ANC men for familiar places in South Africa which they had not seen for years.

Relly was reluctant to comment afterwards about his trip. He privately took the view that he had done his bit as far as the ANC was concerned. The rest was up to the government, as he explained nine months later.

My interest in the thing was entirely in order to develop a judgement about the importance of this crummy Marxism which they purported to advocate. I'm less concerned about who runs South Africa than I am about the form of economic system which prevails. My judgement is that the leadership of the ANC would be more interested in a viable and vibrant South African economy than they would be in the Marxian form of economy. It didn't alter their view that they would nationalise everything in sight but they were people who can be talked to and I am not so rigid about my own point of view that I am not capable of being talked to either.[18]

A Zambian-based official afterwards explained one reason behind the talks. He said the idea was to detach as many Whites from Botha as possible:

Through talks of the kind held in Zambia recently, it may be possible to move some elements away from active support for and perpetuation of the system. Relly and the others have drawn the attention of a portion of African society to the fact that this government is unable to maintain stability in our country. These are people who had illusions that the Botha regime had the answers.[19]

The historic consequences of the meeting and the spectacle of Anglo American on the run was not lost on the commentators. The South African journalist Stanley Uys wrote:

Capitalism in South Africa has now entered the fight for its survival. It faces the risk that unless it can distance itself from apartheid, it will go down the drain with it. For the longer the impasse continues between black struggle and white repression, the more Blacks will see the destruction of capitalism as a precondition of their freedom.[20]

In talking to the ANC for the first time, Relly was representing not only the narrow interests of Anglo and of South African capital. In mining, at least, he can be confident that Anglo's technical and management skills will not be readily dispensed with, in the short term, by an ANC government. The further devastation of Mozambique and Angola after the Portuguese exodus, and the lessons of Robert Mugabe's pragmatic approach in Zimbabwe, have been noted. But the fuel for South Africa's economic growth has come from the outside, from foreign investment and technology. In this respect, Relly was also the messenger-boy for the institutions, the banks and the multinationals of the United States and of Europe that have so much to lose.

The two external factors that give succour to the ANC are voluntary disinvestment and official sanctions. Foreign investment, both direct and indirect, amounted to over £30 billion in 1984, with Britain's £12 billion the largest proportion, just ahead of the United States. American and British investors owned about half of all mining shares, and about 40 per cent of South Africa's manufacturing capacity is held overseas. In some sectors, such as computers, American firms controlled up to 70 per cent of the market. Shell and British Petroleum supplied 40 per cent of the petrol market, and two British banks – Barclays and Standard Chartered – were the largest in the country. The private sector, at least, was still able to raise overseas bank loans with comparative ease, despite South Africa's £17 billion foreign debt. From mid-1982 to the end of 1984, 202 banks of eighteen nationalities made ninety-eight new loans totalling £3 billion, according to research by the World Council of Churches.

European and American multinationals and banks have long argued that sanctions are ineffectual in speeding up reform in South Africa. Speaking in mid-1985 Dr Werner Breitschwerdt, the chairman of Daimler-Benz said: 'We are absolutely convinced that a boycott would be a completely unsuitable way of trying to improve conditions of the black population in South Africa. It would achieve nothing but a further hardening of the present situation.' An executive of Mobil, with one of the biggest US investments, was able to say in 1983: 'Total denial of supplies to the police and military forces of a host country is hardly consistent with an image of responsible citizenship in that country. The great bulk of the work of both the police and military forces in every country, including South Africa, is for the benefit of all its inhabitants.'[21]

But the underlying trend, culminating in the decision of US banks in August 1985 not to roll over short-term loans, has been to disengage, with up to fifty US firms alone pulling out in the year to July 1986. The South African Reserve Bank estimated that between 1976 and 1984 there was a net outflow of capital from the private sector amounting to 1 billion rand and that the level of domestic investment in manufacturing, at constant 1975 prices, had fallen by 40 per cent from 1980 to 1984. In the period of 1983–6, real growth was negative, and on the basis of a 2.8 per cent growth in the population the Bank calculates that real wealth decreased by 4 per cent over the period 1977–85. In its 1986 annual report the Bank said that short-term and long-term capital amounting to 2.64 billion rand had left the country in the first six months of the year. The foreign trade account was dramatically reduced because of oil stockpiling in the event of more stringent sanctions looming on the horizon from the US Congress, from the EEC and from the Non-Aligned Movement led by Zimbabwe. The question that occupied the world's attention – as news leaked out of torture, security forces' excesses in the townships, massive detentions and unbroken resistance – was how long could white-ruled South Africa survive under siege within and without? We would add, does the West really need its fabulous metals and mineral wealth? And what, in all this, will be the role of Anglo? Had not Oppenheimer remarked, only in 1984: 'Have you never noticed how in countries where millionaires flourish, ordinary people themselves tend to live better?'[22]

12

Crossing the River

The international sanctions campaign had small beginnings, going back twenty-seven years in Britain to the founding of the Boycott Movement in 1959, the forerunner of the Anti-Apartheid Movement. It was not until the 1970s that the campaign began to take off. The first significant move was made in 1971 by London's Camden Council, which decided to remove its superannuation fund investments in companies with more than a 10 per cent interest in South Africa. The amount was a relatively meagre £150,000. In the USA the first city to limit its South African investments was Cotati, California, in 1978. By 1985, 121 British local authorities had taken some form of anti-apartheid action. In America, six states and twenty-six cities had a disinvestment policy, and in November 1984 the Free South Africa Movement was launched in Washington with a campaign of civil disobedience that has attracted more support than anything since the protests in the 1960s against the Vietnam War. More significantly, New York City announced in 1984 that it would withdraw its pension fund from banks which lent money to the South African government. This was of an altogether different dimension. Citibank, which managed $3 billion of the fund, promptly complied in February 1985. It was followed by Morgan Guaranty in March. Wells Fargo and the First National Bank of Boston went further, banning all loans to private South African companies.

By March 1985, the *Economist* estimated that $5 billion worth of South African shares had been sold. The momentum of the campaign gathered pace. By the time President Reagan announced a package of limited sanctions on 10 September, reversing his policy of 'constructive engagement', all the major US banks had agreed not to give loans to South African state agencies, and to lend money only for projects which demonstrably benefited all races. In October, the Commonwealth Heads of Government summit in Nassau in the Bahamas followed suit, although most of its sanctions merely formalised existing practices.

By far the most persuasive reason for this exercise in corporate withdrawal was the threat to their domestic business. There is no more graphic example than the case of Phibro-Salomon, Anglo's cherished US money-earner.

Anglo's stake in Phibro-Salomon meant that it was always vulnerable to anti-apartheid pressures. At its 1981 annual general meeting Phibro officers were asked about their South African activities. They replied that they were opposed to any resolution that restricted the South African business because the Johannesburg office acted for 'the procurement of materials that are utilised all over the globe and include platinum group metals, which are supplied from only three sources in the world: South Africa, the Soviet Union and Canada. If these metals were not available sophisticated industry would come to a halt. The entire automotive industry in the US would cease to function because it could not make catalytic converters.'[1] The then chief executive officer, David Tendler, replied to a question about whether Phibro sold oil to South Africa with: 'Unequivocally, no.' There were more questions the next year from two church groups, and a resolution calling on Salomon Bros to end loans to Pretoria. Tendler opposed the resolution, saying that 'to preserve the company's ability to conduct its worldwide business effectively, we have found it essential to remain apolitical.'[2] Phibro executives began to lose patience in 1983 when, in response to further criticism, one replied:

Ownership is continually misunderstood or misinter-
preted despite our efforts at clarification. I feel com-
pelled to tackle this issue today because we have been
asked to vote on another share-holder proposal that is
at odds with the truth. The proposal calls on Salomon
Brothers to stop underwriting bonds for the South
African government, even though the evidence against
this is apparent. The fact is that 72 per cent of the
shares of Phibro-Salomon, a Delaware corporation,
are held in the US. A lot of flak that we have to take on
this issue is, I suppose, attributable to the 26.6 per
cent shareholding that South African-related interests
have in our company. That position reflects a passive
investment made in 1969 in a predecessor company
three times removed from today's Phibro-Salomon.
We cannot control purchase of the company's stock,
nor would we want to. The shares are traded on the
New York Stock Exchange, the ultimate free market.[3]

That year, 1983, the Salomon arm was placed on the
Arab Boycott for its connections with both Israel and South
Africa. This in itself was of little consequence, because of
the uneven enforcement of the boycott. One of the firm's
biggest clients is the London-based Kuwait Investment
Office, which had facilitated Charter's take-over of Anderson Strathclyde in the same year. And in 1981 a South
African government report provided evidence that Saudi
Arabia had secretly sold several large consignments of oil to
South Africa through middlemen.
    At the beginning of 1985 there were more critical pres-
sures. Again they came first from the cities, New York and
Los Angeles. Phibro's municipal underwriting business
stood at £35 billion. In January, Los Angeles said it would
require companies doing business with the city to disclose
their connections with South Africa. In answer to a request
for information from the New York City comptroller,
Phibro-Salomon's chief executive, John Gutfreund, wrote
on 20 February:

Instructions have been given to our oil-trading organisations not to deal in petroleum products for this
destination. It is our present intention to maintain this
policy in effect while the existing social system in
South Africa continues. As a Sullivan Principles signa-
tory, we are pledged to support changes in that system
which will lead to full equality in that country.
Phibro-Salomon is strongly opposed to apartheid policies in South Africa which, we believe, are morally
repugnant and have led to infringements of basic
human and civil rights.[4]

The letter gave Gutfreund's support for the Sullivan
Principles – the voluntary code of conduct for US companies operating in South Africa – a rather hollow ring.
Despite Gutfreund's public views as an anti-apartheid
Democrat, Phibro-Salomon had received a low rating of
111-C for its performance in 1984, indicating that it 'needs
to become more active'. The company did not even file a
report. Gutfreund's decision was formally announced in
May 1985, with an added indication that the company
would neither trade in South African securities nor make
any new investments there. Fears about losing municipal
business were confirmed in early August, when Salomon
lost out on a bid to finance a $20 million waste and energy
recovery project for Los Angeles.

On 22 August Phibro-Salomon, the twelfth largest corporation in the United States of America, announced that it
was pulling out of South Africa, closing its Johannesburg
office and refraining from any dealings with South African
concerns. Phibro-Salomon blandly said that the decision
would have no 'material impact' on its business.[5] The
Johannesburg office, with a staff of fifty, handled some of
the products of several South African industrial and mining
heavyweights, including Anglo's Highveld Steel. Besides its
shipments of oil, precious metals and steel, annually shipped 159,000 tons of various mineral ores to Japan alone.
Phibro-Salomon's departure, according to Gavin Relly,
made very little difference. The Johannesburg staff simply

resigned and formed their own trading company. Producers and customers could breathe again. But for how long?

In 1986 the West formally and with some reluctance adopted a broad, if piecemeal, range of sanctions. The EEC, despite Mrs Thatcher's strictures, banned imports of South African iron and steel. Overriding President Reagan's veto and perhaps looking to its black constituency, the US Congress banned food, coal, uranium, steel, the double-taxation agreement and South African Airways' landing rights. In order to beat the 12 November congressional deadline on new investment, two of the biggest US companies, General Motors (GM) and International Business Machines (IBM), arranged for their subsidiaries to be bought out by the local management, who would continue to buy GM components and IBM computers through franchise agreements. Both corporations also signed buyback agreements. Other US companies have followed suit. Of the hundred or so companies which had 'divested' by 1987, less than twenty actually closed down operations. GM continues to send its parts from Opel in Germany and Isuzu in Japan; Coca Cola has simply moved its plant to neighbouring Swaziland, from where it will export to South Africa; IBM has guaranteed computers to the new 'independent' company for three years and spare parts for five.

The popularity of this approach was picked up in 1987 by the Urban Foundation. Facing a vanishing US funding base and sensing US corporate reluctance to lose their valuable market share, it launched a proposal with the approval of the US Treasury to help companies preserve their South African stake while formally divesting. Or, as the Foundation put it, it had discovered 'the potential for maximising tax and financial advantages in the exit transaction from South Africa while accomplishing desirable social responsibility goals'. One option was for departing companies to cut their losses by selling their subsidiaries to the tax-deductible US office. Another, looking suspiciously like sanctions evasion, involved the setting up of overseas companies by the Foundation in tax havens, which would then act as go-betweens in transferring funds and technology to the formally-divested subsidiary. The Foundation also offered to hold companies in offshore trusts until such time as US sanctions were repealed.[6] Companies were not the only ones to seek a way out of sanctions: ten months after they had agreed to ban iron and steel imports, West Germany and the UK were still importing these products, with the UK taking 202 million rand worth in the first seven months of 1987.

None the less, sanctions hit hard. The American corporate presence halved to about 170 companies, with direct investment dropping from a high of $2.4 billion in 1982 to less than £1 billion at the end of 1987. By mid-1987, 21 out of 52 state legislatures, 72 cities and 14 counties had adopted some form of anti-apartheid measure, and the state of California had divested $10 billion worth of shares of companies with stakes in South Africa. Twenty-five industrialised countries had imposed sanctions; even Israel, with its hand forced by US legislation, banned investment, loans, oil exports and new defence contracts. The economy began to feel the pinch: in 1986, growth was a limping 0.5 per cent, and in 1985 and 1986, despite the imposition of a two-tier exchange rate, 15 billion rand fled the country. With the abolition of the tax credit for US companies at the end of 1987 – with a predicted cost of $43 million in two years – the talk was of a massive exodus of the remaining US firms. Meanwhile, ICI was under attack by British local authorities, who were threatening to divest their £40 to £50 million pension funds invested in ICI because of its 38 per cent stake in AECI, now planning to build an oil-from-coal plant in South Africa. De Beers was forced to create a new category of shares so that American investors could comply with the US ban on purchases of South African stock after 2 October 1986. In the wake of Consgold's intervention to keep Newmont, a black member of the House of Representatives proposed hearings on South African mining interests' holdings in the USA, and even legislation to ban such investments. And although Salomon Brothers was the largest investment bank dealing in asset swaps, it was refusing to trade in South African debt, priced in 1985 at 71 per cent of face value, the same as that of Chile.

On the defensive, Anglo's public response ranged from Zach de Beer's more sophisticated plea not to separate the 'Siamese twins' of economic progress and political reform to Relly's blunt attack on Australia and Canada for their 'duplicitous and cynical morality' in supporting sanctions since they would be the obvious beneficiaries of any halt to South African steel, coal, iron or uranium exports. But it was an incident in mid-1987 which really showed the thinness of Anglo's liberal veneer. When COSATU wrote an open letter to employers asking for support following the bombing of its head office, Relly replied:

> We cannot be expected to treat sympathetically the appeals for support of those, including trade unions and trade union federations, who promote sanctions and disinvestment, the more so when such advocacy is part of a wider political programme inimical to the very survival of the free enterprise system of which we form part.[7]

Clearly, a raw nerve had been touched. But to what degree has Anglo truly been affected by sanctions? Its uranium, agricultural products, coal, iron and steel have now been effectively banned from much of the West. Its key products, however, have been securely protected. Anglo, the South African government and its Western supporters have long argued that the industries of the 'free world' are dependent on South Africa's minerals and metals. Any major disruption of supply would place the West at the mercy of alternative Soviet supplies. Accordingly, in the 1986 US sanctions, ten key minerals were excluded from the mandatory sanctions list. Of these ten, which contribute four billion rand a year to South Africa's income, five minerals – antimony, asbestos, diamonds, platinum and vanadium – are monopolised by Anglo in their production, refining and marketing, and its prize commodity, gold, had been left completely untouched by sanctions legislation.

Yet the threat still exists. While the West argues that its

mineral supply must be guaranteed, a look at the eight most important commodities, all controlled by Anglo apart from chrome and manganese, shows that the reality is very different.

Asbestos South Africa produces about 5 per cent of the world's production which includes the deadly blue asbestos which has taken such a heavy toll of the lives of miners who extract it. Third World countries which cannot afford substitutes are the main markets. Its disappearance, in the long run, would be a distinct advantage to all concerned.

Diamonds Industrial uses for diamonds include polishing and cutting. Their use in bearings and pivots declined with the introduction of the electronic timer. The De Beers cartel under sanctions conditions would inevitably weaken, releasing stocks and encouraging production, both in mines and artificial diamond factories outside South Africa. Only gem-quality stones would be in short supply.

Antimony South Africa produces 15 per cent of world output as concentrated ore. In metallic form it is used as a minor additive to the lead in lead-acid batteries. Its other use is as a flame retardant. Both uses have declined in recent years. Calcium has replaced it in some batteries, notably those made by General Motors. Since it gives out toxic fumes under heat it has been designed out of aircraft and cars. In addition, the Chinese have found they have a mountain of the ore. They now dominate the market, having brought the price down from $8,000 a ton in the early 1970s to $2,000.

Vanadium Almost all of the world's vanadium is used as a hardening agent in various steels. It is similar in its application to molybdenum, which can be used as a substitute in many cases. In the oil boom of the 1970s, vanadium was used in oil pipe lines but it was found on the new Alaskan field that the metal could not withstand the severe conditions of the permafrost. Molybdenum was substituted and, with massive over-production, its price fell by a tenth. The increased demand for vanadium in softer climates also created a plentiful supply and the USA holds about 2 per cent of world annual production as a stockpile. China has recently expanded production and many other producers have spare capacity.

Platinum South Africa produces about the same quantity of platinum group metals as the Soviet Union and between them they provide about 90 per cent of the world's supplies. However, the Soviet ores contain 70 per cent palladium to 20 per cent platinum, while in South Africa the reverse obtains. There are four other metals in the group – rhodium, ruthenium, iridium and osmium. Platinum is the most important for cracking and re-forming organic compounds in the petro-chemical industry and for use in anti-pollutant catalyst convertors in cars. Stocks are low compared with other metals, although the USA keeps a strategic stockpile of six months' supply for its own use. The fact that the price went over $600 an ounce in August 1986 showed its sensitivity to South African events. But there are industrial savings to be made, principally through recycling scrap from auto catalysts which have been mandatory in cars in Japan and the USA since the early 1970s. Japan is the largest user for jewellery and would undoubtedly redirect stocks for industrial use. The price would go up, but as in the gold boom of 1980 people will begin to sell even their trinkets. Here Soviet supplies could be crucial but Soviet platinum, like gold and diamonds, already finds its way on to the market through the pricing understandings with the South Africans.

Chromium There is a major surplus of all three types of ferrochromes. The USA has two to three years' supply, partly because of the slump in the steel business. Only stainless-steel production would temporarily suffer as this uses the low-grade charge-chrome largely from South Africa. However, nickel, titanium and molybdenum can be used as substitutes for chrome content and stainless steel can often be replaced by aluminium.

Manganese Again, as this is used in steel, there is a plentiful supply and large stocks. The USA has as much as South Africa produces in one year.

Gold In terms of sanctions this is the key. If all the gold in Fort Worth was sold the metal would be worth the price of lead. If enough was released on to the market, bringing the price down to, say, $250 an ounce, much of South Africa's gold industry would be unprofitable. However, as most gold trading is not in the physical metal but on paper, it could still be bought and sold around the world – as long as real stocks are actually held in a neutral and responsible place so buyers know that in the final analysis they can get their bullion. Switzerland or Hong Kong could be possibilities.

These, then are the jewels of the Anglo economy. What would Anglo's reaction be if greater sanctions were imposed on South Africa? Would it press its far-flung international network into service to ensure the survival of a siege economy and with it white power? The answer must be an unequivocal yes. Eighty years of bold acquisitiveness and political timidity will not be changed overnight. No amount of liberal pleading by Relly or furtive globe-trotting by Harry Oppenheimer to reassure investors can disguise their collaboration. It is now too late for them to challenge the state in those areas such as wages, trade-union recognition and training and promotion which were never constrained by apartheid laws. In fact, Anglo is already well prepared to come to the aid of Pretoria, just as it has done in times of crisis before.

There is more than just a set of plans to be dusted off when sanctions really threaten the country's life blood. Anglo has a well tried and tested sanctions-busting operation in place with its concealed Swiss metal-trading agencies, its freight network and the secretive companies that De Beers and the CSO use to channel the diamond trade. As the Thirion Commission discovered, it is extremely difficult for even quasi-judicial investigators to find out exactly what De Beers is doing. Tracking down the obscure international web of brass-plates is a formidable task, especially those like Management and Technical Services (MATS), which is registered in Liberia. A 1980 report for this company was among those discovered by the squatters in Anglo's Amsterdam office in 1986. It shows assets of US$25 million, mainly in loans and quoted company shares, fee income of $160,000 and interest received of $1.1 million. Who paid the fees or who was charged the interest is nowhere explained, and the report does not even identify the ultimate owner of MATS or explain why this company sits in Liberia owning such large assets. It is only through other sources, in this case the Angolan government, that we know MATS' role as a service company which administers non-De Beers diamond sales. A major clandestine operation such as the diamond cartel provides the perfect base from which to organise finance and service a sophisticated sanctions-busting plan.

Just as important are the connections through Anglo's international business, connections from Johnson Matthey and Engelhard to its well endowed exploration activities that buy up sensitive mineral rights. In many respects it can be argued that Anglo has moved internationally in ways calculated as much to buy influence and intelligence as investments. The directors of Minorco, for example, seem to have been pulled in for their political clout as well as for their expertise. The Rohatyns, Frasers and Hambros of this world do not come cheaply but they do have extremely useful friends. So the Anglo empire can easily cope with the range of insubstantial sanctions imposed by the West. It can guarantee to maintain the country's mineral exports and will scour the world to do so. Enough foreign exchange can be earned for all essential imports, and Anglo's transport system can help ensure that they continue to slip into the country. The state will take care of its military needs and oil.

More immediately, Anglo has extended its interests by picking up cheaply the multinationals' cast-offs, like Barclays National. The group's mainstays of gold and platinum have actually benefited from the threat of sanctions as prices have risen and the opportunity to pick up Western investors' discarded gems has simply added icing to the cake. This process has benefited the state by turning what could have been an unmitigated disaster into a controlled transition from which both the rule of apartheid and Anglo emerge paradoxically strengthened. The government is, in effect, dependent on South Africa's major corporations to carry out the rationalisation of industry.

South Africa's white minority has been so wealthy in past years, even relative to the richer Western industrialised countries, that it has been worth while for many old US and European multinationals such as the General Electric Company (GEC) to maintain their manufacturing operations there even when this did not fit a global view of their business. In a sense, the richness of the white market and low wage rates allowed industry to survive despite being fairly backward, and so the multinationals could remain in the country with only minimal reinvestment, their aim being to keep a foothold in the hope that a political settlement would eventually be achieved. In turn, this meant that the overall pace of economic concentration was slowed as the multinationals, although not investing heavily, still sought a share of South African markets for their subsidiaries. Since those subsidiaries were usually fully controlled, their competitors did not even have the option of taking them over to buy their market share. This not only retarded the pace of concentration, it also meant that South African experience of managing integrated local manufacturing units was more limited than would otherwise have been the case.

The South African regime must now take much more seriously the possibility of harsher sanctions being applied which will cut off a large part of the country's imports. This can happen directly, as when the USA banned exports of computer equipment for use by the police or military. It can also happen indirectly, as a consequence of partial sanctions reducing the price South Africa receives for its mineral exports. However unlikely, this is the situation the government must be prepared for, and that means moving the economy towards much greater self-sufficiency. This can be attained either by using the machinery of state to impose the change, by nationalising and legislating to control production and markets, or by encouraging the private sector to induce it. Because they claim that the defence of

apartheid is essential in the defence of Western free enterprise, President Botha and his henchmen have little choice
but to adopt the latter approach. On 7 November 1986,
Botha convened for the third time since coming to power a
convocation between the government and South Africa's
business leaders. The twin themes of the conference were a
new inward-looking economic strategy which had been
recommended by the Economic Advisory Council, and
discussion of a proposal to sell off large parts of the
economy currently owned by the state. Both demonstrated
Botha's dependence on the management of South Africa's
largest corporations to pull the country through sanctions.
And although the chair of AAC, Gavin Relly, demonstrated
the group's dissatisfaction with the pace of change by
pleading 'prior engagements', this certainly did not prevent
a number of Anglo representatives including Zach de Beer
from attending a conference that was notable for its avoidance of the key political issues. 'We were working on the
basis that apartheid has already been abandoned,' one
participant said afterwards, completely ignoring the racial
divisions epitomised in the conference's whiteness. 'No-one
asked about the release of Nelson Mandela.'[8] Zach de Beer
ventured that there had been 'a great deal of constructive
discussion', and awareness that solutions had to be political
as well as economic.

While Anglo clings to the remnants of its liberal image, it
continues to be pivotal for the survival of the white state, a
role whose importance will only be enhanced by national-
istic economic strategies and privatisation. Such short-term
opportunities may well in fact become the irresistible carrot
whereby the regime quietens its leading business critic. The
South African government is now only too well aware of its
dependence on the Anglo group, and of its inability to
control Anglo's executive directly. For once, liberalism in
the South African context has afforded those espousing it
considerable protection from the long arm of the South
African state. As the largest privately owned corporation
with many US shareholders, apparently bravely endorsing
freedom for all people within South Africa regardless of

race, Anglo is now the embodiment of the American administration's idealised vision of capitalism: fighting to be fair and free. Botha knows that to try to control Anglo by threats or force would be entirely counter-productive, and could possibly be fatal to his attempts to steer a narrow course between the West's abhorrence of naked racism and its delight at easy profits. He also knows that Anglo's real desires lie not so far from his own, and that the temptations of the lucrative favours to be disbursed at a time of large-scale privatisations may be more than enough to keep the group's leaders muted.

In many respects Relly's non-appearance at the economic summit, and Zach de Beer's presence, showed exactly the lengths to which Anglo's leadership will go to oppose the regime's efforts to maintain white supremacy. After Oppenheimer himself, de Beer has always been the politician in Anglo; he is the only group executive to have come into the company from politics, rather than dabbling in parliament from a position in the business. Despite his seniority, loyalty and experience, he is not numbered among the key business decision-makers, as the Consgold take-over showed. But as chairman of the LTA construction company he displayed his talents. Winning large state-funded construction contracts such as new roads and airport facilities is about the most political business in any country in the West, because of the sums of money involved and the high visibility of the projects. In all likelihood Relly would have always been rather out of his depth, given his background as a career business aide to the Oppenheimers. It is one thing to fence publicly with the President and his friends when you have a background of immense wealth and parliamentary experience as Harry Oppenheimer did; quite another when you are a company man like Relly. While his absence explicitly denied approval of the government's policies, it also gave de Beer a stronger negotiating stance. In truth the snub was no more than a flea bite for Botha, but the rationale was classic Anglo – the well-tried image of disapproval, tempered by the practice of co-operation.

Relly's 1986 chairman's statement was a piece of prose

that in earlier days Harry Oppenheimer would have been proud of:

> I believe that the unbanning of political parties and the freeing of political prisoners will not be sufficient to get the constitutional negotiations properly underway, nor to minimise the threat of sanctions. The residual elements of apartheid as well must be expunged from the statute book. I would urge the government there-fore publicly to commit itself – as it did with the Pass Laws – to repeal the Group Areas Act, Separate Amenities, Population Registration and the Lands Act within a fixed time. Once that goal is in sight, negotiations could begin on the framework of a new constitution which would establish and guarantee the rights and freedoms of all people *so admirably set down by the State President earlier this year* [emphasis added].[9]

This was not the only genuflection to the President, and Relly went on to undermine his own critique of government policy. Botha, he said, had 'kept to his commitment to press ahead with his reform programme, notably by repeal-ing the Pass Laws and system of influx control that had been applied to black South Africans for well over half a century. . . . Taken together with the extension of freehold property rights to black people, the opening for trading and investment purposes of central business districts to all South Africans and the restoration of citizenship to many black South Africans, they constitute a major step forward towards the abolition of statutory apartheid and the nor-malisation of our society. Among the international commu-nity, where lack of trust and cynicism also prevail, appreciation of what the State President has achieved tends to be further inhibited by a simplistic view of our prob-lems.'[10]

So Relly ends up on the rickety fence, playing to the international audience, both condemning the failures of the regime and pleading forbearance for it. Yet it was just such an approach that led to the ill-fated tri-cameral parliament, spurring the unrest of 1984 and onwards.

Across at De Beers at the same time, Ogilvie Thompson was offering his diagnosis which suggested that the black unrest had been encouraged not only by rising black expectations but also by 'the attitude of excitable people in the international community'. To his mind, the Commonwealth Eminent Person Group, which recommended harsher sanctions, was to blame. 'There is no question,' he said, 'that it was the adoption of more punitive sanctions by Western nations that caused the Government to call a halt to reform initiatives.' Nevertheless, writing in his annual report before the Whites-only election, he optimistically anticipated that the results would show a desire among the white community to move towards accelerated reform and negotiations with Blacks without preconditions, other than the renunciation of violence. The chairman of De Beers could not have been more wrong, for the Progressives were routed and replaced as the official opposition by the right wing Conservative Party. Like Relly, he would have his shareholders believe, against all the evidence, that the National Party and the majority of Afrikaners were capable of relinquishing power. But Ogilvie Thompson was able to hold out the certainty of some cheerful developments to coincide with the centenary of De Beers in 1988. Besides the 53 million rand that year from the Chairman's Fund for educational and training projects he pointed to the several more million for the Harry Oppenheimer Institute for African Studies at Cape Town University and the Harry Oppenheimer Chair of Human Rights at the University of Stellenbosch. This largesse has to be compared with a 1987 cash reserve in AAC alone of 2,300 million rand.

Some analysts of the Anglo empire have argued that it has acted like any other multinational – maximising profits, avoiding tax where it can and protecting its interests in foreign countries by economic threats or accommodations. But Anglo's peculiar position within South Africa and the cultural links of the Oppenheimers have also obliged it to adopt another role. Its social conscience, tinged perhaps with guilt as well as a pragmatic understanding of its long-term economic interests, has prompted it to take the business lead in eroding apartheid's restrictions on the labour market. The decisions to allow trade union organisation and to break with the Chamber of Mines' wages policy have undoubtedly had a positive impact on the confidence and power of the black working class.

Following Tony Bloom's example, the new head of JCI, Pat Retief, has also come out in favour of a universal franchise and black majority rule. 'I do not believe that we can solve our problems by looking at protection for minority rights,' he says.[11] This belated endorsement of unconditional black majority rule has yet to percolate through the hierarchy of Anglo management and will probably never do so as long as the likes of Relly, Ogilvie Thompson and Harry Oppenheimer himself are still in fundamental control. Relly cannot bring himself to the same conclusion, but in his routine fudging he does consistently call for the abolition of the Group Areas Act, one of the last bastions of grand apartheid. As for Harry Oppenheimer, he did not inherit and develop a dynastic empire from the splendid isolation and fastness of the Brenthurst estate with any view to relinquishing it to the uncertainties of a black-ruled and inevitably left-wing government.

The question has been raised: could they have done more? Ernest Oppenheimer may have had some decent impulses, after the fashion of a nineteenth-century liberal such as Lord Lever, who built the innovatory model workers' town of Port Sunlight near Liverpool. But Ernest was also a fiercely ambitious entrepreneur in a business noted for its ruthlessness. To combine this with such public opposition to a political and labour system that served him so well smacked of a profound hypocrisy. We have already noted his ignorance of living conditions in Soweto until just before his death. Having seen them, however, he made money available for housing improvement, and that was in the 1950s. No one would have expected him actually to take on the state; his paternalism found too many echoes in the policies of the National Party.

But for Harry Oppenheimer there were new opportunities and a new political framework created by the internal and international pressures for reform. It is most significant that gold miners' wages were increased in the 1970s because of the rising gold price and the beginning of organised workers' unrest. Anglo has recognised the unions, but the impulse behind their legitimisation by the state and their acceptance by 'progressive' companies was to provide a channel for labour relations that were verging on the anarchic.

Business cannot, however, be seen as the cutting edge of political change in South Africa. That will come from the people. Yet even within the restrictions of the law, Anglo could certainly have made a far greater contribution to the struggle for a democratic as well as prosperous South Africa within its own factories and mines. In doing so the company would have been investing in its own profitability. But it would not take the risks that were being taken by other, foreign multinationals which recognised that they could wield the power of 'good capitalists'. During 1986 a number of American companies decided to flout the law by building integrated residential areas for employees and their families. Gavin Relly knew this and applauded it in an article in *Foreign Policy*, the journal of the Carnegie Endowment for Peace foundation. Much to the dismay of his close political advisers, this article was picked up by the South African press.

So in housing within black settled areas, in wages and related social benefits, in the training and education of black people Anglo could well have taken a more challenging lead. It could have tackled head-on the racism and obduracy of the white Mine Workers Union. It could have improved safety in the mines. It could have rejected the medieval and vicious *induna* system in the compounds. It could have more boldly rejected Botha's divisive reforms before the rest of business became so frustrated that it took the initiative. Anglo could have put more of its money where its mouth was.

Though by early 1988 the talk was only of inevitable

bloodletting, it may still be possible to achieve a peaceful transition to majority rule. Doing so would involve huge risks for Anglo's management. It would mean pushing the government so hard towards a just settlement as to risk severe retaliation – from the shareholders, from the military and from the Afrikaner Right and with only fickle support of the US Congress to rely on. And the worst risk of all is that, after transition, the business may be taken over, lock, stock and barrel, by the new government. Harry Oppenheimer, as the quintessential survivor, would not like that, but he has built his own straitjacket. For the exclusive coterie of men who run Anglo the frequent remark of Bishop Desmond Tutu must be a recurring nightmare: 'We will know who our friends were.'

Appendix
Profile of the
Anglo Group

E. OPPENHEIMER & SON'S CONTROL

At the very top of Anglo, E. Oppenheimer & Son, the Anglo American Corporation (AAC) and De Beers Consolidated Mines are very closely tied together by cross-directorships and shareholdings. These connections mean that AAC and De Beers effectively control one another, subject to the control of E. Oppenheimer (see Table 1).

The combined De Beers/Oppenheimer stake of 46.3 per cent in AAC gives them full control of AAC, especially when hidden family, executives' and intergroup holdings are taken into account. At 34.3 per cent, the AAC holding in De Beers is much smaller, but AAC's stronger resources mean that its control of De Beers cannot be challenged either. This leaves the Oppenheimer company as the dominant shareholder in AAC and De Beers. Its 8.2 per cent stake is equivalent to 13.3 per cent of AAC's issued shares excluding those owned by De Beers. The only other shareholding over 5 per cent is that of SA Mutual Life Assurance, with 7.7 per cent of AAC and 7.3 per cent of De Beers. These shareholdings may seem significant, effectively matching those of the family company. Alone, however, they carry virtually no voting weight, so long as the boards of the two companies support the Oppenheimer family. This is why the close relationship between the

299

TABLE 1

Key cross-shareholdings (per cent)		
	AAC	De Beers
Oppenheimer & Son owns:	8.20	
AAC owns:		34.30
De Beers owns:	38.15	

Key cross-directorships			
	Oppenheimer	AAC	De Beers
H. F. Oppenheimer	D		D
N. F. Oppenheimer	D	DC	DC
H. R. Slack	D	D	
G. Waddell	D	D	
J. Ogilvie Thompson	D	DC	C
G. W. Relly	D	C	D
P. J. R. Leyden		D	D
G. C. Fletcher	D	D	D
Sir P. Oppenheimer	D	D	D

Key: C   chairman   DC   deputy chairman   D   director

Note: These are publicly recorded shareholdings. It is possible that the family company has other, undeclared holdings, quite possibly in De Beers, and there may be further Oppenheimer family connected holdings in both companies.

Oppenheimer family and the entrenched management at Anglo/De Beers is so important.

Below AAC and De Beers, Anglo group companies can be defined in terms of the control that the Oppenheimers' inner cabinet is able to exert over them. They can be loosely divided into four types:

- *Group subsidiaries* are the central companies, which can be controlled directly on a day-to-day basis by virtue of majority shareholdings alone. They form the solid heart of Anglo, within which the rule of the Oppenheimers' inner cabinet is practically absolute. Sometimes the shareholdings will be held indirectly, by a combination of companies which may be quoted or unquoted. That in Premier Group Holdings, for instance, is largely channelled through Premsab Holdings Ltd, which is owned

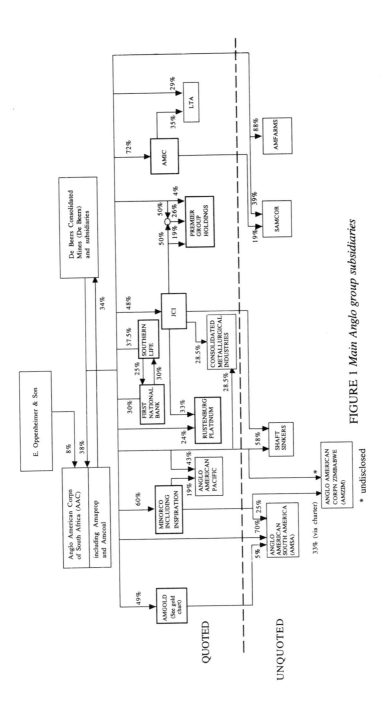

FIGURE 1 *Main Anglo group subsidiaries*

50:50 by AAC and JCI, but classified as a subsidiary of neither, considerably limiting disclosure. Some companies that are just under 50 per cent owned must also be included, since this is a favoured Anglo ploy to maintain a pretence that such companies have some real independence. JCI is one of the best examples of this. In theory, the 48.2 per cent of the company's shares held by AAC and De Beers is insufficient to give full control. In practice it is more than enough, given that the remaining shares are quite widely owned, but some of them fall within Anglo's control anyway. At 30 June 1987, for instance, JCI's directors had direct and family interests in 0.4 per cent of the shares, and the trustees of JCI's share incentive scheme for 'senior members of the staff' controlled a further 3.3 per cent of the shares – making 51 per cent in all. As well as shareholdings such as these, which at least have the virtue of being disclosed in the company's annual report, there are likely to be further, hidden holdings in Anglo's control. Most companies in the group will have some form of pension fund, for instance, and some may have several to cover different grades of staff. These funds will usually own a diversified portfolio of shares, including those of group companies such as JCI. Southern Life Association (SLA) is part of Anglo. It was formed from the merger of Anglo's life assurance company, Amlife, and Southern Life Association, with Anglo taking the largest shareholding in return for Amlife, and Barclays the second largest in return for finance. SLA later built up its shareholding in Barclays to 25 per cent, giving Anglo at least 55 per cent including that holding. However, such shareholdings (like pension fund shareholdings) are often ignored because they are regarded as belonging to the insurance policyholders. SLA's chairman Zach de Beer can none the less cast the votes the shares carry.

- *The 'administered' associates* category includes companies where Anglo's shareholding is significantly below 50 per cent. This is because of the immense power that the entrenched executive of a company wields. In the case of an 'administered' company, Anglo is formally recognised as controlling that company's management on a day-to-day basis. This means that Anglo appoints management, and naturally its choice lies with people whose loyalty rests primarily with the parent, and only secondarily with the company they are running. The split loyalties are not irreconcilable, since it is in Anglo's interest that its 'administered' companies should perform well, producing good profits for other shareholders as well. A loyal management can be relied on implicitly to maintain Anglo's control of an administered associate, and they have the weapons at their command to do so. They can, for instance, keep close tabs on any transactions in their company's shares – which must be notified to its registrar – and ensure that all the directors keep in line and are happy with their relationship with the parent. It all amounts to a well-oiled machine that, in the context of South African financial circles at least, cannot be shifted without the consent of the Oppenheimers' inner cabinet.

• *Controlled associates* are companies that are neither majority owned nor 'administered' by the group, but over which it nevertheless has considerable influence. This is typically the case where Anglo's total shareholding is a dominant one, usually of the order of 20–45 per cent, with the remaining shares quite widely spread between a number of unconnected shareholders. The group is then invariably able, over a period of time which may amount to many years, to establish an entrenched, Anglo-connected management. How closely and the ways in which such companies are linked to Anglo varies enormously. It is affected by many factors, including the degree to which Anglo has established its management control, the extent to which it is viable to let a major associate operate freely as an almost entirely independent profit centre, whether the company is based in South Africa or elsewhere, and sometimes political factors such as the danger of exposing Anglo's dominance of the

South African economy, particular sectors within it or
even, in some cases, a particular sector in the international economy. For example, South African Breweries
(SAB) has to be kept well separated from Anglo because
it is already infamous as a monopolist in South Africa.
Close links with Anglo would only worsen the situation,
leading to tighter controls, and would bring few benefits.
SAB is not a vital supplier to other parts of Anglo, and
can operate effectively as an independent profit centre
without harming Anglo's wider interests. Contrast this
with African Explosives and Chemical Industries
(AECI), an equally notorious monopolist in South
Africa. Anglo needs tight connections here, as AECI is a
major supplier of explosives and chemicals to Anglo's
mines and industrial plants, and has strong boardroom
representation as a consequence. But the Anglo connection here is long established and everyone is accustomed
to it. It also has to be tolerated by the government, which
desperately needs to maintain this strong chemicals and
explosives base, with its crucial technological input from
Britain.

• *Related companies* are companies in which Anglo is
neither a dominant shareholder, nor has management
control, yet where it nevertheless has significant influence. No two cases are identical, and Anglo's relationship with them varies widely as a result.

In the long term, this structure will change. The writing is
on the wall for South African business: international and
domestic political pressure will continue to mount, and the
Oppenheimers' global plans must take this into account. As
international rather than local South African financiers,
they are looking for a safety net outside their home base, as
their recent overseas consolidation shows. They appreciate
the lessons of the Salomon experience – that the South
African connection will become increasingly damaging for
their multinational empire as time goes by. Logically this
would lead to separation of the South African and interna-

tional companies, with the latter emerging as a series of interlinked quoted mini-empires spread around the globe – in Europe, North and South America, Australasia and Africa.

In the meantime, however, the empire remains a single entity. The first three categories above – group subsidiaries, administered associates and controlled associates – are essentially all fully controlled by Anglo. In consequence, they constitute the core companies within the greater Anglo group. The related companies are different in that, although closely and co-operatively linked to the group, Anglo's control of them is not as far as we know totally secured. This is a key distinction, and for this reason the related companies are grouped separately in the following list.

THE ANGLO GROUP COMPANIES

The list below is not intended to be comprehensive: there are simply too many companies and subsidiaries involved, and any such list would be confusing and well out of date before it was completed. The aim here is to describe the operating form of the group, rather than the artificial structure that legal, political, financial and tax accounting requirements impose upon it. The companies are accordingly grouped by the type and location of their economic activity. The group's South African interests are described first, and then its international interests. In each part the core companies are listed first, followed by a separate section dealing with related companies. In the South African section the companies are broken down by sectors and industries, in the international portion by sectors and regions.

Where a company is a subsidiary of a finance house, the name of the parent is indicated as in *Amcoal / AAC*. The status of associates, including the identity of any administering finance house, is given in brackets after the title as in (admin: AAC) or (controlled associate).

SOUTH AFRICA

Core companies

Mining

Despite its wide diversification into other industries and other parts of the world, South African mining still provides the cash-generating heart of the Anglo group. Gold in particular dominates, with platinum, coal and diamonds major profit generators but far less important individually. Because of the nature of the industry, the diamond business is the most self-contained and readily identifiable part of the group, and we therefore begin with that sector.

DIAMONDS

De Beers itself functions solely as Anglo's diamond-mining, trading and selling division. It does have investments outside the diamond industry, including its holdings in AAC, and these make up about 30 per cent of the company's assets (at carrying values) and profits, but practically all of these are controlled by central Anglo management.

- *The Central Selling Organisation* is the name of De Beers' entire international gem-marketing operation, whether carried out under the De Beers corporate empire or in conjunction with others, mainly meaning other parts of Anglo. To back up its marketing operation, the CSO runs full-scale promotional operations in all the main markets for gem diamonds, including the USA and Canada, Brazil, Mexico, Japan, Hong Kong and South-East Asia, Australia, and all the main European countries.
- *De Beers' Industrial Diamonds (Ireland)* markets all of the company's natural and synthetic industrial diamonds and related materials. It has technical advisory centres in London, Dusseldorf, Milan, Tokyo, Hong Kong, Bombay, Melbourne and Sao Paulo. Boart International, an Anglo industrial company, is a major international user of industrial diamonds for making diamond-tipped tools and cutting bits (see below).

- *De Beers Consolidated Mines* is the parent and operates all the South African mines, large parts of which are operated under lease from the South African government.
- *Consolidated Diamond Mines of South Africa (CDM) (Proprietary)* operates the Namibian mines spreading up the coastline north from the Orange River, providing mainly valuable gem diamonds. Output was increased by 50 per cent in 1986.
- *De Beers Botswana Mining (Debswana)* owned jointly with the Botswana government, operates the Botswanan mines of Orapa (commissioned 1971), Letlhakane (1976) and Jwaneng (1982).
- *De Beers Industrial Diamond Division (Pty)* manufactures industrial diamonds through: Ultra High Pressure Units in Springs, SA and Shannon, Eire; and Scandiamant Aktiebolag in Sweden (both 50 per cent owned).

Mine production figures give no indication of value as this is so dependent on quality. Only De Beers assesses this, and does not publish the figures, so the mines cannot really be compared. De Beers does not provide overall turnover figures for the synthetic diamond or industrial natural diamond business. As a result, no real measure of the whole business is available.

TABLE 2
De Beers' vital statistics

Employees	25,000	including the CSO
Turnover	$3,075m.	CSO sales worldwide 1987[1]
Turnover	R 6,300m.	CSO sales worldwide 1987[1]
Assets	R16,006m.	declared 31.12.1986[*2]
Pre-tax profits	R 1,515m.	declared for 1986*
Profits/employee	R60,600	
Minimum wage	R 4,896	basic*
Av. mineworker's wage	R10,260	including overtime and allowances*

*Figures as claimed by De Beers.

Notes:
1. Excludes non-CSO sales, which are not quantified.
2. Includes investments at market value of R8,999m., mainly in non-diamond Anglo group companies such as AAC, AMIC, Minorco, etc.

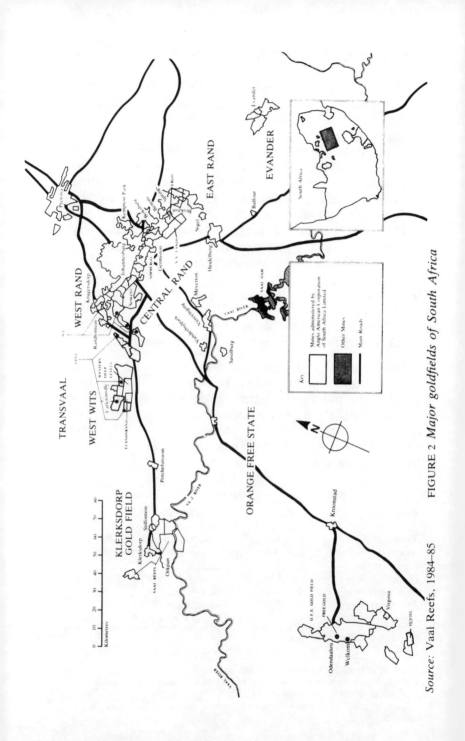

TRANSVAAL

WEST RAND

CENTRAL RAND

EAST RAND

EVANDER

WEST WITS

KLERKSDORP GOLD FIELD

ORANGE FREE STATE

Key
Mines administered by Anglo American Corporation of South Africa Limited
Other Mines
Main Roads

Kilometres
0 10 20 30 40 50 60 70 80

N

Pretoria

Kempton Park

Johannesburg

Krugersdorp

Randfontein

Soweto

Germiston

Brakpan

Springs

Benoni

Boksburg

Nigel

Heidelberg

Meyerton

Vereeniging

Vanderbijlpark

Sasolburg

VAAL RIVER

VAAL DAM

Balfour

Evander

Potchefstroom

Klerksdorp

Stilfontein

Orkney

VAAL REEFS

VAAL RIVER

Kroonstad

O.F.S. GOLD FIELD

FREE GOLD

Odendaalsrus

Welkom

Virginia

HJ.O.U.L.

Carletonville

WEST DEEP LEVELS

South Africa

FIGURE 2 *Major goldfields of South Africa*

Source: Vaal Reefs, 1984–85

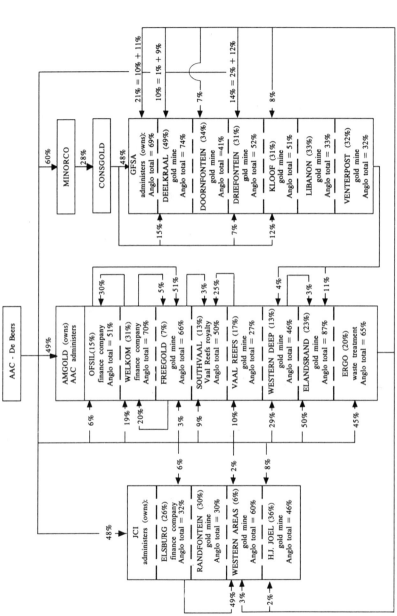

FIGURE 3 *Anglo's hold on South Africa's gold*

GOLD

Gold in particular provides the profit bedrock of the whole Oppenheimer empire. In fact, Anglo controls such a large part of South Africa's gold-mining industry that it has to maintain a complex corporate structure for this part of the group for political reasons. For a start, AAC administers four gold mines, among them the two largest in South Africa, producing between them 40 per cent of South Africa's mined gold and 51 per cent of its uranium. This makes AAC officially the country's largest gold-mining house. Anglo's second core mining house, Johannesburg Consolidated Investment (JCI), is small by comparison, ranking fifth in terms of gold production. It administers only two mines, the smaller of which is a marginal one nearing the end of its working life. But between them AAC and JCI control 47 per cent of South Africa's gold and 71 per cent of its uranium production. It is the dominant position of these two companies alone that prevents Anglo consolidating its hold over South Africa's second largest mining finance house, Gold Fields of South Africa (GFSA), which runs six mines producing a further 23 per cent of the gold and 2 per cent of the uranium. Instead, GFSA has had to be run by proxy for Anglo by the London-based Consolidated Gold Fields (Consgold; see below). This unique relationship in Anglo terms leaves GFSA's relationship with Anglo well hidden, even though it is 70 per cent owned by Consgold and AAC together. To avoid sanctions, Consgold has arranged to transfer part of its interests in GFSA to the Rembrandt Group, run by Oppenheimer's old pal Anton Rupert. But, at the same time, Consgold has been careful to keep effective control of the South African mining house by retaining over 48 per cent of the shares.

Overall, this leaves Anglo in control of 70 per cent of South Africa's gold mine output and 74 per cent of its uranium output (Table 3).

The mines

Free State Consolidated (admin: AAC/Amgold). Until recently, AAC ran four mines in the Orange Free State, all clustered in a strip around the town of Welkom 172 miles to the south-west of Johannesburg. These mines – Free State Geduld, President Brand, President Steyn and Western Holdings – already shared a joint tailings treatment plant, the Orange Free State Joint Metallurgical Scheme (OFS-JMS). Then, in February 1985, AAC announced that the mines would be merged to create what rapidly became known as 'Anglo's super-mine'. It took another year of corporate manoeuvring and negotiating government approval before the new mine, called Freegold, came into existence.

The biggest gold mine in the world, Freegold is almost three-quarters larger than the next South African gold mine in terms of workforce, and two and a half times larger in terms of output. The discrepancy is the result of Freegold's relatively low grades, an average of 4.3 g/ton in 1987, in turn due to the age of the mines on which it is based. They were begun in the late 1940s, and are described as mature mines, meaning that the richest ores have been removed. They are none the less classified as 'better-quality mines' with a life of 15–20 years, and Anglo hopes to be able to extend this as a result of the merger, and will doubtless aim to do so by cutting the workforce in the longer term. The mine sprawls across the area around Welkom in the Orange Free State and completely dominates gold mining there, producing almost twice as much gold as all the other mines put together.

Vaal Reefs Exploration and Mining Company (admin: AAC/Amgold). South Africa's second largest gold mine and the largest uranium producer (almost 2,000 tons of uranium oxide in 1986) is located on the Vaal River near Klerksdorp, with a second lease area to the north mainly for uranium. Another 'better-quality' 15–20-year life mine, but with a significantly better grade, at 7 g/ton, than Freegold, its workforce is proportionately much smaller but nevertheless

TABLE 3
Anglo's South African Gold and Uranium Mines, 1986

	Gold				Uranium		Employees (1986–87)
	Kg.	Revenue Rm.	Working cost Rm.	Profit Rm.	Kg.	Profit Rm.	
AAC							
FS Consolidated (North Region)	53,365	1,442	886	556			
FS Consolidated (South Region)	53,124	1,443	858	586			
OFS-JMS/FG	2,743				529,811		
Freegold total	109,232	2,885	1,744	1,142	529,811		112,238
Elandsrand	11,836	321	140	181			8,678
Vaal Reefs	81,501	2,222	909	1,313	1,930,044	131	51,378
W. Deep Levels	37,200	1,011	437	575	n.a.	18	27,552
JCI							
Randfontein	27,059	697	347	350	600,498	17	14,670
Western Areas	16,074	419	354	65	255,211	19	9,682
HJ Joel	—	—	—	—	—	—	400

GFSA

Deelkraal	7,588	205	115	90			7,345
Doornfontein	8,661	236	159	77			11,305
Driefontein Con	59,767	1,628	528	1,100	81,435	8	32,491
Kloof	28,841	790	228	562			17,687
Libanon	8,932	240	138	102			8,849
Venterpost	5,903	161	130	31			8,861
Totals (excluding OFS-JMS)							
Industry	577,218*	15,677	7,966	7,712	3,839,000*	248	454,142
AAC	237,026*	6,439	3,229	3,211	2,185,000*	149	199,846
JCI	43,133	1,116	700	416	600,000	36	24,752
GFSA	119,691	3,261	1,298	1,962	81,000	8	86,538
Anglo	399,850*	10,816	5,228	5,589	2,867,000*	194	311,136
Shares (%)							
AAC	41*	41	41	42	57*	60	44
JCI	7	7	9	5	16	15	5
GFSA	21	21	16	25	2	3	19
Anglo	69*	69	66	72	75*	78	68
Other residue treatment							
ERGO	6,395				150,997		2,539
SA Lands	1,680						343
Vlakfontein	1,033						529

*These figures refer to primary gold producers only, and exclude Harmony (primary uranium and gold), OFS-JMS, ERGO and SA Lands.

314   *SOUTH AFRICA INC.*

very large. Vaal Reefs is also the product of earlier mine mergers, and dates back to the early 1950s. Since inception it has produced 1,479 tons of gold worth R40 billion at current prices and 28,500 tons of uranium oxide. Given recent labour unrest, it is not surprising that the mine's new No. 9 shaft is being used as a group centre to establish a suite of equipment to develop 'efficient mechanised mining methods' (Report and Accounts, 1984). It is all part of the mine's response to the way in which 'the changing economic and socio-political climate will present many challenges to the mining industry in the years ahead' (*ibid.*).

Western Deep Levels (admin: AAC/Amgold). This mine reflects directly the advantages that control of a large financial and industrial empire provide. Anglo may have missed out when it came to the gems of the West Wits goldfield, the Driefontein and Kloof mines, but sheer cash and technical resources allowed Anglo to get at the parts that the other mining houses simply could not reach. Western Deep is, as its name implies, an extremely deep mine. Each of the main shaft systems has a first shaft reaching down 1,930 metres, to mine the first, 'Ventersdorp Contact' reef. At that depth a horizontal chamber is also cut to house winding gear, and another shaft is then cut down from that chamber a further 1,175 metres to reach the next, far richer, 'carbon leader' reef. Yet another chamber and shaft then reach down a further 675 metres to mine the lower part of the reef, which slopes down at an angle of 22 degrees. So the total depth is 3,780 metres, which is more than the height of any mountain in the Pyrenees, and not much less than some of the tallest in the Swiss Alps. It is certainly a considerable technical achievement, and also a very harsh, hot working environment at the bottom, according to the mine-workers who have to suffer it. Nevertheless, the mine has made good profits since Harry Oppenheimer turned the first sods in 1957, with the highest yield, at 10g per ton, of any AAC mine. It is still expanding: a third shaft commenced production in 1986 and has another 40 years' worth of reserves.

Elandsrand (admin: AAC/Amgold). Abutting on to Western Deeps, Elandsrand is AAC's youngest mine, having been incorporated in 1974. The mine reaches 2,875 metres down to the upper, 'Ventersdorp Contact' reef only, the richer lower reef being too deep to mine at this point. Again Anglo's technical and financial resources enabled it to risk the capital necessary to develop the mine. By developing it faster than any deep-level mine in the country before, Anglo could get the gold running and its capital turned into profits much faster. The sub shafts to reach the mine's full depth were only completed in 1984–85, and full capacity was only reached in 1987.

Randfontein Estates (admin: JCI). This mine is in three sections spread across the West Rand goldfield to the west of Soweto, touching on its borders at points. (True to form as one of the worst employers in the industry, JCI's annual report maps out the mines and the white cities and towns around, such as Johannesburg and Westonaria, completely omitting Africa's biggest city lying on their doorstep.) Randfontein's age is now showing, and with falling yields, JCI is trying to maintain profits here and at Western Areas (see below) by mechanising at the expense of the workforce. This led to disputes and the victimisation of mineworkers at both mines by the company in 1987.

Western Areas (admin: JCI). Western Areas gold mine lies directly to the south of the Randfontein mines, with only a short distance separating it from Randfontein's Cooke section. This is a marginal mine with a below 4 g/ton yield. Falling yields notwithstanding, each worker produced 1.5 kilograms of gold in 1986–87, worth 41,400 rand, or approximately ten times the minimum wage. As a result, management hopes that mechanisation and more pressure on the workforce will lead to a profits recovery.

HJ Joel (admin: JCI). This new mine, lying to the south of AAC's giant Freegold complex in the Orange Free State, is still under development at a total budget of over 1 billion rand. Output will build up to reach capacity in 1991, and the mine should yield 7,800 kgs of gold annually for 25 years – but could well achieve more.

Driefontein Consolidated (admin: GFSA). Formed from the merger of the East and West Driefontein mines in 1981, this is truly the jewel in South Africa's mining crown. Driefontein is only the third largest gold producer, behind AAC's Freegold and Vaal Reefs, yet outstrips them both in terms of profits by a considerable margin. It does so by virtue of high ore grades averaging 11.5g/ton in 1987, or over twice those at Freegold. And despite being the richest mine, Driefontein is also content with being one of the most exploitative of its black workforce, paying significantly less (along with all the GFSA mines) than the other mines for work carried out in conditions as bad if not worse than those elsewhere. The high profits have resulted in ever larger sums being handed over to the South African government in taxes and states' share of profits. These reached well over half a billion rand in 1984, before the gold price exploded with the rand's slump in 1985. This was 140 per cent more than the Freegold mines and 50 per cent more than Vaal Reefs paid that year, with the Dries' smaller capital spending accounting for only a small part of the difference. East and West Driefontein still publish separate working figures because they have differing tax rates. The yield of these and other rich mines is reduced noticeably when profits are high, in order to extend their life.

Kloof (admin: GFSA). At almost 15g/ton in 1986, Kloof is the richest mine in South Africa in terms of grade of ore mined, richer even than Driefontein Consolidated. Located just to the east of the latter, Kloof is a smaller mine with less than half the output. Nevertheless, the similar grades and employment conditions mean that the profits and taxes paid are proportionally equally obscene. Development of a new, adjacent lease area, the Leeudorn Division, means these profits will continue to flow for years ahead.

Doornfontein (admin: GFSA). GFSA's remaining mines look poverty-stricken by comparison with their stable-mates. Doornfontein abuts on to AAC's Elandsrand mine and rights belonging to AAC (though GFSA's and AAC's mapmakers seem to differ on this). It is a 'better-quality' mine with a reasonable but declining 5.5g/ton yield and a 15–20-year life, but relatively small, producing just under one-third of Kloof's output with a workforce two-thirds as large housed in hostels described by their residents in 1984 as the worst in the region. This and the low wages ensure that good profits are still made. Substantial spending on a new shaft (and hostel) should increase profits significantly in the longer term.

Libanon (admin: GFSA). Lying immediately to the north of Kloof, this mine has a grade which, at under 5.1g/ton, is only just over one-third that of its neighbour. However, development around a shaft commissioned in 1983 should maintain the mine's steady flow of dividends to its owners.

Deelkraal (admin: GFSA). This mine lies to the west of AAC's Elandsrand mine, and is targeted on the same 'Ventersdorp Contact' reef. The mine was started later and development was slower, so that the sub-shaft was only commissioned in 1985–86 and output will continue to expand. No taxes are payable at present owing to the various reliefs available, and the company had a 'tax loss' standing at R78 million in 1987 so that none will be payable for some time.

Venterpost (admin: GFSA). The smallest of GFSA's gold mines, Venterpost abuts the northern edge of Libanon, marking the end of a classic chain from strong to weak that begins with Kloof. It is a marginal mine, with a grade below 4g/ton and the smallest output of any GFSA mine. It is quite vulnerable to any deterioration in the gold price or increases in working costs. Of late, though, the former has been working in its favour, and shareholders have received large and unexpected bonuses as a result.

Tailings treatment
Anglo has four tailings treatment companies, which re-treat
the waste, often from now defunct mines, to extract the
residual gold and/or uranium. One is OFS-JMS, which was
set up, financed and supplied by the four mines that now
constitute Freegold. The other three are separate companies.

East Rand Gold and Uranium – ERGO (admin: AAC).
This company was established with new plant in the 1970s
to recover gold, uranium and pyrite from some of South
Africa's older mine dumps on the East Rand goldfield
immediately south-east of Johannesburg. It has since
expanded to three plants and is uprating its original plant so
that lower grades will be economically viable.

*South African Lands and Exploration – SA Lands (admin:
AAC) and Vlakfontein Gold Mining Co (admin: GFSA).*
Both these operations are based on former mines using
existing plant to re-treat both their own and other mines'
waste dumps.

GOLD FINANCE
There are a number of gold finance companies in the group.
These are purely financial vehicles, run by their respective
mining houses, with no significant trading activity, and so
have no real existence. There are three types.

- *Lease or royalty* These companies usually cede their
  mineral rights to another mine on a 'with profits' basis,
  which means revenues will fluctuate according to the
  success of mining in that area. They may as a result be
  classified as separate mines, though they do not trade.
  Their income must be added back to that of the main
  mine when comparing net profits. *Afrikander Lease*
  (admin: AAC) and *Southvaal Holdings* (admin: AAC) are
  both mined as part of Vaal Reefs.
- *Share-holding* When mines merge, some 'mining' companies are left holding nothing but shares in the main

mining company that results. In Anglo's case such companies include:

Orange Free State Investments – OFSIL (admin: AAC) holds 51 per cent of Freegold.
Welkom Gold Mining Co. (admin: AAC) holds 30 per cent of OFSIL and 5 per cent of Freegold.
Elsburg Gold Mining Co. (admin: JCI) holds 49 per cent of Western Areas.

● *Gold finance* These companies hold a wider portfolio of shares, including non-Anglo and sometimes non-gold shares. Their size varies enormously, but even Amgold, the largest, has no real existence outside of its administrator AAC, contrary to the impression the glossy annual report generates. Anglo's gold finance companies include:

Anglo American Gold Investment – Amgold (admin: AAC) has investments in many mines valued at R7.9 billion in all in 1987.
New Central Witwatersrand Areas (admin: AAC) has R54 million of shares.
DAB Investments (admin: JCI) has a R61 million portfolio of mainly mining shares.
New Wits Ltd (admin: GFSA) has portfolio valued at R246 million in 1986.

There are other companies in this category such as AAC's *Ultra Deep Levels* and GFSA's *Selected Mining Holdings*, but these are subsidiaries of other group companies and so their interests are included elsewhere.

Industry organisations
Anglo mines and mining houses also have shares and participate in industry-wide organisations such as the Rand Refineries, the Chamber of Mines, the International Gold Corporation, the Nuclear Fuels Corporation of South Africa and The Employment Bureau of Africa (TEBA). Naturally the Anglo mines' domination of the industry is reflected in these organisations, but political and labour

relations considerations necessitate that the group keeps an ultra low profile at this level, leaving its administration to the harder-line parts of Anglo and the industry.

OTHER MINING

Anglo's other mining interests may not generate as much income as gold, diamond and uranium, but they nevertheless play an important part. The relative importance of individual minerals to the group can fluctuate remarkably widely. Over a number of years up to mid-1985, for instance, coal was a rising star, but the oil price slump of early 1986 followed by international sanctions set its prospects back significantly. Meanwhile, however, platinum was on the ascendant, with sales revenues rapidly overtaking those of coal. This was because the combination of a declining rand (a lower proportion of coal output is exported) and a price that soared beyond that of gold both worked in its favour simultaneously. The past few years have also seen the base metals mines, such as copper and nickel, at a very low ebb, with little prospect of a significant recovery except as a consequence of an exceptionally low value for the rand for the South African mines.

One of Anglo's industrial companies, Highveld Steel, also operates a mine. Since this is an integral part of the industrial operation, it is dealt with in that section.

Platinum group metals

1986 could not have begun better for Anglo's platinum producer, Rustenberg Platinum Mines. Already the low rand and rising platinum prices meant that sales and profits for the previous six months were up 54 per cent and 93 per cent respectively on the levels of a year earlier. Then miners at its most important competitor, Impala Platinum, went on strike on the first day of 1986, and Impala proceeded to sack them. The platinum price kept heading upwards, as it became apparent that Impala would lose a great deal of output while recruiting and training a new workforce. Rumours were soon circulating that Impala was having to buy platinum elsewhere to meet its contractual commitments. Those supplies would have to come from Rustenberg directly or indirectly, which would be another favour owed by the Nationalist government and their supporters to Anglo. At the same time, Anglo's international platinum refining and marketing companies, Engelhard Corporation in the US and Johnson Matthey in the UK, were doubtless notching up large benefits in either cash or kind from former Impala customers who found themselves short of supplies. So out of what amounted to disaster for Impala's black workforce, Anglo emerged with not only an extremely healthy bank balance but also very large, though well-hidden, political credits.

South African platinum mine-owners are much more secretive than the gold mine-owners. This is because there are only three of them, they control 83 per cent of supplies to Western markets (a large part of the rest comes from the USSR), and platinum is one of the government's classified minerals.

Rustenberg Platinum Holdings (admin: JCI). Rustenberg operates three major and one smaller platinum mines, which also produce significant quantities of other group metals – palladium, rhodium, ruthenium, iridium and osmium – as well as some gold, silver, copper and nickel. The company has a base metals refinery at Rustenburg and precious metals refineries, developed and operated in conjunction with Johnson Matthey using the UK company's technology, at Wadeville in South Africa and Royston in the UK. Johnson Matthey is Rustenberg's sole marketing agent, and there are substantial long-term direct sales contracts with Engelhard Corporation.

Capacity (estimated)	1.25m. oz platinum group metals p.a.
Turnover	R2,216m. before commissions 1986–87
Turnover	R2,073m. after commissions 1986–87
Market value	R6,516m. June 1987
Pre-tax profits	R955m. declared for 1986–87

Northam Platinum (admin: GFSA). This is a platinum prospect which is 52 per cent owned by GFSA, lying 'down dip' from the Amandelbult platinum mine. GFSA is now planning to spend R1,000 million to develop a mine with a capacity of 350,000 oz of platinum group metals per annum, which will further strengthen Anglo's position as the dominant platinum producer. Start-up is scheduled for 1991.

Coal

The coal market in South Africa is distinguished by the high level of state control, mainly aimed at maintaining a wide divergence between the price of coal directed into the domestic market and that exported. In 1984, for instance, the average export price was R45/ton, compared with R14/ton on the domestic market. Coal is the second largest mining industry in terms of turnover, but the third largest mineral export, because three-quarters of coal produced goes to the domestic market, a large part of it to supply the state's Electricity Supply Commission (Escom) to generate electricity, much of which in turn is supplied to the gold and other mines.

Anglo again is by far the largest producer overall. It has three main coal-mining companies, one administered by each mining house in the group, which together form one of the largest private-sector coal-mining groups in the world. And its most important customer is Escom, for which Anglo's mines and industry in turn form the most important customer.

Anglo American Coal Corporation – Amcoal/AAC. Under the Amcoal label, AAC runs 13 collieries in Transvaal, the Orange Free State and Natal, together with associated facilities such as a rapid-loading facility for coal trains. The key to profitable coal mining in a country such as South Africa with a low, controlled domestic market price lies well beyond getting the coal mines in the first place. Coal is a high-volume, low-unit-value mineral, so reducing the cost of extraction and then moving huge volumes of it to the customer is crucial. It is here that AAC's large-scale and technically advanced operations had big pay-offs. Over the five years 1982–87, for instance, the cost per ton of AAC's coal rose only 64 per cent against an inflation rate of 99 per cent. Over that period there was a 7.5 per cent cut in jobs and a 20 per cent increase in sales volume. With that sort of performance, it is small wonder that AAC collieries' profits rose rapidly during the first half of the 1980s. Although hit hard by sanctions and falling world prices subsequently, an increasing share of the crucial Escom market – which takes 65 per cent of Amcoal's output – has limited the damage.

Year to 31 March 1987	
Employees	25,147
Turnover	R1,182m.
Pre-tax profits	R417m.
Group assets	R1,848m.
Profits/employee	R16,580

Gold Fields Coal/GFSA. This operation was only created in early 1986 in its present form when GFSA finally succeeded in a battle that had lasted for over a year to gain court and shareholder approval for the merger of Apex Mines and Clydesdale (Transvaal) Collieries. GF Coal has three collieries, and jointly owns a fourth with Gencor's Trans Natal Coal.

Year to 31 December 1986	
Turnover	R185m.
Net profits	R26m.
Coal sold	7,917,000 tons

Tavistock Collieries (admin: JCI). JCI has three fully owned collieries and a fourth that is jointly owned with the French oil company Total. Full accounts are not published, only a summary.

Year to 30 June 1985	
Pre-tax profits	R62m.

Vierfontein Collieries (admin: AAC). This AAC-administered company has one colliery supplying the Vier-fontein power station.

Turnover	R21m.	year to 31 March 1984
Pre-tax profits	R1m.	
Gross assets	R6m.	31 March 1984

TABLE 4

Anglo coal in South Africa, 1985 ('000 tons)

Company	Escom	Export	Other	Total
AAC/Amcoal	22,581	11,200	3,515	37,296
AAC/Vierfontein	800			800
GFSA/Gold				
Fields Coal:	12,385	1,529	1,227	15,141
JCI[2]	n.a.[3]	1,899	3,518	5,517
Anglo totals	35,766	14,628	8,360	58,754
S.A. totals	59,500	44,700	64,800	169,000
Anglo share	60%	33%	13%	35%

Notes:
1. Includes output of joint venture with Gencor's Trans Natal Coal.
2. Includes output of joint venture with Total Exploration South Africa.
3. Included in 'other'.

Base metals

The group has relatively few South African base metals mines, though some base metal interests are linked into industrial companies. Moreover, Anglo has neither large chrome nor manganese mines, two important South African base metals. It did build up a large share in SA Manganese Amcor, the world's largest integrated producer of manganese, chrome ores and ferro-alloys, in the expectation of being able to secure control in the longer term. The government thwarted its hopes by making the state steel-maker, Iron and Steel Corporation (Iscor), pass control to the Afrikaner-connected General Mining and Finance Corporation (Gencor). Anglo is left with a large and redundant shareholding, and no real prospect of entering either of these areas where South African mineral output provides a large part of Western supplies.

Antimony: Consolidated Murchison (admin: JCI). Jointly managed with the small Anglo-Vaal mining house, this is the only South African antimony mine, and produces gold

Year to 30 June 1986	
Output	12,060 tons antimony concentrate
	838 kg gold
Turnover	R42m.
Pre-tax profits	R11m.
Tax	R0.3m.

as a valuable by-product. JCI complains that its profits are being hit by Chinese producers 'who discount prices unnecessarily'.

Copper, lead, zinc, silver, tin. Apart from Zaaiplats Tin, an AAC subsidiary, these mines are all run by GFSA. Their output for 1986 was as follows:

Company	Output tonnes	Turnover R'000
Zaaiplats Tin/AAC	198 tin (1984)	3,835 (1984)
Rooiberg Tin	1,684 tin	23,000
Zinc Corp SA	86,517 zinc	107,456 (1984)
O'Okiep Copper	28,587 copper	82,000 (1985)
Black Mountain Mineral	31,365 zinc	119,000
	5,133 copper	
	92,965 lead	
	125 silver	
(See also Namibia: Tsumeb Corporation)		

Industry and commerce

Anglo's major acknowledged industrial grouping is the Anglo American Industrial Corporation (AMIC). This is another mainly paper operation, since AMIC is administered by AAC: its trading operations are mainly directed from AAC headquarters and run locally as individual profit centres. In fact, in terms of size and profits the non-AAC-administered companies such as South African Breweries and Premier are the more important. Then there are companies such as Shaft Sinkers and the South African Motor Corporation (Samcor) which, while directed straight out of AAC's head office, are not formally administered by AAC. As a result, none of the different annual reports provide a summary of Anglo's dominant industrial role any more than they do of its role in gold or other minerals.

IRON, STEEL AND ENGINEERING

This sector forms a vital, basic supplier to the mining industry, and to gold mining with its great depths and complex geology in particular. The mines need heavy steel equipment to do everything from building headgear, lift cables and cages to tools and equipment for drilling the rock for blasting, then moving and crushing the ore and extracting the metal. This demand provided the base for Anglo's investment into this sector, but the group has moved on to wider investment here as elsewhere.

Scaw Metals (admin: AAC). Scaw casts, rolls and engineers iron and steel products ranging from steel bar and huge balls and rings for pulverising mills to railway wheels. Its customers, include Escom and South African Railways as well as the mining industry.

Employees	4,000	1986
Pre-tax profits	R57m.	1986
Net assets	R262m.	1985
Profits/Employee	R14,250	including income from Haggie

Highveld Steel (admin: AAC). Highveld mines its own ore to produce iron, steel and vanadium rich slag in a large integrated steelworks and to supply its Vantra division which extracts vanadium pentoxide directly from ore. In addition, its Rand Carbide and Transalloys subsidiaries produce ferro-alloys and manganese alloys. Newmont Mining retains an interest in Highveld.

Year to 31 December 1986

Employees	7,430 average
Crude steel produced	865,500 tons (1985)
Vanadium slag	57,340 tons (1985)
Vanadium pentoxide	n.a.
Ferro-alloys	190,937 tons (1985)
Exports	R373m. 56% of sales (1985)
Total sales	R816m.
Pre-tax profits	R98m.
Gross assets	R746m.
Profits/employee	R13,190

Boart International (admin: AAC). Boart is a very large and international manufacturer and supplier of mining tools and equipment in particular and of diamond and carbide tools for industry generally. Its international strength derives from its roots in South Africa's large mining industry coupled with utilisation of De Beers' boart – the diamonds that are more valuable for their cutting ability than their appearance. As a result, this company is an important industrial money-spinner for Anglo.

Year to 31 December 1986

Employees	11,000
Profits	R81m.
Net assets	R327m. (1985)
Profits/employee	R7,365

Consolidated Metallurgical Industries – CMI (admin: JCI). This company provides Anglo with a back-door entrance to the South African chrome extraction business. Using Japanese technology, Anglo has built the world's largest plant to produce granulated ferrochrome for CMI at Lydenburg in the Eastern Transvaal. The ore is drawn from the mines of other mining houses at the moment, but JCI controls 'very substantial' chrome ore deposits within 70km of the plant, ensuring a long-term supply of ore. Essentially AAC is now well placed to strengthen its position in chrome, since it can process the ore economically into a premium product, and also has the reserves to ensure that ore prices remain reasonable.

Year to 30 June 1987	
Output	150,000 tonnes per annum
Turnover	R137m.
Net profit	R43m.
Gross assets	R125m.

Lennings/JCI. Lennings is a diversified engineering group with foundries, machine shops and fabricating plants selling to the railways, mines, agriculture and industry.

Year to 30 June 1987	
Turnover	R321m.
Pre-tax profits	R11m.

CHEMICALS AND EXPLOSIVES

African Explosives and Chemical Industries – AECI (controlled associate). This company is one of the major industrial groups in South Africa in its own right. Set up by De Beers in 1924 as a main supplier of explosives to the South African mining industry, AECI has thrived on its monopoly ever since. The company now dominates the plastics and chemicals industry there, as well as retaining a 95 per cent hold on the commercial explosives market. With Britain's ICI as a co-owner with Anglo, AECI has ready access to that company's chemicals technology.

Year to 31 December 1985	
Employees	26,600 at year end
Exports	R233m. 10% of turnover
Sales	R2,340m.
Pre-tax profits	R162m.
Taxation	R53m.
Gross assets	R1,966m.
Profits/employee	R6,090

CONSTRUCTION

Anglo's interests in the sector have developed out of its mining needs. They have to be run independently of AAC since tax finance provides such an important element of mine finance.

LTA Limited (admin: AAC). This is the largest construction company in South Africa. It does considerable work for group companies, including building mineshafts, hotels and office blocks, but derives an even larger part of its business from the state. While it mostly services the state by building major roads and bridges, the company works for every part of government – building new hospitals or the Post Office's Pretoria headquarters, for instance.

Year to 31 March 1987	
Employees	30,000 (1984)
Turnover	R1,065m.
Pre-tax profit	R7m.
Gross assets	R355m.

Shaft Sinkers (admin: AAC). This company provides a design and construction service for excavation work for both mining and civil engineering industries, from tunnelling to constructing the main shaft for new mines.

VEHICLES

AAC/South African Motor Corporation – Samcor (admin: AAC). This is South Africa's second largest car manufacturer. Ford has now handed its 24 per cent shareholding over to the employees but still provides components and know-how. The company produces Ford, Mitsubishi and Mazda vehicles. Because of the large losses it has

1984 (pre-merger) results:	
Cars sold	31,948
Commercial vehicles	13,688
Loss	R88m.

suffered in an over-supplied industry, Anglo has had to keep its car company hidden behind joint AAC/AMIC ownership, but in 1987 Samcor made its first profits – while cutting employment from 10,000 to 4,500.

McCarthy Group (controlled associate). This is the country's main vehicle distributor, with about 100 outlets across the country. Franchises range from Rolls Royce and Mercedes-Benz to Ford and Toyota, as well as Kawasaki and Yamaha motorcycles and other products.

Year to 30 June 1987	
Employees	5,109
Motor vehicles sold	62,700
Motor cycles	7,800
Turnover	R1,309m.
Pre-tax profits	R36m.
Gross assets	R247m.
Profits/employee	R7,046

Komatsu South Africa (admin: AAC). Komatsu has grown very rapidly in recent years to challenge Caterpillar as the world's leading earth-moving and heavy construction equipment supplier. Komatsu SA also supplies forklift trucks and holds the South African franchise for Michelin tyres. All are valuable in Anglo's mining and construction businesses.

PULP, PAPER AND TIMBER PRODUCTS
This is both a major industrial activity for Anglo, and also an important landowning and agricultural interest to add to the farms and sugar estates owned by other parts of the group.

Mondi Paper (admin: AAC). South Africa's largest pulp, paper and board producer, Mondi, is another example of how Anglo's financial and technical resources can be targeted to benefit both the group and the economy. It has recently built a new pulp mill at a cost of R865 million which will replace imports and provide exports, all at a good profit to Anglo and creating 600 jobs (i.e. R1.4 million per job). Mondi also had a substantial timber products business and owns forests in the Eastern Transvaal which supply all parts of the company.

Year to 31 December 1986	
Employees	15,000
Pulp capacity	450,000 tons/year
Paper capacity	500,000 tons/year
Pre-tax & interest profits	R115m.
Net assets	R1,345m. (1985)

HL&H Timber Holdings Ltd (admin: AAC and Rembrandt). Anglo has recently increased its share in this company to 50 per cent, with Rembrandt holding the remainder. HL&H owns and manages large timber plantations, and supplies amongst others Mondi's Richards Bay Mill with timber and is the mining industry's major supplier of pit props.

Year to 31 March 1987	
Net profit	R26m

Natal Tanning Extract (admin: AAC). Owns or leases 102,000 hectares in the south-east of the country for forestry, the manufacture of tanning extract and sugar cane.

Year to 31 December 1986	
Employees	5,500
Production timber	500,000 tons
Sugar cane	140,000 tons
Exports	R39m. (1985)
Pre-tax & interest profits	R14m.
Net assets	R75m. (1985)

FOOD, BEVERAGES AND CONSUMER PRODUCTS
Anglo's dominance of this sector has expanded rapidly in recent years, though it is quite well hidden because the main group companies operate quite independently of both one another and the group's mining houses. This separation from the latter is eminently sensible, given how far removed mining is from mass consumer markets.

South African Breweries – SAB (controlled associate). SAB is a major South African company in its own right, and has a 'powerful position in the mass consumer market' (Report and Accounts, 1987). It has a long-standing monopoly in the brewing industry and has diversified from the base that provided. SAB now encompasses the Southern Sun/Holiday Inn hotels chain; the OK Bazaars, Amalgamated Retail and Edgars Stores supermarket, shop and department store chains with over 1500 sites nationwide; and manufacturing of some consumer products such as footwear, furniture and appliances; as well as its extremely large alcoholic and non-alcoholic beverages business.

Year to 31 March 1987	
Employees	79,100
Turnover	R7,083m.
Pre-tax profits	R437m.
Tax	R122m.
Gross assets	R4,328m.
Profits/employee	R5,525

Premier Group Holdings (controlled associate). Premier is

Year to 31 March 1987	
Employees	31,149
Turnover	R2,690m.
Pre-tax profits	R154m.
Tax	R45m.
Gross assets★	R3,090m.
Profits/employee	R4,943

★Includes investment in SAB of R1,658m.

principally a milling and general food industry company, though it also controls CNA Gallo, with its shops and media activities, the Twins Propan drug company and Southern Seas', Namibian, South African and Chilean fishing operations. Premier also holds the Anglo stake in SAB.

Tongaat-Hulett Group (controlled associate). This is Anglo's 'food, clothing and shelter' company. Built up as South Africa's largest sugar-cane grower and refiner, Tongaat has spread not only into other foods, but also to become one of the world's largest brickmakers and the country's principal aluminium fabricator.

Year to 31 March 1987	
Employees	42,720
Turnover	R2,177m.
Pre-tax profits	R107m.
Tax	R40m.
Gross assets	R1,585m.
Profits/employee	R2,505

Anglo American Farms – Amfarms (admin: AAC). The only Anglo food company administered by a mining house is not surprisingly the one most directly involved in supplying the mines. Amfarms owns many farm and ranch properties, and produces grain, cattle, vegetables, fruit, dairy products, sheep, pigs and wine.

PUBLISHING
Anglo controls the two main English-language publishing groups in South Africa.

Argus Printing & Publishing (controlled associate). The largest newspaper group in Africa, Argus also shares control of the CNA Gallo music, books and newsagents group with Premier. Argus publishes the Johannesburg *Star*, Cape Town *Argus*, Durban *Sunday Tribune*, along with eight other leading newspapers, and has investments in

several major South African media companies, including
Times Media.

Year to 31 March 1987	
Turnover	R843m.
Pre-tax profits	R51m.

*Times Media Limited – TML (formerly SAAN) (controlled
associate).* Publisher of the *Rand Daily Mail* before its
closure, Times Media is now concentrating on financial
journalism – with *Business Day* and the *Financial Mail* –
and the *Sunday Times* and *Cape Times*. The company is
moving closer to the Argus group, using its printing works
in Johannesburg and sharing offices in London.

Year to 31 March 1987	
Turnover	R134m.
Net profit	R10m.

Industrial finance

*Anglo American Industrial Corporation – AMIC (admin:
AAC).* AAC lists AMIC as a 'principal finance and investment company' (Report and Accounts, 1985), yet AMIC
appears at first sight to be very much an active industrial
group with many subsidiaries and a large trading turnover.
AAC's view is the correct one, with AMIC interspersed as a
financial vehicle geared to the capital markets between the
major parents AAC and De Beers and the operating industrial companies. Its figures therefore have to be used
carefully to avoid the danger of double counting the figures
for companies such as Highveld Steel and LTA.

Year to 31 December 1986	
Employees: in subsidiaries	43,500
in associates	158,700
Total sales	R3,138m.
Pre-tax profits	R433m.
Gross assets	R5,052m.

Finance and property

In the past, Anglo's principal financial assets used to lie with its mining houses, and AAC in particular. These handle their administered companies' cash as well as their own, and have large investments besides, so that the mining houses stood alongside South Africa's larger banks in terms of the resources available to them. Although this is still the case, Anglo's purchase of three important financial institutions in the 1980s, Barclays National Bank (now First National), Citibank and Southern Life Association, means that its financial assets are now not only much greater but also dispersed across more institutions. Anglo thus has a veritable battery of weapons aimed point blank at South Africa's financial markets.

First National Bank of Southern Africa (formerly Barclays National). This is by far the most important of Anglo's financial companies, being South Africa's largest bank. The connections with Anglo are long established, with six Anglo directors sitting on Barclays National's (Barnat) board in 1985 when it was supposedly controlled from the UK. They included Gordon Waddell and J. Ogilvie Thompson, who is Barnat's vice-chairman. Together the Anglo directors made up one-quarter of Barnat's board, a greater number than from Barclays Bank itself, Barnat's then parent.

As the UK company came under steadily greater divestment pressure, Anglo was their natural choice to take over control of the South African operation. The closeness of the relationship was shown in the Southern Life/Amlife merger. Barnat played a major role in creating this new financial institution for Anglo, taking 30 per cent of the new SLA itself. This was followed by a Barnat rights issue in which AAC and De Beers' stake in Barnat rose to 25 per cent and SLA's to over 7.5 per cent, and finally by the sale of Barclays' entire shareholding in Barnat to AAC, De Beers and SLA. At this point the longer-term intentions behind the Anglo- and Barnat-backed formation of SLA were revealed. First National is now owned 22.5 per cent by AAC, 7.5 per cent by De Beers and 25 per cent by SLA, making 55 per cent in all, but SLA itself is controlled jointly by AAC and First National. Anglo got what it wanted at a very low price.

Year to 31 December 1986	
Employees	25,134
Operating income	R2,793m.
Pre-tax profit	R302m.
Tax	R141m.
Total assets	R20,604m.
Profits/employee	R12,015

Anglo American Corporation – AAC. Apart from Amcoal, much of AAC's resources is invested in shares, mainly in group companies. As so many of these are quoted, these investments are quite liquid. In addition, AAC has large property holdings through Amaprop (see below).

Year to 31 March 1987	
Quoted investments	R23,560m. market value
Deposits and cash	R2,313m.
Investment property	R670m.* 'market' value
Total	R26,544m.

*Excludes property purchased by Amaprop on behalf of others such as group pension funds.

Gold Fields of South Africa – GFSA

Year ending 30 June 1987	
Quoted investments	R7,131m. market value
Deposits and cash	R36m.

Johannesburg Consolidated Investment – JCI

Year ending 30 June 1987	
Quoted investments	R4,598m. market value
Deposits and cash	R519m.
Investment property	R35m. 'market' value
Total	R5,152m.

Anglo American Properties Ltd (Amaprop)/AAC. Amaprop was South Africa's fourth most highly valued property company in 1987, with a market value of R193 million, only R80 million less than that of the leader. The company owns large properties in the city and suburban centres of South Africa's major cities, as well as some township properties and hotels. Its subsidiary Carlton Centre Ltd owns and operates Johannesburg's prestigious Carlton Centre hotel, office and shopping centre.

Year ending 31 March 1987	
Pre-tax profits	R26m.
Properties at valuation:	R597m.
Johannesburg	
Carlton Centre	R197m. (1985)
Other	R138m. (1985)
Pretoria	R70m. (1985)
Durban	R31m. (1985)
Cape Town	R28m. (1985)

Southern Life Association – SLA (controlled associate). Southern Life is the fourth largest life assurance company in South Africa, only slightly smaller than Liberty Life, Anglo's partner in the Premier/SAB take-over. SLA's creation cemented the already close links between Anglo and Barclays National Bank: its shares are now owned by AAC (42 per cent plus 2 per cent convertible), First National (30 per cent plus 5 per cent through pension fund), Amlife and

Year ending 31 March 1987		
Premium income	R859m.	
Investment income	R488m.	
Total income	R1,346m.	
Disclosed profits	R64m.	excluding profits in hidden reserves within life funds
Quoted investments	R3,262m.	
Total assets	R7,723m.	

SLA executive share schemes (3 per cent), accounting for 82 per cent of the shares in all even before other Anglo group interests are brought in. SLA's funds mainly belong to policyholders, which does not prevent them being invested, to some extent, where Anglo needs them. Group companies – AAC, First National and De Beers – form the three largest investments in Southern's portfolio. At present, life assurance funds tend to grow faster than inflation as the individual pension and insurance policies they represent build up towards maturity.

Related companies

There are a number of related companies in South Africa that Anglo does not control absolutely but where its influence is considerable.

Discount House of South Africa. Originally established by Anglo, the Discount House now plays an important role as a financial intermediary that borrows very short-term funds from banks, building societies and mining houses and invests them, typically over a slightly longer term, in government securities. This means it handles huge amounts of money and makes its profits by judging how interest rates will move in the short term and offering and accepting interest rates that vary accordingly. First National also has a holding.

Year to 31 December 1986	
Net profits	R4m.

Bowring Barclays. A big South African insurance broker linked with Marsh & McLennan of New York, this is jointly controlled by AAC and First National.

Year to 31 December 1984	
Profits	R5m.

Haggie Ltd and Rennies Freight Services (Renfreight). These companies are both controlled in partnership with the Afrikaner-linked South African National Life Assurance Co., which Anglo helped to build the mining house General Mining and Finance Corporation. Haggie specialises in manufacturing the steel cable that is so vital for the mines and consequently the joint control benefits all concerned. Renfreight is the main South African surface and air freighting company. Both companies have substantial international operations, Haggie's mainly to supply the mining industries in countries such as Zimbabwe and Zambia, Renfreight having offices and facilities worldwide.

INTERNATIONAL

Anglo's large international investment company, Minerals and Resources Corporation Ltd (Minorco), has a relatively high profile, as its shares and those of most of the companies it invests in are quoted. Minorco provides an accessible guide to some of Anglo's international holdings, but there are a number of others, both direct and indirect. Many of the smaller ones are well hidden, particularly in countries where the South African connection could be troublesome.

Core companies

Mining

NORTH AMERICA

Inspiration Resources (informal admin: AAC). This company was set up in its present form only in 1983, and is the product of a series of unfortunate investments which seem to be continuing to the present. Even in 1984–85, Minorco had to write off $154 million of its investment in Inspiration. Inspiration was formed from Inspiration Copper and Canada's Hudson Bay Mining and Smelting, both principally base metal producers, and it is the base metals side

that has produced most of the losses. Inspiration also has
coal mines, and agricultural chemical interests. It recently
expanded its oil interests by merging Trend International's
oil interests with Madison Resources and Adobe Oil and
Gas, has added Sohio's eastern corn-belt distribution to
Terra Chemicals existing southern and mid-western US
agri-chemicals business, and has added Danville Resources'
forestry and printing business to its stable. However, the oil
and gas were spun off directly to Minorco as they too ran
into losses.

Year to 31 December 1986	
Employment	5,518 (1985)
Revenues	US$1,099m.
Net profit	US$38m.
Gross assets	US$731m. (1985)

LATIN AMERICA
Anglo American Corporation of South America (AMSA)
(informal admin: AAC). This mining and industrial group
operates right across Latin America, with its subsidiary
Ambras (Anglo American Corporation do Brasil) running
the Brazilian activities. Anglo has only recently completed
its acquisition of AMSA, and evidently intends to use it to
build a 'mini-Anglo' in Latin America. AMSA, registered
in Panama, is entirely privately owned by Anglo, and
consequently only limited information is available about its
activities. In Brazil it controls: Mineracao Morro Velho,
with gold mines in Minas Gerais and Bahia producing 5.6
tons of gold in 1985; the Codemin ferro-nickel mine; the
Copebras-Fosfago carbon black, phosphate and fertiliser
group; the Catalao ferro-nobium operations; and investments in the Bozano Simonsen banking, property, mining
and farming group. AMSA owns the Mantos Blancos
copper mine in Chile and the Petrosur fertiliser company in
Argentina.

Year to 31 December 1986	
Net profits	US$33m.

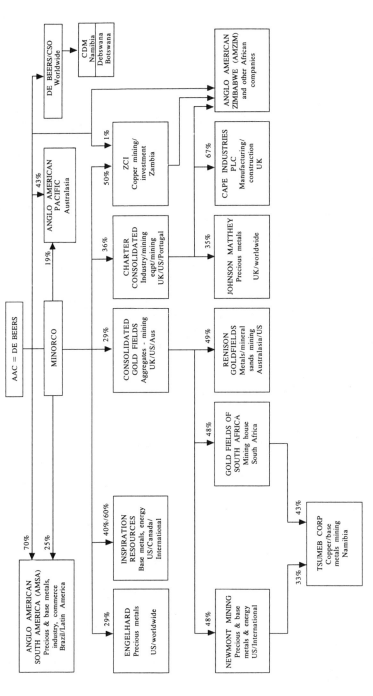

FIGURE 4 *Anglo's International Empire*

NAMIBIA
De Beers Consolidated Diamond Mines of South-West-Africa.
This is Namibia's most important mine, extracting large, very valuable gem-quality diamonds from alluvial deposits along the Namibian coast (see De Beers, pp. 306–307 above).

Tsumeb Corporation (admin: GFSA/Newmont). Namibia's largest base metals mine, Tsumeb was originally set up by Newmont Mining, and was hugely profitable until metal prices slumped in the 1970s. Since then Newmont has become an associate of Consolidated Gold Fields, and GFSA has taken increasing responsibility for its main southern African mines. O'Okiep in South Africa and Tsumeb, in an attempt to stem their losses.

Year to 31 December 1985	
Metal sold	39,058 tons copper
	42,196 tons lead
	97 tons silver
Turnover	R175m.
Net profit	R10m.

ZIMBABWE
Anglo's Zimbabwean mining companies are administered by *Anglo American Corporation Zimbabwe Ltd* (Amzim), which forms a mini-Anglo in Zimbabwe, though it has to be kept discreetly separated from the South African parent for political reasons. Between them these companies cover an important spectrum of the Zimbabwean mining industry, encompassing coal, nickel and copper mining, and ferro-chrome production.

Bindura Nickel (admin: Amzim 69% owned)

Turnover	Z$95.2m.	1985
Net Profits	Z$12.8m.	

Wankie Colliery (admin: Amzim 23% owned)

Turnover	Z$93.4m.	1985–86
Net Profits	Z$17.7m.	

Zimbabwe Alloys (admin: Amzim 65% owned)

Turnover	Z$83.0m.	1984–85
Pre-tax Profits	Z$12.0m.	

BOTSWANA

Botswana's major source of foreign exchange, Debswana is jointly owned by De Beers and the government, and operates three diamond mines (see De Beers, pp. 306–307 above).

Morupule Colliery (admin: AAC). This colliery, which supplies Botswana's power stations, is an AAC subsidiary.

Year to 31 March 1985	
Profits	P502,000
Capacity	480,000 tons per year

Botswana RST. Jointly controlled with AMAX Inc. of the USA, but with Anglo's close links with Botswana giving it a dominant role, this company has a major nickel/copper mine at Selebi-Phikwe. So far the project has proved to be a financial disaster as a result of low base metals prices, and probably remains open only because of the benefits Anglo obtains elsewhere.

Year to 31 March 1986	
Production	18,974 tons nickel
	17,378 tons copper
	163 tons cobalt
Sales	US$53m.
Net loss	US$5m.
Accumulated deficit	US$724m.

AUSTRALIA
Anglo's most important mining interests in Australia come
via Consolidated Gold Fields' control of *Renison Goldfields
Consolidated Ltd*, a substantial quoted mining and industrial
group that also has some interests in the USA.

Industry

UK / USA
Engelhard Corporation. With Johnson Matthey, Engelhard
dominates the international precious metals processing
business. Its main activities are production of precious
metal bars and medallions, precious metals refining and
fabrication and speciality chemicals. Like Johnson Matthey, it handles and refines gold but also specialises in
platinum, particularly for catalysts. Engelhard has long-
term sales contracts with Rustenburg Platinum.

Year to 31 December 1985	
Employees	6,900
Turnover: speciality metals	US$1,624m.
speciality chemicals	US$666m
Total	US$2,290m.
Pre-tax profits	US$71m.
Gross assets	US$1,043m.
Profits/employee	US$10,290

Johnson Matthey (JM). This company is virtually a
transatlantic mirror-image of Engelhard, being the major
UK-based precious metals refiner. Lax management led to
the collapse of JM's bank, but Anglo ended up more tightly
in control than ever with the Bank of England's consider-

Year to 31 March 1987	
Employees	7,454
Turnover	UK£1,221m.
Pre-tax profits	UK£51m.
Gross assets	UK£532m.
Profits/employee	UK£6,842

able assistance. Like Engelhard, JM has plants all over the world. The two are the principal suppliers of catalytic convertors to the US and European auto industries, for instance, and both have plants on each side of the Atlantic to supply their respective customers. Only anti-trust laws prevent closer links between them.

Charter Consolidated. Charter was intended to be Anglo's international investment arm, but has ended up as a mainly industrial group with some strategic investments held on Anglo's behalf. Its subsidiaries make building products, railway-track components and heating, refrigeration and catering products, and include Cape Industries, formerly a major asbestos company, which has been astonishingly adept at extricating itself from the business without paying huge compensation. Charter mines coal, tin and wolfram, but not very profitably on the whole. Strategically more important, Charter owns mining equipment suppliers Anderson Strathclyde in the UK and National Mine Service in the USA. It also holds Anglo's controlling interest in Johnson Matthey and other important Anglo shareholdings.

Year to 31 March 1986	
Employees	12,644
Turnover: manufacturing	UK£260m.
construction	UK£168m.
mining	UK£40m.
Total	UK£506m.
Pre-tax profits	UK£42m.
Gross assets	UK£567m.

ZIMBABWE

Hippo Valley Estates (admin: Amzim). The second-largest listed company in Zimbabwe, Hippo is 41 per cent owned by Amzim. It owns large sugar estates and mills and buys in cane from other farmers.

Turnover	Z$73.0m.	1984–85
Pre-tax profits	Z$11.5m.	

Border Timbers (admin: Amzim). This company grows and processes timber on large estates in Zimbabwe.

Turnover	Z$15.8m.	1984–85
Loss	Z$1.3m.	

Delta Corporation (controlled associate). South African Breweries' Zimbabwean associate, Delta has the largest turnover of any quoted company in the country. Now the Zimbabwean government has taken a majority stake, but Delta still has the old SAB management and sells the same SAB products and services, from beer to hotels.

Turnover	Z$537.1m.	1985–86
Pre-tax profits	Z$23.0m.	

AUSTRALIA

Anglo American Pacific. AAC set up Australian Anglo American as an exploration company in the hope of finding new mines in this political haven. Many millions of rands later, it has ended up with a small industrial minerals processing and marketing company bought from the UK's Steetley Industries, along with a small gold recovery operation. But at least it has now got a quote on the local stockmarket.

Net profits	A$2.6m.	1985

Finance

Minerals and Resources Corporation Ltd – Minorco. As Anglo's main international investment company, Minorco is structured so that its ownership cannot be attributed directly to any one South African company. It is really only a paper company, investing in other companies and not trading on its own account, but it is valuable paper which has the advantage of a Bermuda domicile. Perhaps this is why E. Oppenheimer & Son has a 6.5 per cent direct shareholding, even though Minorco is fully controlled by AAC and De Beers. Minorco has performed dismally so far in its mining investments, and has been rescued only by the good fortune of its investment in Phibro-Salomon. In the process, Anglo has thrown a great deal of good money after bad, despite the promise of the Oppenheimers' golden touch.

Main investments at 30 June 1987		US$m.
Philbro-Salomon	14%	700*
Consolidated Gold Fields	28%	965
Engelhard Corporation	30%	340
Inspiration Resources	58%	260
Adobe Resources Corporation	53%	167
Charter Consolidated	36%	249
Anglo American Corp. of South America	25%	89
Anglo American Investment Trust	10%	144*
Arcata Trust	84%	58
Anglo American Pacific	30%	19
Cash and deposits and other		183
Total		3,174

* Salomon and Anamint have now been sold.

ZIMBABWE
RAL Holdings. This investment bank is a subsidiary of Amzim.

Operating profits	Z$3m.	1984–85

Related companies

Consolidated Gold Fields – Consgold (UK). Consgold is a diversified international mining finance house in its own right. Anglo has two representatives on Consgold's board, but its interest is targeted on Consgold's 48 per cent share in Gold Fields of South Africa (GFSA) and its gold mines. In effect, while its 48 per cent holding should give Consgold

full control over GFSA, Anglo's shareholdings and directorships, added to Consgold's position as an external
investor, mean that the board's control over GFSA is
strictly subject to Anglo's approval. Anglo sweetens the pill
by giving the Consgold board its full support in return for
playing the game on GFSA. Consgold's management is free
to go its own way so far as the rest of its business is
concerned, and particularly the Amey Roadstone construction materials subsidiary with its very profitable public
sector contracts in the UK and USA. Consgold also controls
Renison Goldfields in Australia (49 per cent), and Newmont Mining (48 per cent), the largest US gold-mining
company, which also has base metal mines and oil and gas
interests. Newmont in turn has interests in Tsumeb Corporation in Namibia, O'Okiep Copper in South Africa,
Peabody Coal of the USA and Sherritt Gordon of Canada.

Year to 30 June 1987		
Employees	12,486	average
Turnover	UK£1,118m.	
Net profits	UK£244m.	
Net assets	UK£2,509.5m.	investments at market value
		including GFSA and gold mines
Profits/employee	£19,542	

Salomon Inc. (US). This was one of the most important
companies connected to Anglo. It has two divisions: Wall
Street's prestigious Salomon Brothers investment bank,
which helps raise over $140 billions worth of finance for
governments and blue chip companies each year; and
Philipp Brothers (Philbro), one of the world's largest
commodity trading companies, handling everything from
cargoes of oil to titanium for the US Strategic and Critical
Materials Stockpile. Anglo saw Phibro-Salomon as both a
profitable investment and an excellent source for invaluable
business and political connections. Between them, Salomon
Brothers and Phibro know most of what there is to know
about finance and commodities. What more could South
Africa's largest mining group ask for? But sanctions pres-

APPENDIX: PROFILE OF THE ANGLO GROUP

sure made Salomon too vulnerable, so Anglo had to take its money and run.

Year to 31 December 1985	
Employees	6,300
Revenue	US$27,896m.
Pre-tax profits	US$943m.
Tax	US$386m.
Profits/employee	US$149,680

Rowe & Pitman (UK). The Queen's stockbrokers in the City of London, Rowe and Pitman have long been connected with Anglo. Now the firm has merged with merchant bank SG Warburg, jobbers Ackroyd & Smithers and the former government broker Mullens & Co. to form Mercury International, one of the more powerful institutions in the reshaped City, which will doubtless continue acting on Anglo's behalf.

OTHER INVESTMENTS

The companies described above are only the main parts of the Anglo empire, those that the group controls or with which it has a concrete working relationship. Many Anglo companies described above have a large number of subsidiaries and brand names, and may trade under any of them in any part of the world. These can be further hidden, for with an organisation of Anglo's complexity it is easy to build a large shareholding in many different names or behind a front company which does not have to be revealed. There are in addition many other companies in which it holds investments, some quite large. Some of these are given below, though the list is not comprehensive.

Company	Holding (%)
Gold	
Buffelsfontein	28.86
Hartebeestfontein	22.86
Zandpan	22.20
St Helena	18.55
Blyvooruitzicht	15.15
Loraine	12.22
Beatrix	3.81
Bracken Mines	0.17
Harmony	2.74
Kinross	1.47
Unisel	3.57
Winkelhaak	8.08
Witwatersrand Deep	2.18
Other mining	
Samancor	28.67
Lydenburg Platinum	2.38
Witbank Colliery	0.48
Industry	
Cullinan Holdings	22.95
Toyota SA	21.40
Commercial Union SA	20.00
Lucem Holdings	17.80
BTR (SA)	16.70
Union Steel	13.10
Wesco	10.08
Barlow Rand (Ordinary)	1.36
Barlow Rand (Preferred)	7.21
Messina	8.24
Sasol	6.00
Finance	
Stanbic	2.40
Mining house	
General Mining	5.92
International mining	
British-Borneo Pet.	26.00
Imetal	6.00

Notes and References

1 A Day Out to Carletonville

1. Peter Randall, *Little England on the Veld* (Ravan Press, Johannesburg, 1982), p. 105.
2. Anglo American Corporation of South Africa, Annual Report 1976.
3. *Financial Mail*, Special Survey, 'Inside the Anglo Power House', 14 July 1969.
4. *Financial Mail* Survey, 1974; quoted in Rodney Stares, *ICI in Southern Africa* (Christian Concern for Southern Africa, London, 1977), p. 14.
5. A. P. Cartwright, *The Diamond Company* (Macdonald, London, 1964); quoted in Stares, *op. cit.* (n4), p. 18.
6. Jim Carson, *Space Research Capitalism*, background paper presented to the International Seminar on the Implantation and Reinforcement of the Arms Embargo against South Africa (London, 1-3 April 1981), prepared for the American Committee on Africa and the World Campaign Against Military and Nuclear Collaboration with South Africa, p. 8.
7. Interview with authors, Johannesburg, June 1986.
8. *Ibid.*
9. Barclays Bank statement, London, 14 August 1986.
10. *Financial Mail* Special Survey, Top Companies, 24 May 1985.

2 The Oppenheimer Dynasty

1. *Fortune Magazine*, May 1968.
2. *Star*, Johannesburg, 18 January 1957.
3. *Star*, Johannesburg, November 1965.
4. Randall, *op. cit.* (Ch.1, n1).
5. Interview with authors, Johannesburg, 12 June 1986.
6. *Ibid.*

SOUTH AFRICA INC.

3 Early Days

1. Geoffrey Wheatcroft, *The Randlords* (Weidenfeld & Nicolson, London, 1985), p. 148.
2. Edward Jessop, *Ernest Oppenheimer: A Study in Power* (Rex Collings, London, 1979), p. 328.
3. Quoted in Anthony Hocking, *Oppenheimer and Son* (McGraw-Hill, Johannesburg, 1973), p. 57.
4. Quoted in Sir Theodore Gregory, *Ernest Oppenheimer and the Economic Development of Southern Africa* (Oxford University Press, Cape Town, 1962), p. 88. Gregory's 600-page volume was commissioned by the Anglo American Corporation as an official history.
5. Quoted in Gregory, *op. cit.*, pp. 86-7.
6. Quoted in Gregory, *op, cit.*, p. 116.
7. South African *Hansard*, 2 March 1932.
8. Quoted in Brian Bunting, *The Rise of the South African Reich* (Penguin Books, Harmondsworth, 1969), p. 59.
9. *Ibid.*
10. Quoted in Merle Lipton, *Capitalism and Apartheid* (Gower/Maurice Temple Smith, Aldershot, England, 1985), p.18.
11. G. Clack, 'The changing structure of industrial relations in South Africa with special reference to racial factors and social movements', PhD thesis, London School of Economics, 1962.
12. Jessup, *op. cit.* (n2). Members of the Oppenheimer family and senior Anglo executives refuse to explain or speculate on Ernest's conversion. For many years Anglo had a reputation for being anti-Semitic in its white recruitment policies, and one still occasionally hears this accusation in Johannesburg.
13. Speech to Cape Town diamond conference with the Minister of Mines, 6 January 1932.
14. Speech to De Aar diamond conference with the Minister of Mines, 30 June 1931.
15. Rhodes' second will, entitled 'Confession of Faith', 2 June 1877; quoted in Wheatcroft, *op. cit.* (n1).
16. Ken Luckhardt and Brenda Wall, *Organize or Starve! The History of the South African Congress of Trade Unions* (Lawrence & Wishart, London, 1980), p. 69.
17. Free State Ventures, 13 March 1943; quoted in Gregory, *op. cit.* (n4), pp. 553-4.
18. Speech on cutting the first sod of No. 2 shaft, Welkom Gold Mining Company, 16 April 1947; quoted in Gregory, *op. cit.* (n4), pp. 573-4.
19. *Ibid.*
20. Minutes of the 34th annual general meeting of Anglo American Corporation, 22 June 1951.
21. Quoted in Gregory, *op. cit.* (n4), pp. 415-16.
22. Communication to the copperbelt employees of the AAC Group, 23 December 1953; quoted in Gregory, *op. cit.* (n4), p. 488.

23. Speech to the Duke of Edinburgh's Study Conference on Human Relations in Industry, Oxford, 1956.
24. One of Ernest's frequent letters to his son during the war, written from N'Kana on 28 August 1941; quoted in Gregory, *op. cit.* (n4), p. 473.
25. Quoted in Hocking, *op. cit.* (n3), p. 330.
26. Thirty years later, in 1986, the majority of white South Africans had never been to a black township – Central Television documentary *Back to the Frontier*, 25 November 1986.

4 The Importance of Being Harry

1. *Star*, Johannesburg, 9 November 1951; quoted in Gwendolen M. Carter, *The Politics of Inequality: South Africa since 1948* (Thames & Hudson, London, 1958), p. 309.
2. Speech by Dr J. H. Loock to South African parliament; quoted in Hocking, *op. cit.* (Ch.3, n3), p. 247.
3. *Ibid.*
4. *Star*, Johannesburg, 6 August 1957.
5. Quoted in Hocking, *op. cit.* (Ch.3, n3), p.308.
6. Harry Oppenheimer, *Towards Racial Harmony*, supplement to *Optima*, September 1956.
7. *Rand Daily Mail*, 18 October 1961.
8. Patrice Claude, 'Harry Oppenheimer: Millionaire with a clear conscience', *Le Monde*, in *Manchester Weekly Guardian*, 26 February 1984.
9. Hocking, *op. cit.* (Ch.3, n3), p. 427.
10. Brian Hackland, 'The Progressive Party of South Africa, 1959-1981: Political responses to structural change and class struggle', in D. Phil. thesis (Balliol College, Oxford, March 1984). Deposited in the Bodleian Library, Oxford.
11. Harry Oppenheimer interviewed by Brian Hackland, Johannesburg, 30 October 1978.
12. *Ibid.*
13. Hackland, 'Progressive Party', *op. cit.* (n10), p. 102.
14. *Sunday Times* (Johannesburg), 22 November 1959.
15. Oppenheimer interview with Hackland, *op. cit.* (n11).
16. All of Oppenheimer's reservations are taken from Hackland's thesis, *op. cit.* (n10).
17. Ronald Segal, *African Profiles* (Penguin African Library, Harmondsworth, 1962), p. 25.
18. Hackland, 'Progressive Party', *op. cit.* (n10).

5 From Sharpeville to Soweto

1. Speech to South African Foundation banquet, Cape Town, June 1967; quoted in Bunting, *op. cit.* (Ch.3, n8), p. 356.
2. Anglo American Corporation of South Africa, Annual Report 1961.

3. *Daily Mail*, London, 31 March 1960.
4. Quoted in Hocking, *op. cit.* (Ch.3, n3), p. 369.
5. Quoted in Hocking, *op. cit.* p. 353.
6. Speech in Kitwe, Zambia, 1961; quoted in Hocking, *op. cit.*
7. Quoted in Hocking, *op. cit.*, p. 369.
8. Quoted in Hocking, *op. cit.*, p. 370.
9. Quoted in Hocking, *op. cit.*, p. 373.
10. G. Lanning with M. Mueller, *Africa Undermined* (Penguin Books, Harmondsworth, 1979), p. 457.
11. *Melbourne Herald*, 23 April 1970.
12. Harry Oppenheimer, 'For South African National Unity', *New York Times*, 2 June 1976.
13. Hackland, *op. cit.*, (Ch.4, n10).
14. *Optima*, Vol. 24, No. 4, 1977, p. 216.
15. *Financial Mail*, Johannesburg, 16 February 1979.
16. Urban Foundation annual report, 1985.
17. John Kane-Berman, 'The Search for the Black Middle Class', *Energos*, One, 1980.
18. Harry Oppenheimer, Chairman's Annual Statement, 1981.
19. *New York Times*, 2 June 1982.
20. Report of the Wages Commission of the Students' Representative Council of the University of Cape Town, Sophiatown, 26 September 1975.
21. *New York Times*, 2 June 1982.
22. Gavin Relly, Chairman's Annual Statement, AAC, 1984.
23. *Financial Mail*, Johannesburg, 11 July 1985.
24. *Financial Times*, London, 12 November 1984.
25. Nicholas Oppenheimer, *Optima* pamphlet, 1979.

6 Bringing in the Yankee Dollar

1. *Forbes* magazine, New York, 15 June 1973.
2. William Minter, *King Solomon's Mines Revisited* (Basic Books, New York, 1986), p. 194.
3. Quoted in *Sechaba*, African National Congress of South Africa, February 1967.
4. Quoted in *African Development*, October 1973, Zambia supplement, p. 15.
5. *Fortune* magazine, 7 September 1981.
6. *Financial Times*, 8 April 1981.
7. US Federal Electoral Commission, 7 October 1984.
8. *Business Week*, 17 March 1980.
9. *Economist*, London, 1 May 1982.
10. Anderson Strathclyde brochure to shareholders, 17 March 1983.
11. London *Standard*, 9 April 1984.
12. Charter Consolidated, Annual Report 1986.
13. The following account was assembled by the authors, after inter-

viewing the Amsterdam squatters who stole the documents and analysing the tax-avoidance schemes they revealed.

14. *Financial Times*, 24 January 1987.
15. *Ibid.*

7 The Diamond Conspiracy

1. Osman's chance meeting led to a BBC Television *Panorama* programme on 6 April 1981. See also an account of the Russian diamond trade by Kurt Campbell of the Centre for Science and International Affairs, Kennedy School of Government, Harvard University, in *African Defence Journal*, Paris, March 1986.
2. Waddell's destination was established by the author's inquiries in Johannesburg.
3. Edward Jay Epstein, *The Diamond Invention* (Hutchinson, London, 1982).
4. *Wall Street Journal*, 7 July 1984.
5. Julian Ogilvie Thompson in a speech to the World Diamond Congress, Tel Aviv, July 1986.
6. *Atlantic Monthly*, February 1982, p. 24.
7. *Barron's*, 30 March 1981.
8. Sir Percy Sillitoe, *Cloak Without Dagger* (Cassell, London, 1955).
9. Epstein, *op. cit.* (n3). One of the mercenaries, a Lebanese called Fouad Kamil, launched a vendetta against the Oppenheimers 20 years later, claiming money he had not been paid. He hijacked an aeroplane, believing that Gordon Waddell was on board, and spent some time in a Malawian jail. In 1976 he recruited several English people to threaten the Oppenheimer family in London. They were caught and were convicted at the Old Bailey. Kamil, dubbed 'Flash Fred' by the British press, remained untouched in Barcelona. He later wrote a sanitised version of his anti-smuggling exploits, *The Diamond Underworld* (Allen Lane, London, 1979).
10. *Financial Times*, 9 March 1983.
11. *Los Angeles Times*, 5 December 1981.
12. P. Thirion, *Commission of Inquiry into Alleged Irregularities and Misapplication of Property in Representative Authorities and the Central Authority of South West Africa*, p. 5.
13. *Ibid.*, p. 16.
14. *Ibid.*, p. 17.
15. *Ibid.*, p. 144.
16. *Ibid.*, pp. 184 and 190.
17. Interviews with authors.
18. Thirion *Commission, op. cit.*, p. 271.
19. *Ibid.*, p. 273.
20. *Ibid.*, p. 143.
21. De Beers press statement, 10 March 1986.

8 The Golden Arc

1. *Le Monde*, reprinted in the *Manchester Guardian Weekly*, 26 February 1984.
2. Karl Marx and Frederick Engels, *Selected Works*, Vol. 3 (Progress Publishers, Moscow, 1970), p. 490.
3. *Ibid.*, p. 379.
4. Interview with authors.
5. Department of Trade report: *Consolidated Gold Fields Limited. Investigation under Section 172 of the Companies Act 1948*. 1980.
6. *The Times*, London, 14 April 1980.
7. Interview with authors, June 1986.
8. *Washington Post*, 4 October 1987.

9 Working for Anglo

1. Interview with authors, Johannesburg, October 1984.
2. *Star*, Johannesburg, 18 September 1984.
3. Anglo American Corporation, Annual Report 1985.
4. Caroline Dempster interviewed by authors, 1984.
5. *Star*, Johannesburg, 19 June 1984.
6. Harry Oppenheimer, *The Conditions for Progress in Africa*, The Fourth T. B. Davie Memorial Lecture, University of Cape Town, 6 September 1962.
7. Harry Oppenheimer, *Optima*, 1975, No. 2.
8. Zach de Beer, *Optima*, 1977, No. 2.
9. Charles Barlow, *Guardian*, London, 6 January 1978.
10. Cape *Hansard*, 1984, p. 362 quoted in Luli Callinicos, *Gold and Workers, 1862-1924* (Ravan Press, Johannesburg, 1985), p. 29.
11. D. Hobart Houghton, *Life in the Ciskei*, South African Institute of Race Relations, May 1955.
12. Ann Seidman, *The Roots of Crisis in South Africa* (Oxfam America, Africa World Press, Trenton, New Jersey, 1985), p. 35.
13. *Ibid.*
14. Ernest Cole, *House of Bondage* (Allen Lane, London, 1967), pp. 23-4.
15. *Mining Survey*, The Chamber of Mines of South Africa, No. 3/4, 1982.
16. Francis Wilson, *Labour in the South African Gold Mines, 1911-1969* (Cambridge University Press, Cambridge, 1972).
17. *Workers' Unity*, 9 May 1978, on the Inter-Departmental Committee of Inquiry into Riots on Mines in 1975.
18. Extracts from the report into riots on mines, *South African Labour Bulletin*, Vol. 4, No. 5, September 1978.
19. *Ibid.*
20. South African Labour and Development Research Unit paper, *Conflict on South African Mines, 1972-1979*, University of Cape Town, June 1980.

21. *An Inquiry into the Disturbances on Anglo American Gold Mines, January 1975*, AAC Gold Division archives.
22. *Rand Daily Mail*, 9 July 1983.
23. *Rand Daily Mail*, 24 May 1978.
24. T. D. Moodie, *The Perceptions and Behaviour Patterns of Black Mineworkers on a Group Gold Mine*, Industrial Relations Department, Manpower Resources Division, AAC, November 1976.
25. Quoted in Wilson, *op. cit.* (n16).
26. Interview with authors, October 1984.
27. Wiehahn Commission of Inquiry into Labour Legislation report, May 1979, para 3.35.4.
28. *A Human Resources Audit of Elandsrand Gold Mine following the April 1979 Disturbance*, Chamber of Mines Research Organisation, June 1979.
29. Interview with authors, Johannesburg, June 1986.
30. Jean Leger, *Towards Safer Underground Gold Mining*, Department of Sociology, University of Witwatersrand, July 1985.
31. *Ibid.*
32. E. Rodenwoldt, *Productivity bonuses for black underground workers on collieries and gold mines*, Chamber of Mines, 1982.
33. Leger, *op. cit.* (n30).
34. A. P. Moerdyk, *Developing initiative in the team leader*, Chamber of Mines, 1983.
35. Quoted in Marcel Golding, 'Mass dismissals on the mines: the workers' story', *South African Labour Bulletin*, June 1985.
36. *Ibid.*
37. AAC report, *op. cit.* (n21).
38. Speech recorded by the authors.
39. *Ibid.*
40. R. Laughlin, paper for the joint AAC-NUM project on inter-group violence, May 1986.
41. Interview with authors, October 1984.
42. *Ibid.*
43. *Ibid.*
44. *Rand Daily Mail*, 3 March 1982.
45. *Weekly Mail*, 11 December 1987.
46. *The Financial Times*, 27 November 1987.
47. *Finance Week*, 10-16 December 1987.

10 Playing the Black Markets

1. Supplement to *Optima*, Vol. 32, No. 4, 1984.
2. David Fig, 'Anglo American in Brazil', *Raw Materials Report*, Vol. 3, No. 1, 1984.
3. T. H. Bingham QC and S. M. Gray, *Report on the Supply of Petroleum and Petroleum Products to Rhodesia*, September 1978.
4. *Guardian*, 27 March 1984.

5. Joseph Hanlon, *Beggar Your Neighbours* (Catholic Institute for International Relations and James Currey, London/Indiana University Press, 1986), p. 332.
6. De Beers Consolidated Mines, Annual Report 1979.
7. *Southern Africa: Towards Economic Liberation*, a declaration by the governments of independent states of Southern Africa made at Lusaka, 1 April 1980.
8. Quoted in Fig. *op. cit* (n2).
9. Frank Sergiades, 'Brazil's Golden Aura', *Optima*, Vol. 32, No. 4, December 1984, p. 158.
10. 'Mario Henrique Simonsen', profile in *Optima*, Vol. 30, No. 1, 31 July 1981, pp. 54-5.
11. David Fig, 'Time for Action: Brazil's Economic Relations with South Africa' (University of Cape Town), paper presented to the Third International Congress of the Asociación Latinoamericano de Estudios Afroasiáticos, Rio de Janeiro, 1-5 August 1983.
12. *Sunday Times*, Johannesburg, 12 March 1978.

11 The Lair of the Lion

1. Tony Bloom interviewed by authors, Johannesburg, June 1986.
2. Dirk and Johanna de Villiers, *PW* (Tafelberg, Cape Town, 1984).
3. *Cape Times*, 25 April 1984.
4. Quoted in Elaine Potter, *The Press on Opposition: The Political Role of South African Newspapers* (Chatto & Windus, London, 1975).
5. Quoted in Hocking, *op. cit.* (Ch.3, n3), pp. 479-50.
6. *Finance Week*, 25 April-1 May 1985.
7. *Financial Times* Business Enterprises report on *Rand Daily Mail*, 1983, p. 32.
8. *Rand Daily Mail*, 17 September 1984.
9. Anton Harber, 'Behind Closed Doors', *Work in Progress*, Johannesburg, No. 36, April 1985.
10. *Rand Daily Mail*, 16 March 1985.
11. *Ibid.*
12. *Ibid.*
13. *Guardian*, London, 4 June 1985.
14. *Financial Mail*, 6 September 1985.
15. *Africa Confidential*, Vol. 26, No. 19, 18 September 1985.
16. From authors' interview with Tony Bloom, Johannesburg, June 1986.
17. *Ibid.*
18. Authors' interview with Gavin Relly, Johannesburg, June 1986.
19. Authors' interview, July 1986.
20. *Guardian*, 25 September 1985.
21. *Multinational Monitor*, Washington DC, Vol. 4, No. 11, November 1983.
22. *Le Monde*, in *Manchester Weekly Guardian*, 26 February 1984.

12 Crossing the River

1. Phibro Corporation Post-Meeting Report, 20 May 1981.
2. Phibro Report, 20 May 1982.
3. Phibro Report, 24 May 1983.
4. *Financial Times*, 24 May 1985.
5. *Financial Mail*, 13 September 1985.
6. *Financial Times*, 10 July 1987; *Cape Times*, 23 June 1987.
7. *Weekly Mail*, 24 July 1987.
8. BBC Radio News, 22.30, 7 November 1986.
9. Gavin Relly, Chairman's Annual Statement, AAC, 1986.
10. *Ibid.*
11. *Financial Mail*, 1 January 1987.

Bibliography and Sources

Books, pamphlets and articles

Africa Fund and District Council 27, *Black Workers Under Siege: The Repression of Black Trade Unions in South Africa*, AFSCME, New York, 1984.

Anglo American Corporation, *The Perceptions and Behaviour Patterns of Black Mineworkers on a Group Gold Mine*, Industrial Relations Department, Manpower Resources Division, Johannesburg, November 1976.

Benson, Mary, *South Africa: The Struggle for a Birthright*, International Defence and Aid Fund for Southern Africa, London, 1985.

Blackmore, Kenneth, *Buying Jewellery*, Weidenfeld & Nicolson, London, 1982.

Boyer, Sandy, *Black Unions in South Africa*, Africa Fund, New York, February 1982.

British-North American Committee, *Mineral Development in the Eighties: Prospects and Problems*, report prepared by a group of Committee members on the basis of a document provided by Ian MacGregor with a statistical annex by Sperry Lea, November 1976.

Brooks, Alan, and Jeremy Brickhill, *Whirlwind Before the Storm*, International Defence and Aid Fund for Southern Africa, London, 1980.

Bunting, Brian, *The Rise of the South African Reich*, Penguin Books, Harmondsworth, 1964; revised edition 1969.

Burgess, Julian, *et al.*, *The Great White Hoax: South Africa's International Propaganda Machine*, Africa Bureau, London, 1977.

Callinicos, Alex, *Southern Africa After Zimbabwe*, Pluto Press, London, 1981.

Callinicos, Alex, and John Rogers, *Southern Africa After Soweto*, Pluto Press, London, 1977.

360

Callinicos, Luli, *Gold and Workers 1886-1924*: *A People's History of South Africa*, vol. 1, Ravan Press, Johannesburg, 1985.

Carson, Jim, *Space Research Capitalism*, background paper presented to the International Seminar on the Implantation and Reinforcement of the Arms Embargo Against South Africa, London, 1-3 April 1981; prepared for the American Committee on Africa and the World Campaign Against Military and Nuclear Collaboration with South Africa.

Carter, Gwendolen M., *The Politics of Inequality*: *South Africa since 1948*, Thames & Hudson, London/Praeger, New York, 1958.

Cartwright, A. P. *Gold Paved the Way*, Macmillan, London, 1967.

Catholic Institute for International Relations, *South Africa in the 1980s – State of Emergency*, CIIR, London, 3rd edn, 1986.

Chapman, Leo, *Diamonds in Australia*: *The Fields and the Prospectors*, Bay Books, Sydney, 1980.

Chimutengwende, Chenhamo C., *South Africa*: *The Press and the Politics of Liberation*, Barbican Books, London, 1978.

Claude, Patrice, 'Harry Oppenheimer: millionaire with a clear conscience', *Le Monde*, 26 February 1984.

Cohen, Robin, *Endgame in South Africa*? James Currey, London/Unesco Press, Paris, 1986.

Cole, Ernest, with Thomas Flaherty, *House of Bondage*, Ridge Press, Toronto/Allen Lane The Penguin Press, London, 1967.

Collings, John, *Social Responsibility in South Africa*: *The Work of the Anglo American and De Beers Chairman's Fund* (foreword by Gavin Relly), supplement to *Optima*, Vol. 31, No. 1, October 1982.

Commonwealth Group of Eminent Persons, *Mission to South Africa*, Penguin Books, for the Commonwealth Secretariat, London, 1986.

Counter Information Services, *Black South Africa Explodes*, CIS, London, 1976.

Counter Information Services, *Consolidated Gold Fields PLC*: *Partner in Apartheid*, CIS, London, Spring 1986.

Cunningham, Simon, *The Copper Industry in Zambia*: *Foreign Mining Companies in a Developing Country*, Praeger, New York, 1981.

Davidson, Basil, *Southern Africa*: *Progress or Disaster*? Canon Collins Memorial Lecture given on 7 December 1983; British Defence and Aid Fund for Southern Africa, London, 1984.

Davidson, Basil, Joe Slovo and Anthony R. Wilkinson, *Southern Africa*: *the New Politics of Revolution*, Penguin Books, Harmondsworth, 1976.

Davies, Robert H., *Capital, State and White Labour in South Africa 1900-1960*, Harvester Press, Brighton, 1979.

Davies, David, *African Workers and Apartheid*, Fact Paper on Southern Africa No. 5, International Defence and Aid Fund, London, 1978.

De Beer, Zach, 'Industrial Relations in Free Enterprise Societies and Guidelines for South Africa', *Optima*, Vol. 26, No. 4, 1977(2).

Desmond, Cosmas, 'Sanctions and South Africa', *Third World Quarterly*, January 1986.

De Vletter, Fion, *Migrant Labour on the South African Gold Mines: An Investigation into Black Worker Conditions and Attitudes*, ILO World Employment Programme, Migration for Employment Project, November 1977.

Duignan, Peter, and L. H. Gann, *The United States and Africa: A History*, Hoover Institute/Cambridge University Press, Cambridge, 1984.

Epstein, Edward Jay, *The Diamond Invention*, Hutchinson, London, 1982 (*The Rise and Fall of Diamonds: The Shattering of a Brilliant Illusion*, Simon & Schuster, New York, 1982).

Etheredge, D. A., 'South Africa Gold Mines' Case: Good for Labor and Capital', *Financier*, April 1980.

Fig, David, 'South Africa's Expanding Relations with Latin America, 1966-1976', unpublished paper, Institute of Commonwealth Studies, University of London, May 1978.

Fig, David, 'Time for Action: Brazil's Economic Relations with South Africa', paper presented to the Third International Congress of the Asociación Latinoamericano de Estudios Afroasiáticos, Rio de Janeiro, 1-5 August 1983.

Fig, David, 'Anglo American in Brazil', *Raw Materials Report*, Vol. 3, no. 1, 1984.

Fig, David, 'Theorising South Africa's Foreign Policy: the case for Latin America', Africa Seminar, Centre for African Studies, University of Cape Town, 29 August 1984.

Financial Mail Supplement, *Top Companies*, Special Survey, Johannesburg, 24 May 1985.

First, Ruth, Jonathan Steele and Christabel Gurney, *The South African Connection: Western Investment in Apartheid*, Penguin Books, Harmondsworth, 1973 (Temple Smith, London, 1972).

Frankel, S. H., *Capital Investment in Africa: Its Cause and Effects*, Oxford University Press, London, 1938.

Frederikse, Julie; *South Africa: A Different Kind of War*, Mambo Press, Gweru/James Currey, London/Ravan Press, Johannesburg, 1986.

Friedman, Steven, 'Chamber of Mines' Policy and the Energing Miners' Unions', *South African Labour Bulletin*, Vol. 8, No. 5, April 1983.

Friedman, Steven, *Black Politics at the Crossroads*, South African Institute of Race Relations, Johannesburg, January 1986.

Gall, Norman, 'Gold Rush', *Forbes*, 21 May 1984.

Gavshon, Arthur, *Crisis in Africa: Battleground of East and West*, Penguin Books, Harmondsworth, 1981.

Gifford, Tony, *South Africa's Record of International Terrorism*, Anti-

Apartheid Movement/Stop the War Against Angola and Mozambique (SWAM) (in cooperation with United Nations Centre Against Apartheid), London, September 1981.

Glynn, Lenny, and Elizabeth Peer, 'Felix [Rohatyn]: The making of a celebrity', *Institutional Investor*, December 1984.

Gold Division of Anglo American Corporation, *An Inquiry into the Disturbances on Anglo American Gold Mines January 1975*, 1975.

Golding, Marcel, 'Mass struggles on the mines', *South African Labour Bulletin*, May 1985.

Golding, Marcel, 'Mass dismissals on the mines: the workers' story', *South African Labour Bulletin*, June 1985.

Green, Timothy, *The World of Diamonds*, Weidenfeld & Nicolson, London, 1981.

Green, Timothy, *The World of Gold*, Simon & Schuster, New York, 1970.

Gregory, Sir Theodore, *Ernest Oppenheimer and the Economic Development of Southern Africa*, Oxford University Press, Cape Town, 1962.

Haarlov, Jens, *Labour Regulation and Black Workers' Struggles in South Africa*, Research Report no. 68, Scandinavian Institute of African Studies, Uppsala, Sweden, 1983.

Hackland, Brian, 'The Progressive Party of South Africa, 1959-1981: Political Responses to Structural Change and Class Struggle', Oxford University D. Phil. thesis, 1984, on deposit at Bodleian Library, Oxford.

Hall, Richard, *The High Price of Principles: Kaunda and the White South*, Penguin Books, Harmondsworth, 1969.

Halpern, Jack, *South Africa's Hostages: Basutoland, Bechuanaland and Swaziland*, Penguin Books, Harmondsworth, 1965.

Hanlon, Joseph, *Apartheid's Second Front: South Africa's War Against Its Neighbours*, Penguin Books, Harmondsworth, 1986.

Hanlon, Joseph, *Beggar Your Neighbours: Apartheid Power In Southern Africa*, Catholic Institute for International Relations in collaboration with James Currey, London/Indiana University Press, Bloomington, Indiana, 1986.

Haysom, Nicholas, *Apartheid's Private Army: The Rise of Right-Wing Vigilantes in South Africa*, Catholic Institute for International Relations, London, 1986.

Herbstein, Denis, *White Man, We Want to Talk to You*, André Deutsch/Penguin Books, London, 1978.

Hocking, Anthony, *Oppenheimer and Son*, McGraw-Hill Book Company, Johannesburg/New York, 1973.

Hornsby, A. H., *The South African Diamond Fields*, Chicago, 1874; facsimile edition published by Historical Society of Kimberley and the Northern Cape, Kimberley.

Horowitz, Paul, and Holly Sklar, 'South Atlantic Triangle', North American Congress on Latin America (NACLA) Report on the Americas, Vol. XVI, No. 3, May-June 1982.

Horwitz, Ralph, *The Political Economy of South Africa*, Weidenfeld & Nicolson, London, 1967.

Innes, Duncan, *Anglo American and the Rise of Modern South Africa*, Heinemann Educational Books, London, 1984.

International Defence and Aid Fund for Southern Africa, *Apartheid: The Facts*, IDAF (in cooperation with United Nations Centre Against Apartheid), London, 1983.

International Defence and Aid Fund for Southern Africa, *The Apartheid War Machine: the Strength and Deployment of the South African Armed Forces*, Fact Paper on Southern Africa No. 8, IDAF, London, April 1980.

International Gold Corporation, 'Gold and South African Gold Mines', *Mining Survey*, No. 1/2, July 1985.

International Labour Office, *Apartheid in South Africa*, Special Report on the application of the policy adopted at 1981 International Labour Conference, Geneva, 1985.

Irving, Joe, 'Investment or pure decoration?', *Money Management*, October 1985.

Jaffe, Thomas, 'Prowling the American veldt?', *Forbes*, 22 December 1980.

Jenkins, Simon, 'Destabilization in Southern Africa: Potgieter counter-attacks', *The Economist*, 16 July 1983.

Jessup, Edward, *Ernest Oppenheimer: A Study in Power*, Rex Collings, London, 1979.

Johannesburg Stock Exchange Committee, *The Story of the Johannesburg Stock Exchange, 1887-1947*, Johannesburg, 1948.

Johnstone, Frederick A., *Class, Race and Gold*, Routledge & Kegan Paul, London, 1976.

Jones, Jim, 'Anglo American Latin American venture', *Financial Mail*, 1 January 1982.

Kamarck, Andrew M., *The Economics of African Development*, Praeger Publishers, New York/Washington/London, 1967; revised edition 1971.

Kamil, Fred, *The Diamond Underworld*, Allen Lane, London, 1979.

Kaplan, David E., 'The internationalization of South African capital: South African direct foreign investment in the contemporary period', paper presented to South African Studies: Retrospect and Prospect, University of Edinburgh, 30 May-1 June 1983.

Kaplan, Ruth, *Anglo American Corporation of South Africa Ltd: Investments in North America*, The Africa Fund, New York, 1982.

Kinkead, Gwen, 'Behind the Salomon Brothers buyout', *Fortune Magazine*, 7 September 1981.

Kramer, Reed, 'Harry Oppenheimer: the man behind the financial empire behind the Carter South African Policy', *Seven Days*, 20 June 1977.

Lanning, Greg, with Marti Mueller, *Africa Undermined: Mining Companies and the Underdevelopment of Africa*, Penguin Books, Harmondsworth, 1979.

Leftwich, Adrian (ed.), *South Africa: Economic Growth and Political Change*, Allison & Busby, London, 1974.

Leger, J. P., *Towards Safer Underground Gold Mining*, investigation commissioned by the National Union of Mine Workers, Department of Sociology, University of the Witwatersrand, Johannesburg, July 1985.

Legum, Colin, *Southern Africa: The Year of the Whirlwind*, Rex Collings, London, 1977.

Lelyveld, Joseph, 'Oppenheimer', *New York Times Sunday Magazine*, 8 May 1983.

Lipton, Merle, 'Men of two worlds – migrant labour in South Africa', *Optima*, Vol. 29, 1980.

Lipton, Merle, *Capitalism and Apartheid: South Africa, 1910-84*, Gower/Maurice Temple Smith, Aldershot, 1985.

Local Authority Action Against Apartheid, survey commissioned by United Nations Centre Against Apartheid, published by Sheffield Metropolitan District Council on behalf of the National Steering Committee on Local Authority Action Against Apartheid, March 1985.

Loomis, Carol J., 'The morning after at Phibro-Salomon', *Fortune*, 10 January 1983.

Lucas, G. H. G., and G. J. de J. Cronje (eds), *The Marketing of the International Image of South Africa*, University of South Africa, Pretoria, 1978.

Luckhardt, Ken, and Brenda Wall, *Organize or Starve! The History of the South African Congress of Trade Unions*, Lawrence & Wishart, London, 1980.

Mandela, Nelson, *The Struggle is My Life* (ed. IDAF Research, Information and Publications Department), International Defence and Aid Fund for Southern Africa, London, 1978; new edition 1986.

Maull, Hans W., *Raw Materials, Energy and Western Security*, Studies in International Security 22, International Institute for Strategic Studies/Macmillan, London, 1984.

Mbeki, Govan, *South Africa: The Peasants' Revolt*, Penguin Books, Harmondsworth, 1962; new edition International Defence and Aid Fund, London, 1984.

McGregor, Robin, *McGregor's Who Owns Whom, Purdey Publishing, South Africa*.

Mining Annual Review, published by *Mining Journal*, London.

Minter, William, *King Solomon's Mines Revisited: Western Interests and the Burdened History of Southern Africa*, Basic Books, New York, 1986.

Monopolies and Mergers Commission, *Charter Consolidated PLC and Anderson Strathclyde PLC: A Report on the Proposed Merger*, presented to Parliament by the Secretary of State for Trade, Her Majesty's Stationery Office, London, December 1982.

Murray, Martin, *South Africa: Time of Agony, Time of Destiny*, Verso, London, 1987.

Namibia Support Committee, *British Transnational Corporations and Namibia*, paper presented to the Public Hearings on the Activities of Transnational Corporations in South Africa and Namibia, New York, 16-20 September 1985; NSC, London, 1985.

Nossiter, Daniel D., 'Justice vs. De Beers', Barron's, 30 March 1981.

Nyangoni, Wellington W., *The OECD and Western Mining Multinational Corporations in the Republic of South Africa*, University Press of America, Washington, DC, 1982.

Nyagumbo, Maurice, *With the People: An Autobiography from the Zimbabwe Struggle*, Allison & Busby, London, 1980.

Ochola, Samuel, A., *Minerals in African Underdevelopment*, Bogle-L'Ouverture Publications, London, 1975.

Ogilvie Thompson, Julian, 'An appreciation of Harry Oppenheimer', *Optima*, Vol. 33, No. 1, 15 March 1985.

Oliver, Roland, and J. D. Fage, *A Short History of Africa*, Penguin Books, Harmondsworth, 1962.

Omond, Roger, *The Apartheid Handbook: A Guide to South Africa's Everyday Racial Policies*, Penguin Books, Harmondsworth, 1985.

Oppenheimer, Harry F., *The Future of Industry in South Africa*, address delivered in Cape Town at the council meeting of the South African Institute of Race Relations, January 1950: SAIRR, Johannesburg.

Oppenheimer, Harry F., *Towards Racial Harmony*, supplement to *Optima*, September 1956.

Oppenheimer, Harry F., *Business Prospects in Southern Africa: A view of factors and influences*, AAC Chairman's annual statement; supplement to *Optima*, September 1959.

Oppenheimer, Harry F., *The Conditions for Progress in Africa*, the Fourth T. B. Davie Memorial Lecture, delivered at University of Cape Town, 6 September 1962.

Oppenheimer, Harry F., *Chairman's Statement 1973* (to be read with annual report and accounts for 1972), AAC, Johannesburg, 30 May 1973.

Oppenheimer, Harry F., 'For South African National Unity', *New York Times*, 2 June 1976, adapted from a speech given at Nelspruit, Eastern Transvaal.

Oppenheimer, Harry F., *Prospects for Change in Southern Africa*, address to the Foreign Policy Association, New York, 14 October 1977.

Oppenheimer, Harry F., 'One Man, One Vote in South Africa: It's not the answer', address to Foreign Policy Association in New York, published by South African Department of Information; reprinted *New York Times*, 2 November 1977.

Oppenheimer, Harry F., *Why the World Should Continue to Invest in South Africa*, address to the International Monetary Conference, Mexico City, 22 May 1978; supplement to *Optima*, Vol. 27, No. 3, 1978.

Oppenheimer, Harry F., *Towards a More Just Racial Order in South Africa*, opening address to 50th anniversary conference of the South African Institute of Race Relations, Johannesburg, 2 July 1979; supplement to *Optima*, September 1956.

Oppenheimer, Harry F., *Apartheid Under Pressure*, address to the governors of the Foreign Policy Association, New York, 11 October 1984.

Oppenheimer, Harry F., 'Paths to love or hate', *Sunday Times*, London, 21 April 1985.

Oppenheimer, Harry F., 'The Anglo American Corporation's role in South Africa's Gold mining Industry', *Optima*, Vol. 34, No. 2, June 1986.

Oppenheimer, Nicholas, *Investment in South Africa Today and Tomorrow*, address to *Financial Mail* conference 'Investment in 1980', Johannesburg, 9 November 1979.

Palestrant, Ellen, *Johannesburg One Hundred*, Ad. Donker, Johannesburg, 1986.

Paton, Alan, *Cry, the Beloved Country*, Jonathan Cape, London, 1948.

Pillay, Vella, *The Role of Gold in the Economy of Apartheid South Africa*, UN Centre Against Apartheid, Department of Political and Security Council Affairs, 1981.

Pillay, Vella, *The Crisis of the Apartheid Economy*, 5 October 1985.

Plaut, Martin, 'Report on the Anglo American gold mines', *South African Labour Bulletin*, 2(8), April 1976.

Plaut, Martin, and David Ward, *Black Trade Unions in South Africa*, Spokesman pamphlet No. 82, Bertrand Russell Peace Foundation, Nottingham, 1982.

Prest, Michael, 'The act of liberation that detonated a gold mine', *The Times*, London, 19 December 1984.

Prior, Andrew, 'Managerial ideology: a case study of an incident in a South African gold mine, 13th August 1975', *South African Labour Bulletin*, 3(8), October 1977.

Quigley, Carroll, *The Anglo American Establishment*, Books in Focus, New York, 1981.

Randall, Peter, *Little England on the Veld: The English Private School System in South Africa*, Ravan Press, Johannesburg, 1982.

Relly, Gavin W. H., *Chairman's Statement 1984* (to be read with annual report for 1984), AAC, Johannesburg, 9 July 1984.

Relly, Gavin W. H., *Chairman's Statement 1985* (to be read with annual report for 1985), AAC, Johannesburg, 5 July 1985.

Relly, Gavin, *Light on a Dark Continent*, address given in Canberra, Australia, October 1985; supplement to *Optima*, Vol. 33, No. 4.

Roberts, Brian, *Kimberley: Turbulent City*, David Philip, Cape Town, 1976.

Robson, G. G., *Platinum 1985*, Johnson Matthey, London, May 1985.

Rodney, Walter, *How Europe Underdeveloped Africa*, Bogle-L'Ouverture Publications, London, 1972; Howard University Press, Washington.

Rogers, Barbara, and Brian Bolton, *Sanctions Against South Africa: Exploding the Myths*, Manchester Free Press and the Holland Committee on Southern Africa, London, 1981.

Rosenthal, Eric, *Gold! Gold! Gold! The Johannesburg Gold Rush*, Collier-Macmillan, London/Johannesburg, 1970.

Schmidt, Elizabeth, *One Step in the Wrong Direction: An Analysis of the Sullivan Principles as a Strategy for Opposing Apartheid*, Episcopal Churchpeople for a Free South Africa, revised edition 1985.

Segal, Ronald, *African Profiles*, Penguin Books, Harmondsworth, 1962.

Seidman, Ann, *The Roots of Crisis in Southern Africa*, Africa World Press, Trenton, New Jersey, 1985.

Seidman, Ann, and Neva Seidman Makgetla, *Outposts of Monopoly Capitalism: Southern Africa in the Changing Global Economy*, Lawrence Hill, Westport, Connecticut/Zed Press, London, 1980.

Seidman, Judy, *Facelift Apartheid: South Africa After Soweto*, International Defence and Aid Fund, London, 1980.

Sergiades, Frank, 'Brazil'a Golden Aura', *Optima*, Vol. 32, No. 4, December 1984.

Shipping Research Bureau, *Oil Supplies to South Africa: The Role of Tankers Connected with the Netherlands and the Netherlands Antilles*, Amsterdam, 1981.

Sillitoe, Sir Percy, *Cloak Without Dagger*, Cassell, London, 1955.

Simons, Jack and Ray, *Class and Colour in South Africa 1850-1950*, Penguin Books, Harmondsworth, 1969; new edition International Defence and Aid Fund, London, 1983.

South African Research Service, *South African Review Three*, Ravan Press, Johannesburg, 1986.

Stares, Rodney, *ICI in Southern Africa*, Christian Concern for Southern Africa, London, 1977.

Tegen, Andreas, 'Gold', *Raw Materials Report*, Vol. 3, No. 2, 1985.

Thompson, Clive, 'Black trade unions on the mines', *South African Review Two*, 1983.

Van der Horst, Sheila T., *Native Labour in South Africa*, Oxford University Press, London, 1942.

Van Rensburg, Patrick, *Guilty Land*, Penguin Books, Harmondsworth, 1962.

Van Zyl Slabbert, Frederik, *The Last White Parliament*, Sidgwick & Jackson, London, 1985.

Vogl, Frank 'Investment in South Africa Does Not Help Blacks', *Financier*, January 1980.

Weinberg, Eli, *Portrait of a People: A Personal Photographic Record of the South African Liberation Struggle*, International Defence and Aid Fund for Southern Africa, London, 1981.

Wheatcroft, Geoffrey, *The Randlords: The Men Who Made South Africa*, Weidenfeld & Nicolson, London, 1985.

Who's Who of Southern Africa, Argus Printing and Publishing Co., Johannesburg.

Williams, Basil, *Cecil Rhodes*, Constable, London, 1921.

Wilson, Francis, *Labour in the South African Gold Mines 1911-1969*, Cambridge University Press, Cambridge, 1972.

Wilson, W. D., 'Commitment to growth in South Africa: its responsibilities and human implications', *Optima*, 1975(2).

Wood, Brian, *Briefing paper on activities of Tsumeb Corporation Ltd and Consolidated Gold Fields PLC in Namibia*, Namibia Support Committee, London, 3 September 1985.

Newspapers, magazines, journals

Africa Confidential, London
Barron's, New York
Business Times, New York
Economist, London
Finance Week, Johannesburg
Financial Mail, Johannesburg
Financial Times, London
Forbes, New York
Fortune, New York
Fosatu Worker News, Cape Town
Guardian, London
Investors Chronicle, London
Leadership SA, Cape Town
Mining Survey, Johannesburg
New York Times, New York
Optima, Johannesburg (quarterly review published by AAC and De Beers)
Rand Daily Mail, Johannesburg
South Africa Hansard, Cape Town
South African Labour Bulletin, Johannesburg

Star, Johannesburg
Sunday Times, Johannesburg
Sunday Times, London
The Namibian, Windhoek
The Times, London
Wall Street Journal, New York
Weekly Mail, Johannesburg
Windhoek Advertiser, Windhoek
Work in Progress, Johannesburg

Index

Inspiration Resources, 126, 127–8,
136, 339, 347
Institute of Directors, 97
International Diamond Security
Organisation, 161
International Gold Corporation, 319
International Labour Organisation
(ILO), 196
International Monetary Fund (IMF),
119, 238
IQM. *See* Industria Quimica
Matiqueira
Iracema, 260
Iran, 175, 257
Ireland, 53, 139, 151, 159
Iron and Steel Corporation (Iscor), 38,
324
Isaacs, Barney. *See* Barnato, Barney
Iscor. *See* Iron and Steel Corporation
Isidingo Technical College, 109
Israel, 161, 257
ITT, 26
Ivory Coast, 246, 255

Jackson, Stanley, 165
Jagersfontein, 56, 59
Jahn, Helmut, 22
Jameson Raid, 80
Japan, 147, 154, 156, 250, 283, 306
Jardin, Jorge, 238
Job Reservation Act, 62
Joel, Solly, 56, 59
Johannesburg Consolidated
Investment Ltd (JCI), 28, 34, 35,
38, 46, 50, 147, 172, 178, 215,
268, 302, 310, 315, 319, 328, 336
Johnson, Bill, 249
Johnson, President L. B., 120
Johnson Matthey, 127, 131, 173,
176–8, 179, 290, 321, 344, 345
Jonathan, Chief Leabua, 243
Jordan, Dr Pallo, 275
Jwaneng, 151, 246, 307

Kamil, Fouad ('Flash Fred'), 355n
Kariba Dam, 74
Kaunda, President Kenneth, 101, 123,
255, 263, 275
Kennedy, Senator Edward, 128, 265
Kennedy Onassis, Jacqueline, 144, 158

Kennedy, President John F., 199, 158
Kenya, 246, 255
Khama, President Seretse, 248
Kimberley (informer). *See*
Ramotsetjoa, Daniel
Kimberley mine, 151
Kinross, 350
Kinsley, Clive, 270–1
Kirkland, Lane, 127
Kissinger, Henry, 128
Kloof, 314, 316, 317
Komatsu South Africa, 330
Kotane, Moses, 67
Krupp family, 75

Labour Party, South Africa, 61
Lancashire Steel, 253
Lands Act (1936), 63. 294
Landbank, 38
Lang, Dr Edwin, 39
Lansdowne, Justice, 67
Lawrence, Harry, 87
Lazard Brothers, 43
Lazard Frères, 127
Leadership SA, 275
Le Grange, Louis, 265
Lekhanya, Major General Justin, 244
Lennings, 328
Leslie, Peter, 36
Lesotho (Basutoland), 192, 200, 202,
207, 234, 238, 241, 243–4, 245,
247
Lesotho Liberation Army, 243
Letlhakane, 151, 307
Le Vaillant, Francois, 116
Lever Brothers, 7
Lewis and Marks, 50, 66
Leyden, P. J. R., 300
Libanon, 317
Liberation, 9
Liberia, 132, 139, 161, 189, 289
Liberty Life, 35, 36, 38, 337
Liechtenstein, 132, 139
Livingstone, 116
Lloyd-Jacob, David, 181
Lonrho, 250
Loraine, 350
Louw, Raymond, 272
LTA Ltd, 241, 293, 329, 334
Lucas-Tooth, Sir Hugh Veer Huntly
Duff, 43
Ludwig, Daniel, 34